W9-BKI-553

31242002904267

INSIGHT ⊙ GUIDES

TOKYO

CITY GUIDE

PLAN & BOOK
YOUR TAILOR-MADE TRIP

BRAZIL   CHILE   ECUADOR

TAILOR-MADE TRIPS & UNIQUE EXPERIENCES CREATED BY LOCAL TRAVEL EXPERTS AT INSIGHTGUIDES.COM/HOLIDAYS

Insight Guides has been inspiring travellers with high-quality travel content for over 45 years. As well as our popular guidebooks, we now offer the opportunity to book tailor-made private trips completely personalised to your needs and interests. By connecting with one of our local experts, you will directly benefit from their expertise and local know-how, helping you create memories that will last a lifetime.

HOW INSIGHTGUIDES.COM/HOLIDAYS WORKS

STEP 1

Pick your dream destination and submit an enquiry, or modify an existing itinerary if you prefer.

STEP 2

Fill in a short form, sharing details of your travel plans and preferences with a local expert.

STEP 3

Your local expert will create your personalised itinerary, which you can amend until you are completely satisfied.

STEP 4

Book securely online. Pack your bags and enjoy your holiday! Your local expert will be available to answer questions during your trip.

BENEFITS OF PLANNING & BOOKING AT INSIGHTGUIDES.COM/HOLIDAYS

PLANNED BY LOCAL EXPERTS

The Insight Guides local experts are hand-picked, based on their experience in the travel industry and their impeccable standards of customer service.

SAVE TIME & MONEY

When a local expert plans your trip, you save time and money when you book, even during high season. You won't be charged for using a credit card either.

TAILOR-MADE TRIPS

Book with Insight Guides, and you will be in complete control of the planning process, from the initial selections to amending your final itinerary.

BOOK & TRAVEL STRESS-FREE

Enjoy stress-free travel when you use the Insight Guides secure online booking platform. All bookings come with a money-back guarantee.

WHAT OTHER TRAVELLERS THINK ABOUT TRIPS BOOKED AT INSIGHTGUIDES.COM/HOLIDAYS

Trip to Portugal

Every step of the planning process and the trip itself was effortless and exceptional. Our special interests, preferences and requests were accommodated resulting in a trip that exceeded our expectations.

Corinne, USA ★★★★★

Trip to Vietnam

The organization was superb, the drivers professional, and accommodation quite comfortable. I was well taken care of! My thanks to your colleagues who helped make my trip to Vietnam such a great experience. My only regret is that I couldn't spend more time in the country.

Heather ★★★★★

Contents

Travel Tips

THE BEST OF TOKYO: TOP ATTRACTIONS

At a glance, the Tokyo sights and activities you can't afford to miss, from traditional Asakusa and fashionable Omotesando to relaxing in one of the city's onsen baths or admiring nature in Shinjuku Gyoen.

◁ **Omotesando.** Parading down tree-lined Omotesando, Tokyo's most fashionable shopping avenue, is a must; many of the boutiques are housed in striking modern buildings designed by the world's top architects. See page 132.

△ **Onsen.** Join throngs of locals enjoying a soothing onsen dip at Odaiba's Oedo Onsen Monogatari, a giant modern bathhouse with a nostalgic design, or the more contemporary-styled Spa LaQua. See pages 183 and 208.

◁ **Senso-ji.** Resplendent in red and gold is Senso-ji, the Buddhist temple that's the spiritual core of Asakusa, one of Tokyo's most venerable areas, packed with craft shops and lovely ryokan (traditional Japanese inns). See page 174.

△ **Shinjuku Gyoen.** Tokyo has several beautiful traditional parks and gardens, among which the extensive Shinjuku Gyoen is a standout, combining French, English and Japanese styles of landscaping. See page 122.

▷ **Shibuya.** Be dazzled by the massed crowds and mega-wattage of neon pulsing through Shibuya, the shopping district that's the front of a million-and-one consumer crazes. See page 138.

◁ **Meiji Shrine.** Note the barrels of sake donated to Meiji Shrine and be sure to visit a sake bar to sample the best. See page 137.

▽ **Toyosu.** Seafood does not come any fresher than at the vast new wholesale fish and fresh produce market in Toyosu, where you can enjoy a breakfast or lunch of top-class sushi. See page 203.

△ **Roppongi.** Still a raucous nightlife district, Roppongi has recently evolved into a daytime hub for art and high-class shopping at the Roppongi Hills and Tokyo Midtown complexes. See page 144.

▽ **River bus.** Take a river bus down the Sumida River or across Tokyo Bay towards the man-made island of Odaiba for a different perspective on this port city. See page 231.

△ **Imperial Palace.** Tours are tricky to get on, but making a circuit of the gardens surrounding the Imperial Palace, home to the world's oldest monarchy, provides a green escape at the heart of the city. See page 87.

THE BEST OF TOKYO: EDITOR'S CHOICE

Setting priorities, saving money, unique attractions... here, at a glance, are our recommendations, plus some tips and tricks even the locals won't always know.

BEST TOKYO VIEWS

Caretta Shiodome. A slightly different view of Tokyo from the 46th-floor restaurant level of this modern tower – lunchtime prices are surprisingly low, given the gorgeous bay vistas. www.caretta.jp.
Mori Tower. Not only do you get to stand on the roof of this 54-storey tower to enjoy heart-stopping 360-degree views of the city, but there's also one of the city's best galleries up here. See page 146.
Tokyo Metropolitan Government Office. The free observatory on the 45th floor has splendid views of city landmarks, the bay and – if the weather plays ball – Mount Fuji. See page 118.
Tokyo Skytree. This vertiginous communications tower and complex provides the city's highest observation platform. See page 192.
Yebisu Garden Place. The restaurant plaza on the 38th floor offers great views of the bay and westwards towards Shibuya and also Shinjuku. See page 158.

Breathtaking views from Mori Tower observation deck.

BEST TEMPLES AND SHRINES

Asakusa Kannon (Senso-ji). Tokyo's most visited temple hosts dozens of annual events and festivals. See page 173.
Gokoku-ji. Off the beaten path, this magnificent 17th-century temple has survived earthquakes and fires. See page 113.
Kanda Myojin. This shrine is especially lively on Saturdays when weddings, rituals and festivals are held. See page 185.
Meiji-jingu. An amazing setting in the centre of a forest in the middle of Tokyo. Gravel paths

Statue at Gokoku-ji, one of the few surviving Edo temples.

lead to the shrine, an example of pure Shinto design. See page 137.
Tsukiji Hongan-ji. An architectural curiosity, this large and imposing temple is based on the ancient Buddhist monuments of South India. See page 203.
Yushima Tenjin. Associated with learning and wisdom, and known for its annual plum and chrysanthemum festivals. See page 184.

BEST FOR FAMILIES

Ghibli Museum, Mitaka. Fans of the animated Studio Ghibli movies will not want to miss this charming inventive complex. See page 27.

Origami Center. Learn about this fun and creative paper-folding craft at the place it was invented. See page 184.

Kiddyland. Five floors stuffed with a vast array of toys and cute characters like Hello Kitty and Pokémon.

Mega Web. Part of Odaiba's Palette Town complex; enjoy a giant Ferris wheel, the Toyota City Showcase and a car museum. See page 208.

Tokyo Disney Resort. Mickey and co. are all present at this replica theme park, which also includes the separate water-themed Disney-Sea Park. See page 211.

Tokyo Dome City. A hyperactive amusement park in the heart of the city with a giant roller-coaster, a Ferris wheel and a play area packed with toys. See page 182.

Ueno Zoo. Children will enjoy getting close to small animals in the petting zoo. See page 165.

A mind-boggling array of toys at Kiddyland.

BEST MUSEUMS AND GALLERIES

Edo-Tokyo Museum. The giant exhibition space in Ryogoku recreates Old Tokyo and documents its evolution into the modern metropolis. See page 194.

Japan Folk Crafts Museum. A beautiful wood and stone building that is home to an exemplary collection of folk crafts. See page 141.

Miraikan. Tokyo's best science museum, explaining cutting-edge technology in a way that's accessible to all ages, is appropriately located in futuristic Odaiba. See page 207.

Mori Art Museum. Superior quality art exhibitions, which change every three months or so, are mounted in this massive gallery in Roppongi Hills. See page 146.

National Museum of Modern Art. This impressive museum boasts an extensive collection of Japanese art from 1900 to the present day. See page 90.

Nezu Museum. As if the elegant collection of Japanese and Chinese arts and crafts isn't sufficient, this lovely museum also has one of Tokyo's best gardens. See page 131.

Tokyo Museum of Contemporary Art. On the east side of the Sumida River this mammoth gallery is a great place to get to grips with the contemporary art scene. See page 197.

BEST WALKS

Cat Street. A river long since filled in provides a traffic-free amble from Harajuku to Shibuya past cafés, boutiques and a few old houses. See page 133.

Imperial Palace Gardens. Cut through the heart of the city via the parkland that surrounds its enigmatic palace. See page 87.

Omotesando. Head to Tokyo's premier shopping avenue to admire its collection of modern architecture. At Christmas, the zelkova trees are also strung with twinkling lights. See page 132.

Tsukiji to Tsukudajima. This bayside stroll takes you from the frantic old market to a tiny enclave of the city that evokes the Tokyo of centuries ago. See page 201.

Yanaka's back streets. Start anywhere among the maze of narrow, winding streets that take you through one of the oldest surviving districts of Tokyo – speckled with a cemetery, temples and old houses. See page 168.

The Edo-Tokyo Museum.

Strolling along Cat Street.

Impressive changing sky of uber-elegant Venus Fort.

ONLY IN TOKYO

Cat's House. Nekobukuro in Ikebukuro's Tokyu Hands allows you quality time in a room packed with pedigree kitties. See page 111.

Design Festa Gallery. A visual explosion of colourful art in the backstreets of Harajuku that has taken over a series of old apartment blocks. See page 133.

Maid Cafés. Role-playing waitresses dress up in wacky costumes to serve besotted geeks and curious tourists in Akihabara. See page 188.

Find cats galore at the Nekobukuro Cat's House.

Meguro Parasitological Museum. A museum dedicated to those creepy body invaders; the highlight is an 8.8-metre (29ft) tapeworm removed from a human intestine. See page 157.

Oedo Onsen Monogatari. A giant, fun bathhouse complex in Odaiba, where you can soak in authentic thermal spring water. See page 208.

BEST SHOPPING

Ginza Six. Ginza Six is one of Tokyo's posh shopping emporiums with 241 shops, restaurants and even a Noh theatre in the basement. See page 106.

Isetan. Shinjuku's top-class department store is a reminder that shopping can be a pleasurable experience – it also has one of Tokyo's best food floors. See page 122.

Jusan-ya. Boxwood combs, made by successive generations of the same family since 1736. 03 3831 3238.

Tokyo Midtown. Hyper-elegant shopping complex with a great selection of luxe fashions and an interior design and homewares floor stocking great local products. See page 147.

Tokyu Hands. A fun hardware and DIY store stocked with an endless array of goods. See page 111.

Venus Fort. Designed to resemble an elegant old European city, this mall in Odaiba even has an artificial sky that changes from sunrise to sunlight. See page 209.

BEST PARKS AND GARDENS

Picnic in Yoyogi Park, a favourite with rockabilly devotees.

Hama Rikyu Detached Garden. An Edo-Period stroll garden with a saltwater tidal pond and ancient pine and cherry trees, not to mention a spectacular high-rise cityscape backdrop. See page 204.

Happo-en. Gently sloping down to an ornamental pond, this pocket of greenery is a beautiful backdrop to a famous wedding hall. See page 155.

Institute for Nature Study. This peaceful park recreates the unspoiled habitat of the Musashino Plain, long before Tokyo was built. See page 155.

Kiyosumi Garden. Famous for its extraordinarily beautiful rocks from all over Japan. See page 196.

Koishikawa Korakuen Garden. Although landscaped, the grounds of this Edo-Period green haven have a natural feel. See page 181.

Rikugien. A serene stroll garden with a teahouse, pond and wooded sections of zelkova, cherry and camphor. See page 114.

Yoyogi Park. A generous swathe of greenery popular with families and couples. See page 137.

The stark interior of St Mary's Cathedral.

BEST ARCHITECTURE

Fuji TV Building. One of Kenzo Tange's works, this TV studio and its suspended dome is one of the city's most futuristic-looking structures. See page 207.

The National Art Center. Metabolist architect Kisho Kurokawa's amazing gallery is a monumental work that plays with basic geometrical forms, its facade billowing like a giant curtain. See page 148.

Prada Aoyama. Fluid and luminous, the tinted, diamond-shaped outer panels of this store allow you to peer through the stylish interior. See page 72.

St Mary's Cathedral. This early Kenzo Tange masterpiece is covered in dazzling stainless steel to symbolise the light of Christ. See page 113.

Tokyo International Forum. An imaginative building: Rafael Vinoly's glass chrysalis seems to levitate. See page 103.

21–21 Design Sight. Tadao Ando turns concrete into elegant geometry in this angular exhibition space behind Tokyo Midtown. See page 147.

MONEY-SAVING TIPS

Cheap food and drink. Many bars have a 'happy hour' that in some cases lasts for as long as two hours. Set lunches and buffets in restaurants can be very cheap, often ¥1,000 or less. You can fill up comfortably for under ¥1,000 at dinner or lunch at local fast food joints like Yoshinoya (for *gyu-don*), Matsuya (for *teishoku* and the like) and others.

Cinema tickets. These usually cost in the region of ¥1,800, but on the first Monday of every month or on the first day of the month, cinema entrance at most establishments is ¥1,100. Every Wednesday is also 'women's day' when tickets for women are ¥1,000.

Free views. Take in sky-high panoramas of the city for free at the Tokyo Metropolitan Government Office building in West Shinjuku (see page 118) and from the top of the Yebisu Garden Place (see page 158) in Ebisu.

Grutt Pass. This ¥2,200 pass, valid for two months after being issued, provides free or discounted entry at 80 attractions, including all Tokyo's major museums; see www.rekibun. or.jp/grutto.

Shopping refunds. Some department stores and major home electronics stores offer an 8 percent discount (equivalent to the Japanese consumption tax) on purchases that cost over ¥10,000. Check at the information desk before making a purchase. You will need to show your passport.

Shibuya Crossing.

Senso-ji, Asakusa.

Jellyfish display at Aqua Park Shinagawa.

Children in Tokyo being cared for by nursery staff.

TOKYO ENIGMAS

Tokyo pulsates with an unremitting energy that stems from a tradition of constant change and reinvention. And while this sprawling metropolis is also crowded and seemingly chaotic – even ugly – many visitors find the city strangely addictive.

In submitting itself to repeated sessions of radical urban surgery and reconstruction, Tokyo's remodelled surfaces always seem fresh, managing to escape the rigor mortis that envelops many European capitals. Tokyoites are the ultimate early adaptors, their city a virtual Petri dish for testing the latest in fashion, art and technology. With its attention firmly on the here and now, Tokyo can seem like a city with a short-term memory. Tokyo novelist Masahiko Shimada expressed this preference for the present when he wrote: 'Things that happened yesterday are already covered with shifting sand. And last month's events are completely hidden. The year before is twenty metres under, and things that happened five years ago are fossils.'

Constantly mutating, Tokyo is a difficult animal to classify; a sense of artificiality and impermanence distinguishes it from all the other well-grounded, great cities of the world. Although Tokyo presents the visitor with glimpses of a mode of life that can seem both enigmatic and indecipherable, it need not be so.

The Tokyoite generation in Harajuku.

Tokyo is a city that should be walked. Seen from a train window or the upper floors of an office block, what appears to be a bland mass from afar will, on close-up, afford endless stimulation in the form of surprising oddities and sudden transitions. In this ultra-modern mishmash, street and place names have survived intact from the ancient Edo era, sustaining history and nostalgia through their literary and narrative connections, long after their visible features on the cityscape have vanished. While Tokyo's streets, awash with the gizmos and gadgets of a portable, lightweight electronic culture, crackle with static and blink with neon, there is an older side to the city visible in quiet neighbourhoods of timeworn wooden houses and the leafy compounds of ancient temples and shrines.

A jazzed-up motorbike.

TOKYOITES

Nearly 13.6 million people live within the boundaries of the modern metropolis that is Tokyo. To understand what makes them tick you need to look back to how the city developed, as well as where it's headed.

Today, 150 years after Japan's capital changed its name to Tokyo, you may still hear elderly Tokyoites born and bred in the city referring to themselves as Edo-ko – children of Edo. It's a small, but telling, sign of the pride Tokyo natives take in their city's illustrious past: Edo was the capital's name for over 400 years during which time it became the most populous and one of the most sophisticated metropolises on the planet.

A respect for history and tradition in Tokyo often comes as a surprise to visitors who are only aware of the city as a thoroughly modern metropolis in the process of perpetual change. But Tokyo wouldn't be what it is today without the events of the past and its citizens are keenly aware of that fact and seek to preserve the city's unique spirit be it in the traditional craft shops, a *shitamachi* (Tokyo's 'low city') area such as Asakusa, or the daily rituals observed in thousands of Shinto shrines across the city.

Children make use of Tokyo's public transport.

A crowded city

One thing hasn't changed about Tokyo in centuries: it remains a densely packed urban environment. Within the central 23 wards (Adachi, Arakawa, Bunkyo, Chiyoda, Chuo, Edogawa, Itabashi, Katsushika, Kita, Koto, Meguro, Minato, Nakano, Nerima, Ota, Setagaya, Shibuya, Shinagawa, Shinjuku, Suginami, Sumida, Taito and Toshima) live around 9 million people. As armies of commuters travel into work from the greater Tokyo area and suburbs in the nearby prefectures of Chiba, Kanagawa and Saitama,

Tokyo-to covers 2,187 sq km (844 sq miles). Besides the 23 central wards of the inner city, it also incorporates 26 smaller cities, five towns and eight villages.

the daytime population of the city's core swells to over 11.5 million. You only have to try and get on a train during rush hour to experience this swell of humanity. Buildings are frequently built so close together there is barely any room for sunlight to penetrate windows. And in all the main city shopping

Hygiene-conscious in Shibuya.

areas, crowds predominate: one of Tokyo's most awe-inspiring experiences is when the pedestrian traffic lights outside Shibuya Station turn green and a sea of people flows in all directions across the 'scramble' crossing.

GERM PHOBIC

The Japanese obsession with cleanliness has resulted in some interesting products on the market. Cosmetics maker Shiseido Company has isolated a substance called noneal as the source of body odour in older people. A line of shampoos, lotions and deodorants inhibits the breakdown of fatty acid in skin that creates noneal. Alongside the usual mints, convenience stores sell an array of liquid capsules and other products designed to blast garlic and beer breath, while Elizabeth Arden Japan's Lip Lip Hooray lip balm neutralises compounds that cause bad breath. All manner of surgical masks and antibacterial hand gels and wipes sell well year-round, but especially so during flu season and (for masks) when spring brings with it uncomfortably high pollen counts.

A culture of convenience

Having long lived under such pressure-cooker conditions Tokyoites have become masters of urban survival. There may be a fair amount of pushing and shoving to get on and off crowded trains but, other than that, you'll find Tokyoites almost faultlessly polite and respectful with each other. Locals seem to have an amazing ability to screen out the perpetual cacophony of noise and visual pollution assaulting them on a daily basis on every major shopping street. While the area of land given over to parks and gardens per capita is low, greenery in the form of potted plants and bonsai outside shops and homes frequently helps soften the urban landscape.

It is highly uncommon to see instances of aggression in public, and crime figures remain amazingly low for a city of such a size and density. Tokyo is one of the few cities in the world where a salaried worker can pass out drunk on the street and wake up to find his wallet intact. Temples and shrines stay open day and night without incident or loss. Even the graffiti when it happens (which is rarely) looks artful.

To further ease living, Tokyo has also developed a culture of convenience that is impressive. By and large the city still operates as the collection of independent communities it once was, each insular and self-reliant. There is no need to cross Tokyo to make a purchase as facilities are generally just around the corner. In particular you are rarely more than a few hundred metres/yards from a vending machine or round-the-clock convenience store, or *konbini* as it's known, stocking everything from hot takeout meals, magazines, deodorants and stationery to socks and prophylactics.

The Ogasawara islands are among the many distant islands falling under the control of the Tokyo Metropolitan Government. Over 1000km (620 miles) southeast of Tokyo, they are connected to the mainland only by a 25-hour ferry ride.

Population growth and decline

After a post-war population boom from 3.5 million in 1945 to more than 10 million by the mid-sixties, the population of Tokyo has grown steadily from 11 million in the 1970s to 13.9 million today, or a whopping 38 million including the wider metro area. However, Japan now has a very low birth rate and the nation is actually experiencing population decline. Despite estimates that Tokyo's population will hover at around 14 million until 2025, even this great metropolis is expected to see numbers tail off soon after. If birth rates continue as they are, government figures predict a population of around 12 million by 2050 and less than 8 million by 2100.

One group that has seen a particular increase in numbers are non-Japanese residents. Despite a slight decrease post 3/11, the total population has increased from around 300,000 to 460,000 in the last ten years. These days, Tokyo certainly feels a much more international place than it did, say, one decade ago. Not only are more non-Japanese calling Tokyo home (and many raising multicultural families), more locals spend time living abroad (particularly the young), then feed back into the city the fashions and styles they

encounter. This fascination with foreign cultures also manifests itself in a superb array of restaurants offering every cuisine under the sun from Belarusian to Vietnamese.

Don't be fooled, though, into thinking that Tokyo is anything like London or New York in terms of multicultural diversity. Figures from January 2017 show that Tokyo's expat community accounts for just 3 percent of the city's total population – the most common foreign nationalities being Chinese (199,949), Korean (90,438), Vietnamese (32,334), Filipino (32,089), Nepalese (26,157), Taiwanese (18,568), American (17,578), Indian (11,153), Myanmarese (9,719) and Thai (7,958). Even these numbers are misleading since many Chinese and Korean families have lived in the capital for generations (they just don't have Japanese passports) and to outsiders will appear fully assimilated.

A creative generation

Lack of ethnic diversity aside, you can find in Tokyo as vast range a range of personalities as in any other major metropolis. Japanese from more rural parts of the country and even other

Brightly dressed teenagers in Harajuku.

big cities, such as Osaka and Nagoya, are likely to label their cousins in the capital somewhat aloof and unfriendly, but in a city of Tokyo's size it's commonplace to find plenty of exceptions to this stereotype.

If there's one characteristic that many of Tokyo's inhabitants do share it's an ability to think creatively out of the box and embrace the new. While the ancient capital of Kyoto can be viewed as Japan's wise and sophisticated pensioner, a repository of the nation's traditional cultural values and pursuits, Tokyo lives up to its image as an attention deficit-disordered teen, feverishly chasing the latest trend. The city's crackling energy is fuelled by the highly disposable incomes of young people, many of whom still live with their parents, refusing to start families of their own. Companies are constantly engaged in creating, developing and marketing new products and services to serve these insatiable consumers – at times it can seem as if the city's prime, if not only, hobby is shopping.

Tokyo's youth are always at the cutting edge of fashion.

There's actually nothing new to this. At the height of the Edo era the city experienced a flourishing economy and artistic outpouring that was driven by the merchants and lower ranks living in the *shitamachi* (low city). You only need look at ukiyo-e prints from those times – the snapshots of their day – to see what a colourful, style-conscious place Edo was, with the geisha of Yoshiwara and the kabuki stars of Asakusa setting the tone and driving the fashions. Likewise, young Tokyoites today flick through mountains of glossy magazines and look towards Harajuku's girls and Shibuya's boys to find out what to wear and buy next.

The greying population

It is to Sugamo, though, that you should cast a glance to discern part of Tokyo's future. In this central northern area of the city is Jizo-dori, a street nicknamed *'obachan-no-Hara-juku'* (old ladies Harajuku) because of the predominance of shops catering to pensioners. By 2040, about 40 percent of the population of greater Tokyo will be aged 65 or older – a doubling of the current figure – giving rise to concern as to how welfare services will manage in the future. The bright neon lights of Tokyo's youth hotspots are not about to go out, but the city will surely adapt to accommodate a greying population.

In a few ways it already is. Tokyo failed in its bid for the 2016 Olympics, but the 10-year plan put in place as part of that campaign remains current – especially as the city was later chosen as the site of the 2020 games – one of its eight key goals is for the city to become 'an urban model for a super-ageing society'. The rebuilding of the Mitsubishi Ichigokan (see page 96) and the historic facade of Tokyo Station are also signs of a renewed respect for older elements of the capital and the need for preservation alongside regeneration.

Home sweet home

Land ownership rules in Tokyo, with coordinated town planning and green belt conservation very low on the list of priorities. As a result, small farms operate alongside factories; a neon-lit *pachinko* parlour may stand amid paddy fields. The result is a startling mish-mash of the good, the bad and the ugly, which, while never

Role-playing with light-sabres.

Ways of escape

Tokyoites are busy, active people – even those who are retired seem to have plenty of energy, gathering for trips around the city to cultural institutions or for games of gateball (a kind of croquet) in a local park. The best time to observe, interact with and really get to know the locals, then, is to join them when they are relaxing. Top of the list of favourite pursuits is a boozy night in a bar or *izakaya*, often in the company of fellow workers. Under such alcohol-fuelled circumstances normally reticent, shy people will risk their fractured English to attempt conversation with overseas visitors.

When needing a bit more TLC, some men and occasionally women will head to hostess and host bars where – for a price – they can be sure of attractive, fawning company and having their fragile egos stroked. It has been said the hosts at such bars are no different from shrinks in other countries – professionals who are paid to listen to other people's problems.

The ubiquitous pinball game of *pachinko*, another favourite pastime, can also be viewed as a psychological safety valve: the deliberately

The official retirement age in Japan is 62, but will be raised to 65 by 2025.

broadly pleasing to the eye, is full of interest and always immensely human.

A tiny apartment, be it in a private block or on a state-subsidised estate, is home to the average Tokyoite. As technology improves to cope with the very real prospects of a major earthquake in Tokyo, there continues to be an increase in the number of high-rise apartment complexes (known as mansions, or, if for the extra tall, tower mansions) sprouting across city. Around these, though, there are still many small concrete, brick and wooden houses.

While many people continue to rent homes, a growing number, especially in the inner and outer suburban areas, are buying property, grabbing the opportunity to secure loans while interest rates remain low and land prices in all but the most chic areas of Tokyo continue to decline. Victims of the recession and the decline in traditional Asian family networks of support, Tokyo's ranks of homeless people have also swelled in recent years. They are most noticeable in major rail stations (such as Shinjuku), along riverbanks and in parks like Ueno-koen where their homes made from cardboard boxes and blue tarpaulin tents are kept remarkably neat and tidy.

Tokyoites drinking in a bar.

induced sensory overload in noisy, brightly lit *pachinko* halls is hypnotic and gridlocks players into a mindless world focused purely on gambling. Similarly, you'll often find Tokyoites young and old with heads buried in thick magazines of manga escaping into imaginary worlds.

Ironically, a fantasy made real is how visitors often feel about Tokyo's extraordinary environment. What keeps the city vibrant and alive is the way in which it so richly and confidently reinterprets its own age-old norms and practice as well as imported Western ones. Fads and fashions come and go, as do buildings, businesses and people. The city is a living organism, hungry for change and renewal, and eternally in a state of flux.

MEETING PEOPLE

Japanese people typically bow on meeting each other. It's polite to follow suit, but as a foreigner you are not expected to. Younger people are typically more comfortable with handshakes than their seniors – be gentle as the grip is seldom firm.

Exchanging business cards *(meishi)* is an essential ritual if you're at a business meeting. Since you are expected to give your card to everyone you are introduced to, be sure to bring a copious number with you. If you can, have your name printed in katakana script, so non-English speakers can pronounce it more easily. It is customary to place the cards you receive on the table in front of you, rather than stuffing them away in your pocket immediately. This will also help you remember people's names and positions. It is considered rude to jot notes or scribble on these cards.

Do not be surprised if you are asked many personal questions regarding age, education, family and work. Identity and 'proper' affiliation are very important in Japan. So is dressing appropriately – if you're at any kind of formal meeting wearing a suit and tie is important. The pecking order for seating matters, too. Wait for someone to indicate where your seat is before sitting down.

Manga and anime

From Hello Kitty to the robots of *Neon Genesis Evangelion*, it's impossible to ignore the omni-present images of manga and anime characters across Tokyo.

Manga refers to drawn cartoons, be they the kind of four-panel strips found in newspapers and magazines or the telephone directory-size weekly comic books and the spin-off collections of strips in book form (known as *tankobon*), which are the equivalent of graphic novels. Anime is any animation, Japanese or foreign, for the cinema or for TV; although to non-Japanese fans, who are legion, anime means only animation that's Japanese in style.

The city is the centre of a multi-billion yen industry derived from these hand- and computer-drawn ambassadors of Japanese cool, with areas associated with these creative arts – such as Akihabara (see page 187), Ikebukuro (see page 109) and Nakano (west of Shinjuku) – all attracting armies of Japanese and overseas fans.

The Japanese are brought up on steady diet of manga and anime. Practically every organisation, from the police down, sports a cuddly cartoon mascot, and it's common to see adults reading comic books on the subway and elsewhere. The top seller is *Weekly Shonen Jump*, a magazine aimed at young male readers, which sells around 2.2 million copies per edition.

Some of Japan's biggest grossing movies are those made by Studio Ghibli, the animation studio co-established by Hayao Miyazaki who won an Oscar for his film *Spirited Away*. Miyazaki was the driving force behind the creation of the **Ghibli Museum** in Mitaka (www.ghibli-museum.jp). This beautifully designed set of galleries and exhibitions on the art of animation, to which entry is limited to 2,400 people daily with advanced tickets only, is a must-visit attraction in Western Tokyo for all anime fans.

There are manga and anime aimed at all ages, and on all kinds of subjects. But both media have developed a reputation, not entirely justified, for focussing on sexually lurid and violent topics. The word otaku is mostly used in Japan as a derogatory term for people with pathologically obsessive interests in anime and manga. To some Japanese the term conjures up images of socially awkward losers whose anime and manga obsessions are so great that they take precedent over relationships, personal grooming and hygiene. However to overseas fans, otaku has been fondly adopted as a label to be worn proudly. Many go to events such as the **Comiket** (www.comiket. co.jp/index_e.html), the world's biggest manga convention dedicated to *dojinshi*, or self-published cartoon books. Conscious of

A typical anime character.

the economic benefits of *otaku* patronage, the Japanese government have also jumped on board. Characters such as the blue robot cat Doraemon and Astro Boy have been appointed international cultural ambassadors, and the cosplaying (see page 188) maids of scores of cafés in Akihabara are touted in tourism brochures like contemporary geisha.

DECISIVE DATES

Tokugawa with 16 samurai.

Pre-Edo periods

AD 628
Senso-ji Temple is founded in the Asakusa district.

1180
First recorded use of the name Edo.

1457
Ota Dokan builds a fortified compound at Edo.

1590
Warlord Toyotomi Hideyoshi makes Edo his base.

1600
Tokugawa Ieyasu takes control after defeating rivals in Battle of Sekigahara.

Edo Period (1603–1868)

1603
Tokugawa makes Edo Japan's Capital.

1639
The system of national seclusion is introduced.

1657
The 'Furisode-no-kaji' (Long-Sleeves Fire) devastates Edo, lasting three days and killing a quarter of the city's population.

1688–1704
The cultural flowering of Edo under the influence of the Genroku era.

1703
The 47 ronin incident occurs.

1707
Mount Fuji erupts, covering Edo in a shroud of ash.

A painting of a Japanese tea garden.

Commodore Matthew Perry meeting the Imperial Commissioners in Yokohama.

1742
Floods kill about 4,000 people in Edo.

1780
Edo's population reaches 1.3 million; probably the largest city in the world at the time.

1804–29
The Bunka-Bunsei Period marks the zenith of Edo merchant culture.

1853
Commodore Perry arrives with US naval ships. Japan is forced to accept trade and diplomatic contact; the shogunate is weakened as a result.

1855
The Ansei Edo Earthquake kills over 7,000 in Edo. Floods and epidemics follow.

Meiji Period (1868–1912)

1868
Meiji Restoration returns emperor Mutsuhito to power. The last shogun Yoshinobu retires without resistance. The capital is renamed Tokyo.

1869
Yasukuni Shrine is established for Japan's war dead. Tokyo's first rickshaws appear on its streets.

Emperor Meiji.

Earthquake damage, 1923.

1872
Samurai class is abolished by imperial decree. The first train service runs from Shimbashi to Yokohama.

1874
Tokyo first adopts the use of gas lighting.

1882
Bank of Japan established in the Nihombashi district.

1883
The Rokumeikan, Tokyo's first Western-style building, is completed in Hibiya.

1889
The new constitution is promulgated.

1894
Marunouchi becomes the site of a European-style business quarter known as 'London Town'.

1895
Japan wins the First Sino-Japanese War.

1905
Japan wins the Russo-Japanese War.

1910
Japan annexes Korea.

Taisho Period (1912–26)

1912
Mutsuhito dies marking the end of the Meiji Period. He is succeeded by his mentally ill son Yoshihito.

1918
Japan is hit hard by economic chaos; rice riots occur.

1922
The Imperial Hotel, designed by Frank Lloyd Wright, opens in Hibiya.

1923
The Great Kanto Earthquake kills 140,000. Much of the city is destroyed.

1925
Completion of the Yamanote loop line.

Showa Period (1926–89)

1926
Taisho Emperor dies. Hirohito ascends the throne.

1927
Asia's first subway line opens in Tokyo, between Asakusa and Ueno.

1931
Japanese occupy Manchuria. Japan leaves League of Nations.

1936
Tokyo sees a bloody but unsuccessful military uprising, one of many in the 1930s.

1941
Japan attacks Pacific and Asian targets. Within a year, Japan occupies most of East Asia and the western Pacific.

1945
Tokyo is firebombed and atomic bombs are dropped on Hiroshima and Nagasaki. Japan surrenders. General MacArthur sets up HQ in Tokyo. Start of US Occupation.

1946
New constitution under Allied occupation forces.

1952
The San Francisco Peace Treaty settles all war-related issues; Japan is returned to sovereignty, except for some Pacific islands, including Okinawa. Japan regains its prewar industrial output.

1955
Socialist factions merge to form the Japan Socialist Party; Liberals and Democrats create the Liberal Democratic Party (LDP).

1960
The first demonstrations against the renewal of the US-Japan Security Treaty take place.

Tokyo hosted the Summer Olympics in 1964.

1964
The Summer Olympics are held in Tokyo and the bullet train begins service between Tokyo and Osaka.

1968–9
Tokyo becomes the focus of massive student unrest.

1980s
Japan's economy becomes the world's second most powerful. Banks extend loans to corporations and small companies based on over-inflated land values.

Heisei Period (1989–present)

1989
Hirohito dies; his son Akihito begins the Heisei Period.

1990
The 'economic bubble' starts to deflate, leading to Japan's worst post-war recession.

1991
Kenzo Tange-designed Tokyo Municipal Government Office (Tocho) opens.

Atomic bombs devastated Hiroshima and Nagasaki.

1993
A series of bribery scandals sees the LDP lose election. The new coalition government lasts seven months. Another coalition takes over, led by socialists.

1995
The religious cult Aum Shinrikyo releases sarin nerve gas in the subway system, killing 12 people and sending Tokyo's citizens into a sheer panic.

1996
The LDP returns to power.

1999
Shintaro Ishihara, an outspoken nationalist, is elected as Tokyo Governor.

2002
The FIFA world cup final is played in Yokohama following Japan and South Korea's co-hosting of the soccer tournament.

2003
The opening of Roppongi Hills complex heralds the reinvention of the nightlife district into a chic shopping and arts hub.

2006
Shinzo Abe takes over as prime minister, and almost immediately upsets Asian countries with revisionist comments about Japan's wartime activities.

2007
Shintaro Ishihara is re-elected as governor for a third consecutive term.

Japanese fan at the FIFA World Cup.

2008
The Fukutoshin Line, the 13th on the city's metro, goes into operation.

2009
The LDP defeated in the general election and replaced by the Democratic Party of Japan (DPJ) with Yukio Hatoyama as prime minister.

2010
Naoto Kan of the DPJ becomes Japan's fifth prime minister in as many years.

2011
The Great East Japan earthquake and tsunami in March kills more than 15,000 people in northeast Japan and triggers the Fukushima nuclear disaster. Tokyo is rocked by aftershocks throughout the year.

2012
Tokyo Skytree, the tallest structure in Japan at 643 metres (2,100ft), opens to the public.

2013
Shinzo Abe and the LDP are swept back into power in a landslide victory.

2016
Yuriko Koike becomes the first female governor of Tokyo. Emperor Akihito, in his second-ever televised address, signals his wish to abdicate.

2017
Japanese Parliament passes law allowing the emperor to abdicate.

2019
Emperor Akihito abdicates in July in favour of his son, Crown Prince Naruhito. Japan hosts the 2019 Rugby World Cup, with several matches held at the Tokyo Stadium.

2020
Tokyo hosts the Summer Olympics for the second time in history.

Tokyo Skytree is Japan's tallest structure.

Samurai warriors in Edo. 1603.

CREATING THE EASTERN CAPITAL

The rise of the great shogunates and their samurai
warlords during the Edo Period has instilled in
Japanese culture ways of thinking and behaviour
that persist even in modern Tokyo.

Travelling across the marshy Musashino Plain, future location of Tokyo, Lady Sarashina apparently failed to notice both the imposing riverside temple and the squalid fishermen's huts and nets nearby. The year was 1020 and the 12-year-old girl, her nurse and entourage were on their way to Kyoto after four years in the eastern provinces where her father had served as assistant governor. The journey, however, was not an easy one. The noblewoman recorded in her now-famous diary that the reeds growing across the plain were so high that 'the tips of our horsemen's bows were invisible'.

Four centuries later, the Musashino Plain was still a wild and desolate place. It also held the largest expanse of arable land for the grazing and exercising of warrior steeds. These auspicious natural features were among the considerations that led a minor member of the Taira clan in the 12th century to build a house and fortified compound on the central of five ridges that descended to the bay. He then renamed his family Edo, which means 'Mouth of the River'. After his death, the lands were split up and divided among his sons.

Settlement of the plain

Little was heard of the area until Ota Dokan, a vassal of the Ashikaga shoguns, decided to build a castle above the Hibiya inlet in 1457. Dokan was taking advantage of a confused political climate in which two rival representatives of the shogun in Kyoto claimed dominion over the provinces. Dokan's creation of an efficient, well-drilled conscript army, his

Toyotomi Hideyoshi, the commoner who became general.

People had lived on the Musashino Plain for over 2,000 years prior to the founding of what was to become Tokyo in 1457. From then on, while the emperor held court in Kyoto, Japan's true centre of power was based in Edo.

efforts to drain the marshes along the bay and create the area's first landfills, and his decision to charge levies on goods in transit at the mouth of the river aroused the suspicion and jealousy of his own lord, head of one of the branches of the Uesugi clan, who had his vassal murdered in 1486.

In the century that followed, the powerful Hojo family occupied the site, but they in turn lost control over it after trying to resist the overwhelming forces of the warlord and future shogun Toyotomi Hideyoshi and his powerful ally, Tokugawa Ieyasu. The latter was awarded the eight provinces of the east that included the strategic site of Edo. Despite the insalubrious marshlands that formed the coastal areas and a lack of natural spring water, Ieyasu grasped the potential of Edo. The area's position at the point where the Koshu Kaido (a road connecting Edo with the mountain province of Kai and the eastern route to Kyoto) promised a strategically positive placement.

The Shogun's fortress

Ieyasu made his formal entry into town as shogun in 1603 and wasted little time in constructing an impregnable castle on the site of Dokan's old fortifications and redesigning the city. To keep his lords militarily hobbled and in a constant shortage of funds, Ieyasu introduced

Statue of Tokugawa Ieyasu, founder of the shogun dynasty of the same name.

the *sankin kotai* (alternate residence duty) system, whereby all lords – both Inner and Outer – were obliged to spend two years in Edo before returning to their provinces. Costly processions were also made compulsory for their exits and re-entrances. Financially bled, they were less likely to raise armies of resistance. The families of these lords were also expected to live permanently in Edo in a virtual state of hostage. The security-obsessed Ieyasu took the added precaution of setting up barriers along the trunk roads into Edo, where a strict 'no

> Englishman Richard Cocks, visiting Edo in 1616, was astonished by the scale of its fortress: 'We went rowndabout the Kyngs castell or fortress, which I do hould to be much more in compass than the city of Coventry.'

women out, no guns in' rule prevailed.

Although the castle was still unfinished, labourers, merchants and craftsmen trickled into the new settlement from the provinces, eventually forming the nucleus of Edo's townspeople. Conforming to the strictly enforced division of classes, the newcomers were accommodated on reclaimed land lying between the castle and the sea. The merchants clustered around the bridge named Nihombashi and the waterways flowing into the port, while the craftsmen inhabited Kanda and Kyobashi, areas to the north and south. The system required that each trade or craft should be identified with a specific quarter, plasterers in one area, dyers, smiths and carpenters in another. In practice, however, the system of strict zoning soon broke down as more people poured into the city.

The Long-Sleeves Fire

The final blow to the original plan for segregation came in 1657 with the 'Furisode-no-kaji' (Long-Sleeves Fire), a series of conflagrations that raged for three days. When the fires eventually abated, Edo's population of 400,000 inhabitants had been slashed by a quarter.

If the speed of destruction was astonishing, so too was the successive reconstruction. Firebreaks were created, and to relieve overcrowding, the city was enlarged and temples

Wood block print of fireworks on the Sumida River in the 18th century.

and shrines removed to less populous areas. More land was reclaimed from the sea, particularly in areas to the east of the Ginza, such as Fukagawa, Tsukiji and Honjo. A bridge, Ryogokubashi, was built to connect the new areas east of the Sumida River with the main city. Despite the improvements, fire – poetically called the 'Flowers of Edo' – remained a scourge.

Between 1603 and 1868, no less than 97 major conflagrations broke out.

As the population grew, the good intentions of the town planners were soon disregarded. In the central districts of Kanda, Nihombashi and Kyobashi, open spaces disappeared as tenement huts were set up. These dwellings, occupied by labourers, tinkers, litter-bearers, itinerant

CREATING THE CITY

By the standards of the day, Edo Castle was massive, and when completed in 1636 it was the world's largest, with moats, a canal reaching into the salt flats along the bay and a conduit to transport potable water. Under Ieyasu's orders, earth was transported from the Kanda Hills to the north, and the Hibiya Inlet became the first of Edo's many landfills – a process of transformation that continues to this day.

Further landfills were made to the east, forming the *shitamachi*, or 'Low City', where the commoners, merchants, artisans, labourers, gardeners, and others who worked for the shogun and his entourage, lived. Ieyasu's trusted Dependent Lords – those who had

supported him in his campaigns – were assigned villas between the outer and inner moats; the Outer Lords – those who had taken sides against Ieyasu at the decisive Battle of Sekigahara in 1600 – were consigned land beyond the outer moats in the vicinity of present-day Kasumigaseki and Hibiya. These estates were intended not only as living quarters but also as a first line of defence on the outer edge of the city.

The Sumida River formed Edo's eastern border and along it were sited the shogunate's official rice storage warehouses. At Edo's far northeast, beyond the city limits, lived the *eta* (outcasts), Edo's lowest caste of people who carried out unclean trades such as tanning and butchery.

The approach of the American 'Black Ships' in 1853.

entertainers and clerks from the large dry-goods stores of Nihombashi, were one-storey back-street slums fronting onto alleys often less than a yard wide. Toilets and drinking water were communal.

Rise of the Edo-ko

While Edo continued its inexorable expansion, it was also beginning to create its own distinctive counterculture. A gritty, rambunctious affair, it was closer to entertainment and the life of the people than high art, although that would eventually follow.

Ryogoku Bridge was a good example of how ordinary people requisitioned space for their entertainment. Ryogoku Hirokoji, a broad fire-break leading to the bridge, was known for its outrageous concentration of freak shows, trick-sters, erotic puppets, professional storytellers and models of Dutch galleons and giants, all packed into show tents or jammed behind tea stalls. This area was also the haunt of 'silver and

The largest of Japan's three rice-growing plains, the Musashino Plain, site of present-day Tokyo, was blessed with an excellent river system and was the furthest removed from potential invasion from continental Asia.

golden cats', as the unlicensed prostitutes who staked out this area were known.

Adding to the visible pleasures of Edo were festivals; a love of potted plant fairs, cherry blossom viewing in the spring and great annual summer fireworks displays along the river. By the early 1720s, Edo had become the most populous city in the world. It had developed its own ethos and style, marked by a love of comic verse, ribald and satirical, of haiku (a Japanese verse form) and of the kabuki theatre. This increasingly mercantile society, fixated on the here and now, found in ukiyo-e – woodblock prints of the 'floating world' – the perfect art form to express the transience, the delectable beauty and sadness of existence.

Although the shogunate was generally hostile to Edo's cultural laissez-faire, and periodic crackdowns took place, the cultural life of the irrepressible Edo-ko (Edo residents) proved too resilient. When the flamboyant kabuki theatre was banished to Asakusa, a district already boasting the important Senso-ji (or Asakusa Kannon) Temple and the pleasure quarter of Yoshiwara a short distance away in the rice fields to the north, the area's position as the foremost pleasure district was assured.

The Black Ships

Powerful earthquakes in the Edo region in 1854 and 1855 killed thousands of people and were followed by torrential downpours that caused flooding to low-lying areas. There was also a cholera epidemic, famines and an unprecedented crime wave. These calamities were superstitiously blamed on the appearance of US Commodore Matthew Perry's so-called 'Black Ships'.

The coal-powered vessels *Mississippi, Plymouth, Saratoga* and *Susquehanna* had first dropped

Ukiyo-e woodblock print.

anchor in 1853 in Uraga harbour near Yokosuka at the southwestern end of Edo Bay. Perry demanded that Japan restore imperial rule and open its doors to international trade – for the previous 200 years only the Chinese and Dutch had been allowed to trade with the Japanese and then only under very strict conditions.

Six months later, Perry returned and the Kanagawa Treaty was signed, opening the ports of Shimoda and Hakodate to US trade and guaranteeing the safety of shipwrecked American sailors (previously such foreign sailors had either been imprisoned or killed). This, and another treaty in 1858 granting the US more trade concessions, effectively ended Japan's self-imposed isolation from the world.

The Meiji Restoration

The shogunate's inability to defend the country from the 'Southern Barbarians' shattered its credibility and accelerated its demise. In 1859, the first US consul, Townsend Harris, arrived and set up a mission at the temple of Zenpuku-ji in Azabu. The following year Ii Naosuke, the shogun's senior councillor and the man who had signed the treaties with the Americans, was assassinated outside Edo Castle by 17 young samurai loyal to the Emperor in Kyoto.

The shogun and his military government were so shocked by Ii's murder that they didn't formally announce his death until several months later. But it was too late for the shogun to restore his power. The feudal lords abandoned their residences in Edo and Japan moved towards civil war. The deaths of both shogun Iemochi and Emperor Komei in 1866

WEALTHY MERCHANTS

Many merchants amassed great wealth during the Edo Period and built large, impressive homes made of thick, fire-resistant mud walls covered in tiles, then stucco finished in shiny black paint. At the same time, impoverished samurai were growing more and more dependent on the merchant class to provide them with loans.

Attempting to contain the merchants, the government introduced prohibitions that were cleverly evaded. Forbidden to wear quality fabrics, the merchants lined the inner sections of rough garments in the finest silk; prevented from building homes with more than two stories, they added extra interior levels to the existing structures.

The first American Legation at Zenpukuji, 1859.

spurred on events and by 1868 a coalition of powerful families from the western and southern provinces of Japan had seized control of the capital in the name of the 15-year-old Emperor Meiji.

The last Tokugawa shogun Yoshinobu had resigned the year earlier (he lived until 1913). At the end of 1868 a formal procession led the young Emperor into Edo from Kyoto, and the Meiji Restoration thus began. The city was renamed Tokyo, or the 'Eastern Capital', and the Meiji Period, which was to last till 1912, saw Japan rapidly industrialise and prosper.

Westernisation of Tokyo

In the flurry of excitement and activity at the creation of a new capital and the abolition of the old class system, many of the physical and mental trappings of the old feudal city were swept away. Among the curious foreigners who arrived to see what it was all about was Isabella Bird. The intrepid Victorian travel writer, observed that 'it would seem an incongruity to travel to Yedo [Edo] by railway, but quite proper when the destination is Tokiyo'.

The eastern bank of the Sumida River, the home of the poorer townspeople and impoverished samurai, was the first area of the city where factories and yards were built. Housing conditions along the river and further east were deplorable and exacerbated by flooding. The river could be expected to flood on average once every three years.

A faddish interest in everything Western, from food, clothing and hairstyles, to the new European-style brick buildings that were springing up, was accompanied by the introduction of telephones, beer halls, department stores and gas lighting. New roads were constructed, and tens of thousands of rickshaws, horse-drawn buses and bicycles crowded the streets. Many working people adopted Western clothing – a welcome convenience for the office, shop and factory workers. Men abandoned their topknots, and women, in imitation of the newly enlightened empress, stopped the traditional blackening of their teeth.

Taisho Democracy

Japan's extraordinary Meiji era came to an end in 1912, with the death of the Meiji Emperor. In

Emperor Meiji presides over the first meeting of Parliament, 1890.

accordance with a tradition that stretched back over a millennium, the funeral was a Shinto rite. The hearse that passed through the hushed streets of Tokyo was drawn by five white oxen and escorted by an entourage of bowmen and banner-bearers. Sand was laid over the streets to muffle the sound of the wheels.

During the succeeding Taisho era (1912–1926), the authorities temporarily relaxed their hold on civil conduct, a reaction perhaps to the physically and morally corrupted state of its central symbol, the Emperor Yoshihito. Portrayed as a syphilitic lunatic, partial to bouts of drinking, womanising and eccentric behaviour; the

TODAI: A LIFELONG TROPHY

Britain has Oxford and Cambridge – the US Harvard and Yale. But none comes close to the near-divine status given by Japanese to the University of Tokyo, or Todai. Its graduates are virtually guaranteed excellent career opportunities in the civil service and in top Japanese corporations.

Because of the university's hallowed status – it dates back to 1877 – competition for entry to Todai and other top universities is very stiff; parents place relentless pressure on their children to study very early in life. The proliferation of *juku* (cram schools), which prepare students for compulsory school advancement tests, is testament to the extraordinary emphasis the nation places on education.

In 1992, then-prime minister Kiichi Miyazawa introduced measures to reduce Todai's over-representation in the civil service to less than half of all employees hired by government agencies. One of these measures prohibited graduates attending interviews from revealing their alma mater. Miyazawa's target was achieved in most ministries by 1996, and his efforts also resulted in a decision by several major companies not to consider the university background in hiring new graduates.

However, prejudices die hard, and today, students from the University of Tokyo, despite a reputation in some circles for having had any inventiveness and creativity drilled out of them, are still popularly portrayed as the brains behind the nation.

Ruins left by the Kanto Earthquake.

new emperor was a poor successor to his father. The brief flowering of the so-called 'Taisho Democracy' saw innovation in the arts, political dissidence and the advance of the women's movement, as well as the growth of unions.

The Great Kanto Earthquake

At precisely one minute before noon on 1 September 1923, as charcoal and wood fires and stoves were being lit for lunch, the Great Kanto Earthquake struck. The firestorm that engulfed and destroyed three-quarters of the city and the adjacent area of Yokohama claimed 140,000 lives out of a population of over two million. Aftershocks rocked the city for days and the fires raged on, creating a hellish, charred landscape. The Sumida River was dense with the corpses of victims who had tried to escape the flames by jumping into the river, only to find its waters boiling.

Once again, Tokyo began to reconstruct itself; parks and reinforced-concrete apartments were the most visible responses to the disaster. More people moved into the city, however, swelling its population and putting new demands on its transportation system. Buses and taxis began to appear, and in 1925, the Yamanote railway loop line was completed, enlarging the commuter belt and spurring the expansion of new urban subcentres like Shibuya and Shinjuku.

In the following year, the ailing Taisho Emperor passed away. With the military back at the helm and a highly acquiescent new emperor, Hirohito, generals and officers were the new arbiters of taste.

World War II

Japan's entry into the war made Tokyo the target of air raids whose intensity few could have imagined at the time. The sense of impending doom that hung over the city during the closing days and months of World War II was captured by Robert Guillain, a correspondent for *Le Monde*. Sensing the atmosphere of despair and doom in the city at the time, Guillain wrote, 'The raids had still to begin, and yet, night after night, an obsession gripped the city plunged into darkness by the blackout, an obsession that debilitated and corroded it more than even the appearance overhead of the first enemy squadrons was able to do. Tokyo was a giant village of wooden boards, and it knew it.'

Emperor Hirohito as a child.

Many of the firebombs fell on the civilian populations of Sumida-ku and other wards to the east, during the 102 raids that were launched between January 1945 and Japan's surrender in August. Robert McNamara, then captain in the US Army Air Force – whose name would later be forever linked with the Vietnam War – took part in the planning of the raids, and he recalled later that 'in a single night we burnt to death 100,000 civilians … men, women, and children.' Tens of thousands of residents of Fukagawa also perished that night beneath the fuselages of over 300 B-29s, which dropped lethal incendiary cylinders that the locals nicknamed 'Molotov flower baskets.'

Economic recovery

Reconstruction and economic growth took centre stage in the post-war years, with the US military presence continuing until 1952. By the late 1950s the city was firmly back on its feet, thriving under stable political conditions and a booming economy. The great strides forward were made evident to the world during Tokyo's successful hosting of the Olympics in 1964. However, despite Japan's phenomenal economic

progress since the war, there were growing undercurrents of social unrest that had first come to a head four years before the Olympics when hundreds of thousands of people took to the streets of Tokyo to protest the renewal of the Japan-US security treaty. Later that decade, in 1968 and 69, the city would see more unrest with waves of student protests.

The economy, however, remained the main focus. Fixed exchange rates were dropped in 1971 and, after the Plaza Agreement in 1985, which saw the creation of the Group of Five (G5) countries (US, Japan, West Germany, UK and France) – a coordinated effort to make the US dollar fall in value – the rise of the yen seemed unstoppable. This led to artificially inflated asset values, speculation fuelling the so-called 'bubble economy', and a construction frenzy the likes of which the city had never seen. The inevitable collapse in land and stock values came in 1990, leaving Japanese banks with mountains of bad debts. The 1995 sarin gas attack on the Tokyo subway by members of the doomsday cult Aum Shinrikyo added to the sense of unease that characterised Japan's 'lost decade.'

Rooftop defenders in Tokyo.

> After the Great East Japan Earthquake of March 2011, officials estimated that a 7.3-magnitude earthquake in Tokyo Bay, registering a maximum level 7 on the Japanese intensity scale, could destroy 390,000 buildings and claim 10,000 lives.

Tokyo rising

The pendulum of fortune began an upwards trajectory for Tokyo in the new millennium as the economy again picked up and a reform-minded Prime Minister Junichiro Koizumi came to power. The city successfully co-hosted the FIFA World Cup in 2002, became the focus of global interest in the 'soft power' of Japanese popular culture, and under three terms of governorship by the right-wing, yet popular Shintaro Ishihara, set about – yet again – reinventing its landscape.

The ever-present threat of earthquakes had long dissuaded Tokyo from creating Manhattan-like districts but improved

Mount Fuji can be seen behind Tokyo's impressive skyline.

Tokyo's public transport system heaves under throngs of commuters.

technological know-how now saw developers keener to reach for the skies. The results, from the towers of Roppongi Hills and Tokyo Midtown to those of Shiodome and the refurbished Marunouchi and Ginza districts, stand out in what remains, beyond its very centre, a predominantly flat city.

In 2012 these were all trumped by the Tokyo Skytree, a new communications tower and associated complex rising on the hitherto neglected east bank of the Sumida River – at 643 metres (2,100ft) it is not only the tallest structure in Japan but one of the highest in the world. If the restless remodelling of the city seems to hint at a weak preservation ethic, one must remember that change itself *is* a tradition in Japan. And that renewal is second nature for Tokyo, where almost anything seems possible.

The same principle has recently been reflected in the sporting arena, as the city underwent preparations for two mammoth sports events, the 2019 Rugby World Cup and the 2020 Summer Olympic Games. Some of the 1964-vintage classics were kept, though the old National Olympic Stadium was demolished and – eventually, after a wee bit of controversy – replaced by a new one, along with 11 other brand new sports venues.

Today's Royal Family

The Japanese monarchy is the oldest existing continuous hereditary monarchy in the world, and its head, the emperor, is the symbol of the state.

Royal mania hit a high on 9 June 1993, when tens of thousands of well-wishers turned out for a glimpse of the royal couple, Princess Masako and the heir to Japan's 2,600-year-old Chrysanthemum Throne Crown Prince Naruhito. The bubbly princess had given up a promising diplomatic career to marry Crown Prince Naruhito. Hopes, however, that she would become a 'royal diplomat' who would give a human face in the manner of European princesses to the protocol-ridden Imperial Court were quickly dashed. The initial spontaneity was smartly squashed by the notoriously protocol-ridden Imperial Household Agency, and the princess was soon seen behaving in the self-effacing tradition of female royals.

In December 2001 Masako gave birth to a girl, Princess Aiko. As the practice of crowning a female as Empress was terminated under the 1889 Meiji Constitution, which now limited the throne to male descendants, the pressure on a woman now in her forties to produce a future Emperor has been intense. Although the Agency preferred to keep imperial family problems under wraps, it had not been able to muzzle the reasons for Masako's long absence from public view. Hospitalised first in December 2003 with shingles, a stress-induced viral infection, she was also said to have suffered from a stress-induced adjustment disorder.

Masako's problems were not the first of its kind in the modern history of the court. In 1963, after a miscarriage, Empress Michiko, then Crown Princess, went into a three-month-long retreat at the Imperial villa. The first commoner to marry into the monarchy, she had to deal with hostility for the miscarriage from both the Agency and other royals. In a series of nervous disorders characteristic of royal females, the Empress lost her voice for several months in 1993 due to 'strong feelings of distress'.

The discontent built up inside the Crown Prince Naruhito over the years finally exploded at a press conference on 10 May 2004 during which he made surprisingly blunt comments in defence of his wife and hinted that members of the Imperial Household Agency were involved in repressing his wife's personality and denying her talents.

In 2006 the succession crisis was resolved after Princess Kiko, the wife of the Crown Prince's younger brother Akishino, gave birth to a male heir, Prince Hisahito, now second in line to the throne after his father.

Emperor Naruhito and Empress Masako with their daughter, Princess Aiko.

Crown Prince Naruhito ascended to the throne on 30 April 2019 after Emperor Akihito, now in his eighties, signalled his wish to step down due to health issues in 2016. In 2017, parliament passed the government-approved abdication bill; the Emperor duly abdicated in 2019 – the first abdication in Japan in 200 years – to usher in the Reiwa era.

Sake barrels at Meiji-jingu.

FESTIVALS

The Japanese sensitivity to the character and changes of the seasons is reflected in their festivals. Exuberant *mikoshi* (portable shrine) fights also indicate a willingness to embrace frivolity within the solemn.

One of the great thrills of travelling in Japan – for first-time visitors, foreign residents and Japanese alike – is running across a local festival (matsuri). Almost every day of the year a festival or other celebration takes place in Japan. Seasonal differences are the basis for almost the whole system of festivals; exceptions are observances of historic events, foundings, birthdays and the like.

Yet even the way in which events are feted may take the nature of a seasonal observance, especially if the festival is an old one.

Portable shrines

One basic element in a typical Japanese religious festival is the *mikoshi*, or portable shrine. The god-presence embodied in the *mikoshi* is carried about the village or urban neighbourhood on the shoulders of the young men of the community, although women are increasingly permitted to join, with ritual purification beforehand and much drinking of sake – or whatever other alcohol might be on hand.

A common practice is to jounce the *mikoshi* to express the exuberance of the god. In communities where nearby shrines have festivals on the same day, *mikoshi* fights are a custom. Those carrying one *mikoshi* may try to jostle their way through and 'win' over other *mikoshi* on the same road.

Japanese festivals often bear strong sexual symbolism, whether implicit or explicit. The god of a number of shrines scattered about the country is manifested as a huge phallus, which is carried about the streets at festival time – the most famous of these near Tokyo is

Shinto priests at a ceremony at Meiji-jingu.

Jibeta Matsuri held around Kanamara-jinja in Kawasaki, in April.

Oshogatsu and Obon

The two major observances of the year are Oshogatsu (New Year) and Obon, which is similar to 'All Souls' Day'. Occurring in mid-winter and mid-summer, respectively, both are celebratory occasions that bring the extended family together. Oshogatsu is a series of rituals and observances that lasts many days.

The ending of one year and the beginning of the next is a time of purification and an occasion to start afresh. Although a religious festival, the event is centred on the individual and the family, not the temple or shrine. The mood is calm, optimistic and joyful. It's a time when people catch up with friends and family, most obviously by sending out *nengajo* (New Year postcards) that always seem to be designed on Chinese zodiac motifs and on which people often print a family photo or montage of photos from the past year.

The New Year traditionally starts with a thorough cleaning of the house at the end of December – shoji screens are repapered and worn things replaced – and ends around 5 January. There are different things to do at set times during the festival – special decorations to put up and special food to prepare. The symbolism behind them hinges on the values of longevity, happiness and prosperity. As part of the latter, children receive *otoshidama* – small sums of money (usually not more than ¥5,000) given in decorated envelopes called *otoshidama-bukuro*.

January, February

New Year's Day: *Shogatsu* is a national holiday. People visit Buddhist temples and Shinto shrines to make wishes for the new

Miniature lanterns on sale, Naka-mise.

year. *Osechi-ryori* is eaten during the first few days of the year.

Water Purification Rites: 10 to 12 January at the Kanda Shrine. Young people coming of age during the year use buckets to pour freezing water over themselves and undergo other cleansing rituals.

Coming-of-Age Day: Second Monday of January is Seijin-no-Hi. Women and men aged 20 put on their best kimono and suits for an 'adulthood' ceremony at a shrine, very often followed by a night of drinking.

Votive offerings.

SHINTO IN DAILY LIFE

Shinto, the indigenous animist religion that forms the basis of many of Japan's festivals, also plays a role in the professional and daily lives of Tokyoites.

One of the most common rites is *oharai*, at which the priest waves a wand with strips of paper attached. With this a new car is blessed for accident-free driving and purification rites are held at a construction site or at the completed building. Amulets are popular purchases at shrines. *Omamori*, special talismans, are purchased to ensure good luck, or to ward off evil. Taxi drivers often have a 'traffic safety' talisman dangling from the rear-view mirror of their vehicle.

Hatsubasho: The first sumo tournament of the year goes on for two weeks in January.

Setsubun: On 3 February, this bean-throwing ceremony is held to purify the home. Beans are thrown out the windows and doors to shouts of 'Oni wa soto' (Devils, go out), followed by, 'Fuku wa uchi' (Good luck, come in). Ceremonies are held at various temples and shrines.

Plum Viewing: The most famous spot for this mid-February event is the Yushima Tenjin shrine, with its floral displays and tea ceremonies.

> On Valentine's Day (14 February), it is the custom for women to give men gifts of chocolate. The men get a chance to return the favour on White Day (14 March).

March, April

Girls' Day: On 3 March is Hina Matsuri, when *hina* dolls representing imperial court figures are displayed at home and elsewhere.

Golden Dragon Dance: 18 March in the precincts of Asakusa's Senso-ji (or Asakusa Kannon). A lively event that is repeated at 11am, 2pm and 3pm.

Cherry Blossom Viewing: From early to mid-April is Ohanami, an important spring rite. Japanese picnic, drink and sing under the pink cherry blossoms. Some famous spots are Aoyama cemetery, Chidorigafuchi Park, Sumida Park, Ueno Park and Yasukuni-jinja.

Birthday of Buddha: On 8 April is Hana Matsuri with commemorative services at temples such as Senso-ji, Zojo-ji and Hommon-ji.

Azalea Festival: 10 April to 5 May at Nezu-jinja. Hundreds of the colourful bushes planted here are in dazzling bloom.

Horseback Archery Event: Early-mid April is when *yabusame*, mounted archers in samurai costumes, storm through Sumida Park.

Golden Week: 29 April marks the first day of the Golden Week holiday period.

Meiji Shrine Spring Festival: From 29 April to 3 May (main rituals 2 to 3 May), this colourful celebration features *yabusame* (horseback archery) and other traditional displays.

Japanese carp banners.

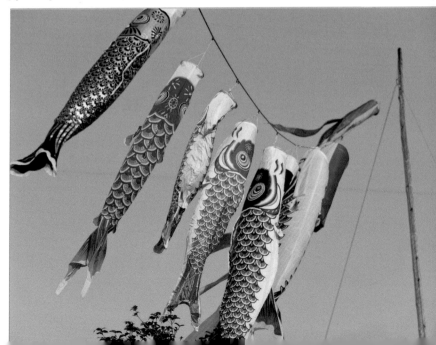

May

Children's Day: On 5 May is Kodomo-no-Hi. Though supposedly for all children, its focus is on little boys. Carp banners are flown from homes where boys reside and it is hoped they will grow up big and strong like the carp – a symbol of strength and manhood in Japan.

Summer sumo tournament: In mid-May, not summer despite the name, catch the 15-day Natsubasho at the Kokugikan in Ryogoku.

Sanja Matsuri: This important festival is one of Tokyo's 'Big Three' traditional events. On the third Saturday and Sunday, Tokyo honours the two brothers who found the image of the bodhisattva (enlightened being) Kannon in the Sumida River and were inspired to found Senso-ji. There are shrine processions, traditional dancing and music at Senso-ji Temple in Asakusa.

Kanda Matsuri: The second of Tokyo's 'Big Three' traditional matsuri. It takes place in mid-May, but only during odd-numbered years. Parades involving around 200 *mikoshi* alongside other floats and people in traditional garb start from the Kanda Myojin.

June, July

Torigoe-jinja Taisai: This night-time festival based at Torigoe-jinja falls on the second Sunday in June, is when the biggest *mikoshi* is carried through the streets of Tokyo.

Tsukiji Shishi Festival: Held in the precincts of the fish market and the neighbouring Namiyoke Inari Shrine, this several-day event is wonderfully boisterous when it culminates on 10 June. Drum performances, portable shrines, sushi-cutting displays and more.

Sanno Matsuri: Held in even-numbered years in mid-June, the third of Tokyo's big festivals culminates after a week of smaller events with a day-long parade that starts at the Hie-jinja in Akasaka.

Iris Viewing: See the irises on the grounds of Meiji-jingu Shrine or at Kiyosumi Teien in full bloom during June.

Morning Glory Fair: 6 to 8 July is Asagao Ichi, when over 100 merchants set up stalls selling flowers at Iriya Kishimojin.

Tanabata Matsuri: 7 July is the only day in the year when two legendary lovers are able to cross the Milky Way to meet. People write wishes on coloured paper and hang them on bamboo

Celebrating the arrival of cherry blossom.

A local deity is paraded around a Tokyo temple.

branches before floating them down a river the next day.

Ground Cherry Fair: From 9 to 10 July, Hozuki Ichi takes place at Senso-ji from early morning to midnight.

Sumida River Fireworks: On the last Saturday in July is Sumidagawa Hanabi Taikai – the biggest fireworks display in Tokyo. The best spots are the Komagata Bridge and between the Kototoi and Shirahige bridges.

August, September

Obon: Mid-August is a time when people return to their hometowns to clean up ancestral graves and offer prayers to departed ancestors.

Koenji Awa-Odori: In this spin-off from the centuries-old Awa-Odori festival in Tokushima, 12,000 dancers take to the streets of Koenji in Tokyo over a weekend in late August for manic dancing that goes on well into the night.

Asakusa Samba Carnival: On the last Saturday in August teams of scantily costumed samba dancers parade through the streets of Asakusa.

Autumnal Equinox Day: Shubun-no-Hi is on 22 or 23 September, a national holiday.

October, November

Chrysanthemum Viewing: Mid-October to mid-November is the time to head for Shinjuku Imperial Garden, Meiji-jingu and Asakusa-jinja shrines and Yushima Tenjin and Daien-ji temples, which are some of the best viewing places.

Shichi-Go-San: On 15 November, this ceremony (literally, 'Seven-Five-Three') has five-year-old boys and three- and seven-year-old girls taken round to visit local shrines, commonly dressed in traditional attire.

December

Gishi Sai: On 14 Dec, a service at Sengaku-ji recalls the famous 47 ronin (masterless samurai) who, on this day in 1703, avenged the death of their master and later committed suicide. They are buried at Sengaku-ji.

Hagoita Ichi: A 'battledore' fair is held at Senso-ji 17 to 19 Dec.

Joya-no-Kane: At midnight on 31 December, every temple bell throughout the country begins to toll. The bells toll 108 times to represent the 108 evil human passions. The public is allowed to join in and strike the bells at two places in Tokyo: Zojo-ji in Shiba Park and Kan'ei-ji in Ueno.

FESTIVALS AND STREET PERFORMANCES

There is always something interesting to see on Tokyo's streets, be it an elaborate religious procession or an impromptu music performance.

Something extraordinary happens to the usually decorous Japanese when they attend festivals, as the customary pro forma manners and inhibitions vanish. Matsuri (festivals) have always been integral to the life of Tokyo, and hardly a week goes by without one. More often than not linked to Shinto religious beliefs and to the honouring of local gods, they can seem more like community street parties, with plenty of food and drink to confirm the impression. If their function is to give thanks, petition the gods for favours and protection, and promote the solidarity of the community, they are also about celebrating the sheer joy of life.

The range of festivals is staggering, from the tolling of bells (108 times as the New Year arrives to atone for the old year's sins) to a more earthy event celebrating how, with the intercession of an iron phallus, a young maiden was saved from the attentions of a razor-toothed demon. The synergetic Japanese have even made Christmas, stripped of any religious meaning, their own. No sooner than the autumn leaves have begun to fall, watch out for Santas in shop windows, fairy lights strung along main streets, and Muzak arrangements of *White Christmas* belting out from cafés. For details of festivals see page 47.

A girl in a 'cosplay' outfit in the Harajuku area.

Medaman-medam street performers eyeball the crowds during a performing arts festival in Yokohama, near Tokyo.

Performer wearing the traditional mask of a fool performs an intentionally funny dance.

Attendants push a float during the Tokyo Jidai Matsuri, a festival held at Senso-ji Temple in Asakusa.

Geisha making a rare public appearance in a temple procession; they are known for their social skills and are adept at singing, dancing and playing music. In fact, the word 'geisha', means 'art person'.

LIFE ON THE STREETS

A performance of butoh in Yoyogi Park.

If a healthy street life means a healthy city, then Tokyo is brimming with vitality. The Japanese may not be exhibitionists, but they can be just as expressive as anyone else. Tokyo street life is a lively spectacle, with a varied repertoire of acrobats, magicians, parading brass bands, even fire-eaters. On weekends, Yoyogi Park (see page 137) hosts rock bands, stand-up comics and buskers singing their hearts out on everything from Elvis to J-Pop. You might even come across a performance of *butoh,* a modern dance form that, depending on your point of view, is either art, or life reduced to tortured gestures and grimaces.

A major secular addition to the city's packed schedule of annual religious street celebrations is Roppongi Art Night (www.roppongiart night.com). From dusk to dawn in late May the infamous nightlife district becomes the stage on which a spectacular series of street performances and public art exhibitions are held. The area's major galleries also stay open through the night.

Saxophonist at a Shibuya street corner.

CUISINE

Japanese cuisine is as much a sensation for the eyes as for the taste buds. Seasoning is minimal and chefs worship at the altar of freshness. The most sophisticated of meals are easy to handle as food is served in delicate portions.

Many Japanese dishes are fish based.

When it comes to number and variety of restaurants, Tokyo has no rival anywhere else on the planet – not even Paris, which, according to the hallowed Michelin Guide, it comfortably trumps in terms of outstanding places to eat. Even in simple eateries, the quality is remarkable; in the best places, it is exceptional. The degree of specialisation is impressive. A sushi shop serves only that. If you want tempura, go to a tempura restaurant. A place serving only *shabu-shabu* may sit next door to another devoted to grilled eel.

Tokyo claims many dishes as its own, from Edomae sushi to the clam-based pilaf known as Fukagawa *meshi*, but it is also a microcosm of the entire country. It is possible to sample the local specialities of any region of Japan, from Hokkaido to Okinawa, without straying past the confines of the Yamanote loop line.

Creative, cosmopolitan tastes

At the same time, Tokyo's sophisticated and cosmopolitan tastes encompass not only other Asian cuisines but also those of Europe, Africa and the Americas. Explore the traditional by all means, but sample the contemporary as well when you eat your way around Tokyo.

Eating out is not as expensive as one would expect it to be, especially with budget-priced lunch sets as low as ¥500 in places. Dinner is more expensive; budget at least ¥2,000 per head if you opt for something more than a simple *teishoku* restaurant or one dish meal. The top places are pricier and can easily go up to

---

MEAL ETIQUETTE

Good table manners – Japanese-style – go a long way. It is bad manners to wave your chopsticks around, use them to point at someone, to spear food or to pull dishes forward. Do not pass food from your chopsticks to someone else's, let alone into their mouths.

Japanese soups and noodles in broth are sipped straight from the bowl. Vigorous slurping is acceptable when eating noodles. Pour soy sauce into the dipping saucer provided, not onto your food (especially rice). It is polite to say 'itadakimasu' (lit. 'I accept') before starting to eat and 'gochisosama deshita' (lit. 'it was a banquet') after every meal.

Seaweed is used extensively in Japanese cooking.

¥10,000 per person or more depending on the type of food and drink ordered; if there is no menu posted at the entrance, look elsewhere.

It is quite possible to eat well in Tokyo without resorting to the ubiquitous fast-food chains. Neighbourhood Japanese diners may have little ambience but prices are low. Noodle shops are found everywhere. Conveyor-belt sushi shops (*kaitenzushi*) are good value and *okonomiyaki* pancakes are fun dining. If all else fails, follow the example of local students and head for convenience stores. They offer good, ready-to-eat snacks and light meals, such as *bento* (lunch boxes) and instant noodles.

If Tokyo lacks anything, it is in choices for vegetarians. A small but increasing number of restaurants, however, are catering to those who cannot afford the vegetarian delights of *shojin ryori* (traditional but expensive temple cuisine). Beyond restaurants that are exclusively vegetarian, however, menus may not always match expectations. A 'vegetarian salad' may be green, but topped with diced ham. Essentially, there are no food taboos in Japan, only preferences. People with diet restrictions may have some difficulty. Tofu and bean dishes are usually a safe bet. Check the plastic samples in restaurant windows as they are generally accurate indicators of what you will be served.

Fresh, naked flavours

The foundations of a typical Japanese meal are rice, a bowl of savoury miso soup, a small plate of *tsukemono* (pickles) and a cup of green tea. The pickles add nutrition and texture, cleanse the palate and assist the digestive process. They can be made from a wide variety of produce including cucumber, turnip, cabbage, eggplant, burdock, lotus root and ginger. Even on their own, these basic elements are enough for a square meal. Usually, however, the staple grain is accompanied or preceded by side dishes.

Unlike Western cuisines, Japanese cooking tends to focus on accentuating the inherent flavours rather than enhancing them with sauces or seasonings. Meals are most commonly based on fish, vegetables, seaweed and tofu. Eggs, meat and fowl are used in lesser quantities, while dairy foods play no part in the traditional diet.

Ingredients traditionally reflect the seasons. Every self-respecting chef tailors his menu to what is at its peak of freshness. Seafood and produce are generally at their best in spring

Be experimental with Japanese food and you'll be rewarded.

The pleasures of *kaiseki*

This celebration of the seasons finds its ultimate expression in the formal cuisine known as *kaiseki ryori*. If time and budget permit, do not pass up an opportunity to sample the exquisite and refined pleasures of such a traditional multi-course banquet. The taste and visual appeal of the dishes are heightened in a setting created to ensure perfect harmony. At the most exclusive restaurants, the dining room is decorated with calligraphy, a seasonal flower arrangement and perhaps a view of a Zen garden with ancient rocks or a pool.

Kaiseki ryori is composed of numerous small courses, some little larger than a mouthful, and each prepared using a different cooking style. They follow a prescribed order. First, a selection of appetisers (*zensai*); next, some sashimi (*nama mono*) and a clear soup (*suimono*). Then follows dishes that have been grilled (yakimono); seasoned with a thick dressing (*aemono*); simmered (*nimono*); steamed (*mushimono*); deep-fried (*agemono*); and dressed with vinegar (*su-no-mono*).

Sake – a wine like drink made from fermented rice – is served alongside the dishes but never with the final course, which consists of rice, a bowl of miso soup and a few pickles. Hot green tea is served alongside, and dessert is usually a small portion of fresh fruit.

Sushi and sashimi

The Japanese love seafood and are enthusiastic about eating it as close as possible to its natural state – either as sashimi, served as raw slices with a dip of soy sauce, usually seasoned wasabi (Japanese horseradish) or on vinegared rice, as sushi.

There are various kinds of sushi, but the best known both in Japan and abroad is the Tokyo style, known as *nigiri-sushi*. The concept of eating small patties of rice topped with cuts of raw seafood originated in the days of Edo. This variety is still also called *Edomae sushi*, because the seafood was all caught in the waters of the bay right in front of the city. Some of the best

Seafood in Japanese cooking is fresh and not disguised by rich sauces.

and autumn, while local gourmets look forward to hearty hotpots in winter and the aroma of broiled eel in midsummer.

Presentation is equally important. Plates, bowls and utensils are made of ceramic, glass, stone, wood or lacquer and are often beautifully decorated and designed. Like the ingredients, they are changed to fit the season for maximum rapport with the food.

Making noodles.

Kaiseki ryori is derived from the formal banquets served as part of the tea ceremony. More than just pleasing the taste buds and filling the stomach, it is a total aesthetic experience.

Bottles of sake for sale.

sushiya (sushi shops) are found near the central fish market in Tsukiji.

There are two approaches at a *sushiya*: either sit at the counter and choose each serving from the seafood arrayed in front of you, or sit at a table and order a mixed selection of sushi (most places offer a variety of set courses). Whichever style you try, the sushi is best washed down with sake – be that chilled in summer or heated in winter.

Good sushi demands that ingredients are of good quality and absolutely fresh. That may mean a dauntingly expensive experience. The alternative is a *kaiten-sushi* shop, where small dishes of sushi pass by on a conveyor belt along the counter, often for as little as ¥100 per plate. These are easy to find all over Tokyo. The atmosphere may lack sophistication and the fish is not from a premium cut, but the outlay will not be excessive and the quality is still good.

Warming winter dishes

One of the pleasures of visiting Japan in the cold season is the variety of hearty stews or hotpots served throughout the winter. Known as *nabe-ryori* (casserole cuisine), every area has its own distinctive variations, many of which can be found in Tokyo's speciality restaurants.

Originating from Japan's northern island of Hokkaido is *ishikari-nabe*, based on salmon and vegetables. *Hootoo*, from Yamanashi Prefecture, includes handmade noodles very similar to udon. In Ibaraki Prefecture, the specialty is *anko-nabe*, made with angler fish. *Fugu-chiri*, from Yamaguchi, in western Japan, features the white meat of the puffer fish. Tokyo's best-known home-grown nabe is *Yanagawa-nabe*, made with dojo (an eel-like loach) cooked in a savoury omelette.

A favourite among locals – and an acquired taste for visitors – is *oden*. Made with daikon, (a radish-like vegetable), potatoes, whole hard-boiled eggs, tofu and other ingredients, this hotpot is one of the standard dishes served at *yatai* street stalls and is even available at convenience stores in the winter months.

Eel, chicken and fugu

The classic dish of summer is *unagi*, broiled eel served on a bed of rice. Since Edo times, this has enjoyed a reputation for imparting energy during the hot and humid days of summer. This belief has some nutritional basis since *unagi* contains more protein than beef.

Popular year round is yakitori, skewers of chicken, often grilled over charcoal, much like the satay of Thailand and Indonesia. Almost every part of the bird is eaten, from the breast to the gizzard and heart. Gourmet versions can be had in upscale restaurants but most people prefer the ambience of the smoky street stalls (check out those under the railway tracks near Yurakucho Station or at the eating and drinking alley Omoide Yokocho in Shinjuku).

If you like a frisson of fear with your food, you will enjoy the dangerous delicacy known as fugu (puffer fish). The flesh of the fish is safe for eating, but its internal organs are so poisonous that it can only be prepared by licensed fishmongers or skilled chefs at licensed restaurants. If ingested, the toxin paralyses the

A delicious noodle-based dish.

Tempura is popular in Japan.

nervous system, eventually leading to heart failure. Once the chef has removed all the dangerous parts, along with the spiny skin, fugu is served as sashimi, sliced so thinly the pattern of the plate shows through the translucent slices. Fugu-sashimi is a great delicacy with a subtle flavour. The rest of the fish goes into a casserole that is served with a spicy dip.

Oodles of noodles

Noodles are the original Japanese fast food. Wholesome, filling, quick to prepare and even quicker to eat, they make a good light lunch or dinner. Just as often, they are eaten as a simple snack to keep energy levels up.

There are three main types: thin, greyish-brown soba noodles made with buckwheat flour; chunky udon, made from white wheat flour; and ramen, yellow noodles also made from wheat flour. Ramen is usually served with a hot savoury broth, while soba and udon are equally popular either hot or cold.

Noodle shops range from venerable establishments that have been in business for generations (Kanda Yabu Soba is the prime example) to cheap and cheerful stand-and-slurp counters on the platforms of railway stations.

Soba noodles are sure to satisfy your hunger.

soy sauce, mirin (sweet sake) and *katsuobushi* (shaved flakes of dried bonito), together with wasabi (Japanese horseradish) and thinly sliced scallions. Prepared like this, it is known as *zaru-soba*. The same noodles may also be served with lightly battered and fried tempura-style shrimp and grated daikon.

In colder weather, soba is more often eaten with a hot broth, topped with tempura, *sansai* herbs, wakame seaweed, deep-fried tofu (*kitsune*) or with a raw egg cracked into it (*tsukimi*). The classic dish, however, is *kamo-nanban*, in which the hot broth contains slices of rich duck meat and sliced leeks.

While soba is favoured more in northeast Japan, the central mountains and around Tokyo, the heartland for udon is Nagoya, Osaka and the western region. The wheat-flour noodles are a cold-weather favourite, served in a hot soy-based broth with scallions and a variety of toppings. A thinner udon, known as *hiyamugi*, is eaten chilled in summer.

The classic hot-weather noodle is the fine vermicelli known as *somen*, served chilled with strips of omelette, shrimp and green vegetables and a sesame-flavoured dip. It is a light, refreshing treat on a hot summer day.

Despite its Chinese roots, ramen has become an honorary part of the Japanese diet. It is served in a very hot broth (that can be soy, miso or pork-bone based), typically with pickled bamboo, chopped scallion and slices of *cha-shu* (roast pork). The best ramen places attract hour-long queues for what amounts to little more than five minutes of noodle slurping.

The best soba is *te-uchi*, freshly prepared and chopped by hand to order. This typically has a buckwheat content of 80 percent, with just 20 percent wheat flour to add bulk (in cheaper, mass-produced noodles, the proportions are reversed). Buckwheat is not just a nutritious source of vitamins, but also contains plenty of dietary fibre. Top-quality soba needs little seasoning. It is cooked, chilled and served on a bamboo tray, accompanied by a dip made from

GOOD SPOTS FOR FOOD HOUNDS

Whether you fancy Japanese, Chinese, French or Italian, there is never a shortage of eating options anywhere. Generally speaking, Ginza is for upscale eating; Shimbashi for raucous salarymen; Shibuya for young people; and Aoyama, Azabu and Roppongi for anyone who appreciates chic, contemporary cuisine. Akasaka has a good cross section of choices, while Shinjuku has it all, from designer bars to insalubrious dives.

Apart from noodle and *kaiten-zushi* shops, most restaurants close between lunch and dinner. English-language menus are not common, but many eateries, especially those in tourist areas, have plastic food displays in their windows or have picture menus. The restau-

rant floors of department stores usually offer a good selection of local and foreign fare.

In the evening, *izakaya* (restaurant-pubs) are a reliable source for reasonably priced local food and alcohol, and plenty of ambience. They sometimes identify themselves with a string of red lanterns hanging over the door. *Izakaya* don't do full-course meals and there is no pressure to eat quickly. Order beer, sake or *shochu* (a vodka-like spirit), and sample a few dishes such as sashimi, grilled fish, yakitori or tofu. If you want to splurge, luxury hotels like the Mandarin, Park Hyatt, Ritz Carlton and the like, all have highly rated restaurants and English-speaking staff.

Socialising in an izakaya bar.

TOKYO AFTER DARK

Evenings are when the neon-clad capital comes alive. There is much to see, hear and do, whether your taste tends towards the traditional or the new. You can catch a rousing kabuki play or dance the night away at an ultramodern club.

Tokyo's neon-spangled streets, as night descends, are an irresistible invitation to come out and play. While the older generation are enjoying a kabuki performance, the city's youth may be catching the latest hit movie or gyrating at a Shibuya hip-hop club. The variety of entertainment can be bewildering – what follows is a brief introduction. For more information check out Time Out Tokyo (www.timeout.com/tokyo), which has listings for all current events.

Commercial sex in Tokyo spells big bucks and many 'pink' businesses trade openly; however, the spread of Aids has led many establishments to close their doors to non-Japanese patrons.

Kabuki performance in Tokyo.

Traditional and modern music

Gagaku: Literally meaning 'elegant music', gagaku, is the same today as it was at least 1,500 years ago. Orchestral pieces are played on wind instruments such as the shakuhachi (bamboo flute), string instruments, gongs and drums; when singing and dancing are added it becomes known as *bugaku*. Most gagaku is based on music imported centuries ago from Korea, India, China and Southeast Asia. There are occasional outdoor performances at some shrines, or at the National Theatre.

Hogaku: This refers to Japanese music in its entirety, from *minyo* (folk songs) accompanied on the shamisen (a banjo-like instrument) to contemporary *enka* (ballads) and J-pop

– exuberant and youthful Japanese pop music. While concerts of the latter two musical forms are common, it is rare to come across more traditional music performances; one place where you can listen to live shamisen music is the Asakusa restaurant Waentei-Kikko (www.waentei-kikko.com).

Japanese theatre and dance

Noh: This minimalist theatre form has its origins in religion. Aristocratic patronage led to the development of its characteristic form from earlier temple plays. The aristocrats demanded esoteric poetry, sophisticated language and a

Checking the programme for samurai drama.

refined simplicity of movement, precisely what you see now six centuries later. It is difficult to describe *noh* – words like ethereal, inaccessible and subtle spring to mind. Fortunately, English translations are available. Catch *noh* performances at the National Noh Theatre and the Cerulean Tower Noh Theatre.

Kyogen: Many people much prefer kyogen, comic interludes designed to provide light relief between *noh* performances. Some last only 10 minutes and present amusing situations based on folk tales and Buddhist parables. Universal human foibles are represented, much like in Shakespeare.

Bunraku: This traditional art form can be traced back to the 7th century, when itinerant Chinese and Korean performers presented semi-religious puppet plays. Bunraku is adult theatre and deals with themes such as revenge and sacrifice, love and rejection, reincarnation and futility. Each major puppet is manipulated by three operators, a logistic marvel in itself. The idea is that the audience ignores the shuffling around of these silent professionals, concentrating instead on the puppets themselves, which are roughly one-third human size. The real

tour de force, though, is perhaps the narrators, the *gidayu* performers, who speak, gesture and weep from a kneeling position at stage left. The National Theatre is the best venue for bunraku.

Kabuki: Japan's most splendid theatre form is kabuki. Difficult to categorise, kabuki includes elements that are similar to opera and ballet. The word kabuki, which translates as 'song-dance skill', with no mention of theatre, in the early 16th century, also came to mean 'avant-garde' and referred to all-female performances, often of a licentious nature. The Tokugawa shogunate took exception to this and, in 1629, banned female performers. This started the all-male tradition that continues today, actresses being allowed only for certain special events.

Kabuki developed into its present form during the 17th and 18th centuries when it was theatre for the Edo masses. The main kabuki theatres are the National Theatre, the Shimbashi Embujo and the Kabuki-za theatre in Higashi-Ginza. Full programmes can span 10 hours, with generous intervals for tea drinking and socialising; it's usually possible to buy tickets for just one act of around an hour.

Butoh: This avant-garde dance form, conceived by Tatsumi Hijikata and Kazuo Ohno

Bugaku combines gagaku music with action.

Store has regular performances at the 'live house' Crocodile.

Classical concerts: Fine concert halls include Suntory Hall, Casals Hall and Orchard Hall at the Bunkamura complex in Shibuya. Next to the concert hall, Tokyo Opera City – a mammoth skyscraper and arts complex near Shinjuku – is the New National Theatre. Smaller adjoining theatres offer ballet and drama.

Pop and rock: Tokyo has long had a fevered pop and rock music scene where the stars of J-Pop, such as Hikaru Utada and Ayumi Hamazaki, can be heard alongside top international acts. Concerts take place most nights at venues ranging from the enormous Tokyo Dome and the Budokan to more intimate 'live houses' such as Club Quattro and Liquid Room, which sprinkle Tokyo's trendy youth districts.

Jazz: There are hundreds of small jazz clubs and coffee shops featuring all styles from swing to free jazz. Many performers have had great success abroad, notably saxophonist Sadao Watanabe and trumpeter Terumasa Hino. Likewise, many American jazz greats visit Japan regularly, performing at nightclubs such as the world-class Blue Note Tokyo, the Pit Inn and B-Flat. Another highlight is the annual Tokyo

> *Kabuki actors were the rock stars of feudal Japan and are still hugely respected performers today. Many of the plots of plays hail from bunraku (puppet theatre) and contained social comment and satire.*

in the early 1960s, is more popular abroad than it is in Japan. Its basic message stresses inhumanity, desperation and nihilism – a devotion not to physical beauty and harmony but ugliness and discord. The best places for viewing *butoh* are the Setagaya Public Theatre and the *butoh* company Dairakudakan's Studio Kochuten in Kichijoji.

Western influences

Western theatre and comedy: Translations of foreign plays and hit musicals imported from London or New York are very popular. Most are performed in Japanese by Japanese dancers and singers. Lyrics, however, are often sung in English. A handful of drama and comedy groups performing in English call Tokyo their home, the longest running being the Tokyo International Players. The Tokyo Comedy

A street restaurant in Shinjuku.

> Tokyo's largest clusters of love hotels – where rooms are rented for a few hours (called a 'rest' stay) or overnight – are in Kabuki-cho (Shinjuku), Maruyama-cho (Shibuya) and next to Uguisudani Station near Ueno.

Jazz Festival (www.tokyo-jazz.com) usually held at the beginning of September.

Karaoke: In the 1970s, Japan gave karaoke to the world. Even if not all the world is thankful, singing along to music videos is here to stay. Karaoke, meaning 'empty orchestra', is either masochistic or sadistic, depending on your tolerance level and on which side of the microphone you are. It is a popular stress reliever and a bonding platform for co-workers or friends. There are karaoke bars in Roppongi and other central locations offering thousands of songs in English (and other languages) targeted at English-speaking foreigners and Japanese who wish to bone up on their English.

Bars and clubs

With its liberal alcohol laws and tolerance of public drunkenness, Japan is a barfly's paradise. Innocents entering the wilds of nightlife hubs Roppongi and Shinjuku will be dazzled by the dizzying array of watering holes. The city's constantly morphing mass of bars and clubs range from the tiniest hole-in-the-wall bar to flashy see-and-be-seen mega discos. Since the 1990s dance culture explosion, Tokyo has incubated

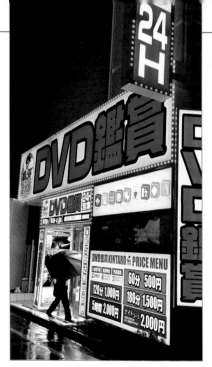

A DVD shop in the Kabukicho district.

a sophisticated club culture on par with New York and London.

Japan's answer to the corner pub is the *izakaya*, the small roll-up-your shirtsleeves restaurant-bars where Japan's army of salarymen go to unwind after work. You can always find *izakaya* near train stations, ranging from mom-and-pop affairs to chains such as Tsubohachi and Watami.

Over the last decade there has been a surge in English-Irish pubs, such as the chains The Dubliners and The Hub, with the Japanese broadening their drinking tastes from the home grown lagers of Sapporo, Kirin and Asahi to British-style beers. These establishments allow homesick tourists to quaff a pint of Bass or Guinness. For a better quality brew, there are also a steadily growing number of bars specialising in craft beers made in Japan and overseas, such as Baird Brewery's Taprooms in Harujuku and Meguro, Goodbeer Faucets in Shibuya, and Beer Club Popeye in Ryogoku.

Dozens of miniature DJ bars devoted to rock, reggae, hip-hop, techno, house, garage

THE ART OF THE GEISHA

Geisha are female performers who sing, dance, play silly games and serve sake with finesse. In Tokyo there are very few true geisha left, and that's why one has to pay a lot – cash, no credit cards – for their company. Usually they perform in exclusive private restaurants (*ryotei*), in Tokyo's *roku kagai* (six flower districts) of Akasaka, Asakusa, Kagurazaka, Mukojima, Shimbashi and Yoshicho (Nihombashi), for expense-account businessmen and politicians. There are, however, occasional chances for lesser mortals to see the geisha in their finery: at parades, such as the Sanja Matsuri in May, and at special performances of Japanese dancing, or *buyo*, at theatres including the Shimbashi Embujo.

A DJ mixes tunes at a nightclub.

and other styles provide Tokyo's spin-masters the chance to hone their technique, and patrons a venue for that most ancient of youthful preoccupations – dating and mating. Tokyo's clubs are similar in nature to its DJ bars with one difference – size. Bigger venues such as Womb and The Room in Shibuya, and Ageha in Shin-Kiba play host to top touring DJs spinning the latest sounds from Europe and the US. For hard-core clubbers, there are after-hours parties that often stretch past noon on weekends. Check out Time Out Tokyo (www.timeout.com/tokyo) to find out about events.

ALL SINGING AND DANCING TAKARAZUKA

The most accessible and unique forms of modern Japanese theatre are the plays, musicals and revues performed by the all-female theatre troupe Takarazuka. This seven-hundred strong company's first performance was back in 1914 when it was the brainchild of department store and railway mogul Ichizo Kobayashi. He had the idea that Japanese audiences might like Western-style operas and musicals, but he wanted to give his productions a local twist, so he adopted the glitz and glamour of kabuki as well as its single sex rule – only this time it would be women performing both male and female roles.

Kobayashi's vision has proved an enormous and enduring success. Thousands of young girls apply to join the Hyogo Prefecture-based troupe each year and the company's established performers are treated like superstars by armies of adoring and predominantly female fans – in fact, it's estimated that more than 90 percent of each Takarazuka audience is female. Particularly popular are the male impersonators *(otoko-yaku)* who embody an idealised, highly camp form of manly traits. The invariably over-the-top shows – anything from *West Side Story* to *The Rose of Versailles*, which is adapted from a classic manga about Marie Antoinette and has become Takarazuka's most famous production – are performed at the Takarazuka Theatre in Hibiya.

FASHION AND DESIGN

The ceaseless innovations in fashion and product
design coming out of Tokyo reflect the chaotic
diversity of the city, and the world's attention
has been caught by their potent mix of simplicity,
asymmetry and irreverence.

*Walk down Takeshita Street in Harajuku to see the
latest fashions.*

The easy co-existence of the traditional
and the contemporary in Tokyo is one
of the city's most refreshing features. The
Japanese have long demonstrated a rare syn-
cretic genius in borrowing and adapting from
their own culture and elsewhere, and then
retooling and recodifying these materials into
something uniquely Japanese.

The willingness to accommodate any number of seemingly conflicting ideas, beliefs and
styles – drawing strength, in fact, from polarities
– partly explains why it is so easy for Japanese
consumers to move on to a new development in
fashion and design so quickly, without apparent
regret or sentimental attachment to older models. A willing collusion exists between consumer
and designer, with both sides understanding
that new models are only provisional and soon
to be superseded. Durability is not the virtue
being marketed: of-the-moment perfection is.

> For a study in Tokyo's very latest (and
> invariably colourful) teen fashions, take a
> stroll along Takeshita-dori in Harajuku or
> explore the Shibuya 109 building. New
> designs come and go here in a heartbeat.

Deconstruction in fashion

It is no accident that the concept of deconstruc-
tion in fashion – the idea of effecting asymmetry while maintaining balance – was born
in Japan. Haute couture examples are seen in
a coat with no armholes; sleeves of different
lengths sewn tightly to the body; dresses with
sewn-in humps. These attempts to transcend
the logic of symmetry are echoed in other art
forms: ikebana (floral arrangement), which
rejects symmetry as unnatural, and *shodo* (calligraphy), in which the young are taught to pay
attention to the empty spaces of a page just as
readily as the inked ones.

When Rei Kawakubo's controversial catwalk
creations debuted in front of an entrenched and
sceptical European fashion establishment nearly
30 years ago, it marked more than the birth of
a new star. Faced with her success, the Western

A model at the Kimono Fashion Show.

fashion scene was forced to accept the unusual beauty of distortion in shape and cut, and the world grudgingly began to admire this new concept of beauty. Asymmetry as a viable fashion movement was born, and Tokyo gained the reputation of an innovative fashion trailblazer.

Who's who in Tokyo fashion

Ask the general public about Japanese fashion today and they will likely throw out the names of long-established Japanese couture pioneers: Yohji Yamamoto, Issey Miyake and Kawakubo (whose best known brand is Comme des Garçons). Those more *au fait* with Japan's current fashion scene will also know about Tsumori Chisato, Kosuke Tsumura and Takahashi Jun – designers who have also captured the attention of the fashion capitals of Paris, Milan, London and New York – and brands such as Undercover, Head Porter and A Bathing Ape. Outside this new fashion establishment, more daring and ever-younger designers, shops and labels are springing up.

Tokyo's grassroots designers, like those of any other fashion capital, are firmly grounded in the chaotic diversity of the metropolis. Young and streetwise brands like Factotum, Yoshio Kubo,

Visvim, Fumika Uchida and Wacko Maria are all on the radar of the city's top fashionistas.

Tokyo as fashion centre

Japan's post-war generation approached fashion from a position of cultural insecurity. For them, 'Made in Japan' labels at the time bore the stigma of poor quality and lack of style and status, while the opposite was true of American and European products. Today's fashion conscious are more knowing and multifaceted. At one end of the spectrum are Tokyoites who think nothing of blowing an entire month's salary on high-end designer goods and international labels. Among these imports, brands such as Louis Vuitton, Prada, Gucci, Fendi and Paul Smith reign supreme. At the other end of the scale, are young people who identify strongly with various fashion tribes defined by distinct looks and influences, such as the 'Gothloli' (standing for 'gothic Lolita') style mixing dark menace with an antique innocence, or the Shibuya girls who slavishly follow the bleached blonde, suntanned style of J-Pop star Ayumi Hamasaki.

Regardless of which subculture they subscribe to, Japan's young consumers are becoming ever more discerning about quality, and this is helped by relatively high disposable incomes and extensive media coverage. Twice a year, Tokyo plays host to the fashion world during the spring/summer and autumn/winter collections unveiled during the Tokyo Fashion Week (http://jfw.jp). As domestic and international fashion cognoscenti turn out to see some of the biggest names in design, these shows, organised by the Council of Fashion Designers (CFD),

---

THE KIMONO

The kimono as we know it today originated in the Edo Period (1600–1868), although descriptions of various versions of the garment can be found in classical Japanese literature that dates back more than 1,000 years. Sewn from a single piece of material, high-end kimonos are made of silk, although they also come in cotton, wool and linen fabrics. The one-size-fits-all kimono is relatively easy to make and is simply adjusted to fit a customer's measurements.

A woman cannot put on a formal kimono without assistance and must enlist the help of a professional dresser or a knowledgeable member of the family.

A woman tries out a solar-power mobile fan in a Tokyo department store.

provide an opportunity for fashion's movers and shakers to showcase their newest creations.

Viewings are not easy for the general public to gain access to, and strong connections are required for those who want to peek at Tokyo's fashion czars. Standing room is available at certain shows, which are worth attending for their glamorous atmosphere as well as the designs themselves. The collections are shown all over the city and locations are decided just before each season. Those who enjoy the trappings of the fashion world – streets teeming with models, cafés catering to sophisticated purveyors of style and a nightlife brimming with attractive, well-groomed people – will not be disappointed.

Hi-tech, hi-culture designs

Tokyo is unquestionably Japan's design mecca. Unfortunately, the popular Tokyo Design Week, once held every October, was cancelled in 2016; the de facto replacement, Designart (http://design art.jp), also held in October, hasn't been as successful, but still showcases inspirational product designs at shows, exhibitions and stylish parties all over the city.

MECHANICAL FRIENDS

Gimmicks, gadgets and gizmos, objects that are both innovative and fun have been around for a long time in Japan. Whereas Westerners tend to anthropomorphise animals, the Japanese have the habit of personalising objects, superimposing human qualities on them that promote a comfortable, almost intimate co-existence in both the workplace and at home. This fondness is evident in Japan's early spring-operated dolls.

Karakuri ningyo (mechanical dolls), first appeared in the 18th century, and were made for both pleasure and amusement as well as a design spectacle. Testifying to the excellence of Japan's mechanical technology in the 17th century was the intricate *chahakobi ningyo*, a tea-serving doll. Besides its novelty value, the fact that it was required to carry a bowl of green tea without spilling a drop, hints at the exacting mechanics involved in the doll's conception.

A happy symbiosis with tools, machines and gadgets has made the transition from dolls to life-like robots a relatively small conceptual step. The basic ideas, aesthetics and skills required to develop today's humanoid robots – creations that embody bipedal ambulation technologies unrivalled in the world – were already in place long before Honda developed its Asimo 'mechanical assistant', or Sony their popular Aibo robot.

At other times of the year it's simple enough to encounter great local product design by trawling trendy shopping complexes such as Omotesando Hills (designed by Tadao Ando) or Tokyo Midtown's floor of contemporary interior design stores. A preview of the latest concepts in electronic goods is available at the showcases for Sony in Ginza and Panasonic in Odaiba. Also not to be missed is Tokyu Hands, a department store with branches across Tokyo (the best two in are Shinjuku and Shibuya) that specialises in providing the raw materials for a million and one design projects – anything from making your own clothes to your own house!

Insatiable quest for the new

The average Tokyo home stocks a continuous series of replaceable products. 'Big Garbage' day, a pre-arranged time for the disposal of furniture and appliances, provides trash pickers with a veritable treasure trove of functioning electronics and interior goods as households chuck out the old to make room for the new.

Industrial design in Tokyo can be shoeboxed into four categories: miniaturisation, the element of fun, disposability and minimalism. Miniaturisation is most evident in the world of technology. Japan has long been praised for its ability to make Western ideas better, faster and ever smaller. While such products spread quite easily around the world these days, triumphs of Japanese miniaturisation have included Sony's famed Walkman, and Nintendo's classic hand-held video games.

Fun with product design can be seen in items such as shocking pink vacuum cleaners or ironing boards encrusted with plastic jewels and glitter; mundane household products transformed by urban fantasy.

Minimalism versus clutter

Perhaps one of the biggest paradoxes in Japanese design is its association, in the Western mind, with minimalism. The austere sparseness of the tatami room is increasingly confined to temples, traditional ryokan, minshuku hotels and the imaginations of tourists. In their daily lives, most Japanese cannot afford the luxury of empty space.

In Tokyo, where rent is often astronomical, small homes are filled to bursting with clothes, toys and collections of *mono* (objects) that reflect a hectic and fast-paced city life. In his highly recommended photo book, *Tokyo Style*, Kyoichi Tsuzuki brilliantly demonstrates the character of the modern Tokyo dwelling.

One often gets the feeling that whether stripped down to the elemental beauty of its ancient aesthetics or dressed up in the gaudy glow of its crowded entertainment districts, Japan's capital city is searching and finding, then searching again, for the design ideal.

Imported brand Louis Vuitton.

ARCHITECTURE

Tokyo's skyline is like a drawing on an immense whiteboard that can suddenly be erased and replaced by something completely different. The city's astonishing penchant for rebuilding is reflected by its mishmash of architectural styles.

Contrasting architectural styles in Tokyo.

If Tokyo ever possessed a blueprint showing everything in its ordained place, it has vanished without a trace in the face of countless natural disasters that have been visited upon the city with an almost Old Testament wrath.

There are historical antecedents, though, to suggest that the erasing of the past is not altogether involuntary. Long before Nara, Kamakura, Kyoto and, finally, Tokyo became permanent seats of power, it was the custom to demolish entire capitals with the enthronement of a new emperor. Today, economic imperatives rather than ritual purity are the catalysts for pulling down buildings. Japanese architecture has always – and to a far greater extent than elsewhere in the world – been linked to the fluctuations of the economy and the progress of technology. This has led to intense periods of creative activity followed by the abrupt shelving, in some cases, of entire projects.

An urban laboratory

Tokyo is a permanently unfinished cityscape driven as much by pragmatism as human needs. Deprived of the cosy illusion that anything could ever be permanent, Tokyoites have voiced little objection to seeing their city transformed into the world's foremost urban laboratory. With Tokyo's sights firmly set on 'the now and the next', there is little compulsion to dwell on the past: a condition ideal for aspiring architects eager to make their mark.

The problem of how futuristic buildings can be adapted to an existing, older urban landscape is resolved by simply ignoring altogether the aesthetics of coordination. New structures are inserted into the body of the city as if they were random but coincidentally harmonious pieces in a giant jigsaw puzzle, the result being a constantly surprising patchwork.

The organic labyrinth

The city's original 17th-century master plan comprised a series of concentric rings radiating from Edo castle, which combined the interests and needs of defence, commerce and geomancy. Only the faintest traces of this grid remain under the modern mire of spontaneous urban expansion.

Watanabe Hitoshi's 1932 Wako Building.

Organic growth has replaced the civic model in a city where plots of land generally take precedence over streets. Any transport infrastructure linking these sites had to be superimposed on the existing mass, in the form of elevated or buried expressways, train and subway lines. The result is a layered complexity that seems to obey organic rather than structural codes.

Japanese architects

Tokyo's early Meiji- and Taisho-period architects were strongly influenced by Western models and by the European architects and

Monorail tracks in Tokyo.

teachers such as Josiah Conder – he designed Nikolai Cathedral and the rebuilt Mitsubishi Ichigokan – and Conder's student Tatsuno Kingo, responsible for the grand redbrick Tokyo Station, which was renovated in 2012. The Showa Period saw more experimentation: Watanabe Hitoshi's 1932 Wako Building on one corner of Ginza Crossing is a good example. Architect Ito Chuta turned to Asian culture for the inspiration for his Tsukiji Hongan-ji in Tsukiji, and to ancient Shinto forms for Meiji-jingu in Harajuku. Contemporary architects, such as the world-famous master Tadao Ando, have their own unfettered vision. Ando's Collezione building in Omotesando is a prime example.

Beyond their obvious functional purposes, the more experimental of Tokyo's buildings are design catalysts that can also be read as discourses on aesthetics and the role of modern architecture. The Aoyama Technical College in Shibuya, designed by Makoto Sei Watanabe, is, for example, a bizarre yet compelling construction of a sci-fi-like montage of poles, lightning rods, water tanks and posts that creep almost organically over the building's surfaces. Other Shibuya constructions, such as the Bunkamura, Shibuya Beam and the Hikarie Building all seem somewhat tame by comparison.

One of Kenzo Tange's final additions to the Tokyo skyline was the headquarters for the

Fuji-Sankei Communications Group, better known as Fuji TV Building, in Odaiba. Its 'corridors in the sky' – connecting walkways that link the two main towers – and a titanium-panelled silver sphere positioned in between, give the impression of a building resembling a widescreen TV. This is no coincidence, as the building houses both Nippon Broadcasting and Fuji Television.

Foreign architects

Flexible building regulations and the vision of developers combined with deep financial pockets have encouraged many foreign architects to work in Japan. Rafael Vinoly's majestic Tokyo International Forum, for example, is a premier culture convention centre in Yurakucho. Comprising four graduated cubes, encased in granite, abutting a high, tapering trajectory of glass and steel, it is aptly named 'Glass Hall'.

The striking Prada fashion boutique in Aoyama also generates a new architectural experience. Origami-like surfaces and vertical planes form an exoskeleton where there is no separation between the structure itself, its surface and the interior space. The drama of the building is most evident at night, when the glass skin, latticed frame and interior lighting turn the whole building transparent.

Kenzo Tange's Fuji TV Building in Odaiba.

Kenzo Tange's Yoyogi National Stadium.

Philippe Starck's distinctive design touch is evident at Super Dry Hall in Asakusa, with its giant rooftop sculpture, officially called Flamme d'Or, but which looks like a giant golden blob of toothpaste, or worse – some locals refer to the structure as 'unchi biru' (turd building). In contrast, Sir Norman Foster found inspiration in the design of the torii (shrine gate) for his Century Tower near Ochanomizu – *ten torii* appear to be piled on top of each other on the building's facade.

NEW MILLENNIUM DESIGNS

Tokyo embraced the new millennium and its architectural possibilities without so much as a moment's hesitation. Highlights from the first decade of the century include **National Art Centre**, Kisho Kurokawa's glass facade inspired by cliffs and seashores; **Prada Aoyama**, which dazzles like a greenish yellow spacecraft at night; **Mikimoto Ginza 2**, Toyo Ito's design inspired by jewel boxes, which glitters through randomly positioned, cell-like windows; and Tadao Ando's **21_21 Design Sight**, whose plunging triangular rooftops look like wing tips balanced on sheets of glass; and most obvious of all, the towering **Tokyo Skytree**, which soars 634 meters (2,080ft) above Tokyo's east end.

Some foreign architects have become so enamoured of Tokyo and its design possibilities that they have relocated here, including British architect Benjamin Warner whose glass Audi Forum looks like a giant iceberg that just happened to float down Meiji-dori. Fellow Brit Mark Dytham, and Astrid Klein from Germany are also longtime Tokyo transplants whose practice Klein Dytham created Uniqlo's flagship store in Ginza.

A sci-fi city

Contrasting with Tokyo's techno-aided verticality is a counter-tendency to burrow deeper into the earth's surface. Tokyo already has a considerable underground life. In addition to the world's largest subway system, which is still vigorously expanding, miles of subterranean corridors connect train lines and concourses with countless underground shopping malls. Tokyo Electric Co. has operated a power station under a Buddhist temple for decades; and an Asahi television studio, built 20 metres (66ft) below ground in Roppongi, operates a simulated downpour behind the announcers when it rains above ground.

In William Gibson's sci-fi novel, *Idoru*, skyscrapers in Shinjuku are hatched from an organic building substance that seems 'to ripple, to crawl slightly... a movement like osmosis or the sequential contraction of some sea creature's palps.' This is not as far-fetched as it sounds. Tokyo, with its natural propensity to shed old skins, has become ideal place to test new building materials and concepts. Witness Chanel's store in Ginza, its entire facade composed of hundreds of thousands of computer controlled LEDs; or the nearby Uniqlo flagship building, whose facade is also made up of a matrix of illuminated cells, whose luminosity can be individually controlled to produce different patterns. However, the sci-fi effect is perhaps best appreciated from an arena which uses only glass for visual impact – the fantastic atelier gallery atop Ginza's Hermès store.

Perpetual change

Japanese contractors, particularly the big five – Kajima, Takenaka, Taisei, Obayashi and Shimizu – have played a key role in transforming Tokyo's appearance. The design and construction management within these companies work closely with their own cutting-edge research laboratories.

21_21 Design Sight near Tokyo Midtown.

With their immense financial resources, these companies have been called 'the richest powerhouses of advanced technology in the world.'

Where building values are only one-tenth the asset value of the land, it is hardly surprising that the urban building stock undergoes constant change. The downside, of course, is a city with no memory, or at best, an inaccuracy-prone collective memory.

As with the structures in Italo Calvino's novel, *Invisible Cities* – a spider-web of 'ropes and chains and catwalks suspended in the air' – Tokyo knows that its edifices are not built to last. As a highly corporeal, perpetually embryonic city, it is ideally suited, however, to a transition in which, from its monuments to its lean-to shacks, the mortality of its structures is keenly sensed.

KENZO TANGE'S VISION

No other architect has left his mark on Tokyo more than Kenzo Tange (1913–2005). His style is writ large across the city, not only in his signature Yoyogi National Stadium, where the 1964 Olympic Games were held, or the controversial Tocho building in Shinjuku, but also in such projects as St Mary's Cathedral in Mejirodai, the Aoyama's United Nations University and the 1996 Fuji TV Building in Odaiba. Tange's ambitious 1960 proposal to impose a vast grid system on Tokyo was never implemented, however.

The company he founded is responsible for one of the most striking additions to Tokyo's skyline: Mode Gakuen Cocoon Tower, a 50-story college building in Shinjuku.

THE ART OF LANDSCAPING

Compact, organised and highly introspective: words which stereotypically describe the Japanese might just as well be applied to their gardens.

As a fully developed art, gardening in Japan can be traced to its introduction from China and Korea during the 6th century. The balance between nature and man-made beauty, with water and mountain as prototypical images, are the principles that form the basis for the traditional Japanese garden.

Artfully blended with ponds, gurgling brooks, banks of irises and moss-covered rocks, carefully contrived Japanese gardens are objects of quiet contemplation. 'In order to comprehend the beauty of a Japanese garden,' the 19th-century writer Lafcadio Hearn wrote, 'it is necessary to understand – or at least to learn to understand – the beauty of stones.' This is especially true of Japanese Zen gardens. Essentially, there are three types: stroll, pond and so-called flat gardens. The dry-landscape garden, the *karesansui*, is the best example of the latter Zen-style garden.

The idea of confined space combined with the Zen idea of discovering limitless dimensions in the infinitely small saw the creation of the *kansho-niwa*, or 'contemplation garden,' created as both tools for meditation and works of art. Carefully framed like a scroll, they are intended to be appreciated like a painting that changes with the seasons and the quality of light.

Traditional Japanese gardens often feature serene ponds containing koi fish.

Vermilion-painted arched bridges are a traditional feature of Japanese gardens and suggest a link between heaven and earth. One of the most famous red bridges is Nikko's Shin-kyo.

Originally used to light the way to temples and shrines, stone lanterns are now a popular and characteristic feature of Japanese gardens.

Tidal waters fill the three ponds at Hamarikyu Gardens beside Tokyo Bay. A wisteria-covered trellis, a teahouse, peony and cosmos fields, and a plum tree grove are other features of the garden.

A carved stone basin filled with water is used by tea ceremony guests to cleanse themselves before entering through the garden to the teahouse.

BLUE-BLOODED BLOOMS

A chrysanthemum bloom.

In Japan, the cultivation of exhibition chrysanthemums is considered an art form. *Kiku* (chrysanthemums) were first introduced from China in the late 7th century, though legend has it that the first flowers materialised from the necklace of Izanagi, the legendary father of the gods. Heian courtiers were known to drink *sake* tinted with the flower petals in the 9th century.

In the 13th century, the 16-petal chrysanthemum was adopted as a symbol of the Imperial household, and used as design motifs for clothing, on sword blades, banners and on official documents.

Blooming late in the year, the flower is a symbol of longevity. In November, many of Tokyo's gardens and temple grounds become venues for the Kiku Matsuri (Chrysanthemum Festival). *Kiku-ningyo*, life-size dolls representing court ladies and historical figures, are fashioned out of the chrysanthemums. Connoisseurs of the flower look for uniformity, enhanced by subtle differences; colours should be lively but not vulgar.

Raked stones at the Raikyu-ji Zen Garden.

The 54th-floor observation deck at Mori Tower in Roppongi.

Tokyo's skyline at sunrise.

Koishkawa Botanical Gardens.

Boat trips take in the cherry blossom.

INTRODUCTION

A detailed guide to Tokyo and its surroundings with principal sights numbered and clearly cross-referenced to maps.

For all its modernity, Tokyo is a city steeped in the past. In its backstreets and in the crevices between its post-modernist architecture and elevated expressways lie hundreds of temples, shrines, stone steles, Buddha images and statues. Parts of Tokyo – its formal gardens, remnants of old Edo Period estates, teahouses, restaurants and craft shops run by generations of the same family, and schools dedicated to the traditional arts – are easily sought-out time capsules. At first glance, the world's largest city resembles a formless, oversized suburb. Closer examination, however, reveals concentrated patterns and order to the chaos.

The sprawling, lit-up city of Tokyo by night.

For administration purposes, the centre of the city is made up of 23 special wards, or *ku*, which are segmented into districts that are sub-divided into numbered sections called *chome*. Individual buildings, blocks and mini-zones that fall within their parameters are numbered separately (see page 233). Combining with the 23 *ku* to form *Tokyo-to* (Tokyo Metropolis) are another 39 municipalities west of the centre and two island chains to the south.

Prayer cards at Gokoku-ji Temple.

Good maps are an essential part of Tokyo life. Only important streets, the city's main thoroughfares, have names. Addresses are seldom written in English. Adding to the confusion is the fact that buildings are usually assigned numbers according to when they are built; numbers are therefore often unsequenced. Smartphones are the usual modern-day solution, and are a (predictably) useful tool for navigating addresses here.

Tokyo has an extensive bus network, but its routes are often convoluted or plagued by traffic congestion. By far the easiest way around the city is to use the underground Tokyo subway (made up of nine Tokyo Metro and four Toei Subway-run lines) and the overground Japan Railways (JR) trains such as the Chuo, Keihin Tohoku, Sobu and Yamanote lines. This last route takes roughly an hour to complete a full loop around the inner city, with almost all the main sights, as well as Tokyo's major hotels and nightlife spots, located inside or near one of its 30 stops. Tokyo's 13 subway lines intersect at all but a few of the stations on the Yamanote Line. Helpful maps can be found inside stations or at their exits.

ADACHI-KU

Senjubashi
Minamisenju
Minamisenju
Minamiwakabacho
Arakawawanichome
Arakawakuyakushomae

TAITO-KU

Machiya
Machiya
Machiyanichome
Mikawashima
Nishi-Nippori
Shimmika-washima
Minowa
Iriya
Kototoi-dōri
Asakusa
Asakusa Kannon/ Senso-ji ★
Asahibro Honsha (Super Dry Hall)

SUMIDA-KU

Kiyosumi
Kiyosumi-dōri
Kokugikan (National Sumo Stadium) ★
Kotobuki
Ryōgoku
Expressway No 7
Kinshicho

Ogubashi-dōri
Nippori
Nishi-Nippori
Tabata
Sendagi
Nezu
Uguisudani
Ueno
Inarichō
Tawaramachi
Kuramae
Asakusabashi
Higashinihombashi

Sugano
Komagome
Tōdai-mae
Yushima
Yushima
Hongō-sanchōme
Suehirochō
Okachimachi
Takaokachimachi
Kodemmacho
Ryōgoku

Tokyo Kokuritsu Hakubutsukan (Tokyo National Museum)
UENO-KŌEN
Ueno
YANAKA REIEN

BUNKYO-KU

Tokyo Daigaku (Tokyo University)
Nezu
Yushima
Kasuga
Suidōbashi
Suidōbashi
Akihabara
Iwamotochō
Bakurochō
Bakuro-Yokoyama
Ningyōchō

Nishigaharayonchōme
Nishikoshinzuka
Sugamoshinden
Shinkoshinzuka
Kōshinzuka
Sugamo
KYU-HAKUSAN-EN
RIKUGI-EN
KOISHIKAWA-SHOKUBUTSUEN
Kōrakuen
Tokyo Dome (Tokyo Dome City)
Sotobori-dōri
Kōbinata
Myōgadani
Iidabashi
Suidōbashi
Ochanomizu
Awajichō
Kanda
Ochanomizu
Ogawamachi
Jimbōchō
Kudanshita
Kanda
Ochanomizu

KŌKYO-HIGASHI-GYOEN
KŌKYO (Imperial Palace)
Kōkyomae-Hiroba
Uchibori-dōri
Tokyo
Kyōbashi
Yūrakuchō

CHIYODA-KU

Yasukuni-jinja ★
Iidabashi
Ichigaya
Ishigome
Kagurazaka
Ushigome-Kagurazaka
Ushigome-Yanaginochō
Ichigaya
Kojimachi
Hanzōmon
Sōmei Reien

Ōtsuka
Shin-ōtsuka
Higashi-Ikebukuro
Higashi-Ikebukuro
ZŌSHIGAYA REIEN
Gokoku-ji ★
Gokokuji
Kishibojinmae
Expressway No 5
Edogawabashi
Waseda
Kanda
Ushigome-Yamagichō
Akebonobashi
Yotsuya-sanchōme

TOSHIMA-KU

Mukōhara
Zōshigaya
Zōshigaya
Kishibojinmae
Gakushuinshita
Waseda
Kanda
Wakamatsu
Nishi Waseda
Yotsuya

KITA-KU

Kanamechō
Senkawa
Kawagoe-kaidō
Kitaikebukuro
Ikebukuro
Ikebukuro
Yamate-dōri
Shin-ōme-kaidō
Zōshigaya
Zōshigaya
Mejiro
Takadanobaba
Takadanobaba
Meijiro-dōri
Higashinagasaki
Shiinamachi

SHINJUKU-KU

Omokagebashi
Nishi Waseda
Higashi-shinjuku
Shinjuku-gyoemmae
Shinjuku-sanchōme
Shinanomachi
Sendagaya
Yoyogi

SHINJUKU GYOEN

Geihin-kan (Akasaka Detached Palace)
Toyokawa Inari-jinja ★
Aoyama-dōri
Aoyama-itchōme
Gaienmae
Aoyama

Seitoku Kinen Kaigakan (Meiji Memorial Picture Gallery) ★
Meiji-dōri

Nishi-Ōkubo
Shin-Ōkubo
Seibu-Shinjuku
Shinjuku
Shinjuku
Shinjuku-sanchōme
Yoyogi

Shimotakaidō
Higashi-Kitazawa
Meijiro-dōri

Takadanobaba
Shimo-Ochiai
Nakai
Ochiai
Higashinakano
Ōkubo
Nishi-shinjuku
Nishi-shinjuku
Tochōmae
Tokyo Tocho (Tokyo Metropolitan Government Building) ★
Shinjuku
Shinjuku
Minami-Shinjuku
Sangūbashi
Ōme-kaidō
Hatsudai
Hatsudai
Expressway No 4
Kita-sandō
MEIJI-JINGŪ (INNER GARDEN)
Sangūbashi
ate-dōri

The elegant Niju stone bridge at the Imperial Palace.

IMPERIAL PALACE, MARUNOUCHI AND NIHOMBASHI

Little is left of the once formidable imperial compound, but its grounds offer leisurely exploration in the heart of Tokyo. Here too are the city's main business districts of Marunouchi and Nihombashi, interspersed with fine museums and glitzy shops.

At the historic and topo-graphic core of a city strug-gling to accommodate 13.9 million people, lies, quite unexpect-edly, a sublimely empty space – the grounds of the Imperial Palace, home to the Japanese Emperor and his family, the world's long-est unbroken line of monarchs. This once impregnable compound occupies a 110-hectare (280-acre) expanse of green – its innermost folds the habitat of rabbits and pheasants, its outer ring of moats and bridges the home of turtles, carp and gliding swans.

This idyll of meticulously con-trolled ecology is deceptive. The pal-ace, sitting at the centre of a district that also includes the National Diet Building (see page 94), a num-ber of key ministries, the Supreme Court and the Metropolitan Police Quarters, remains a fortified citadel at the core of establishment Japan, nourishing as it has always done the centres of power. Very little remains of Ieyasu's fortress. However you can get a very good impression of the medina-like ground plan for his cas-tle and the city that grew around it by exploring the concourse of moats, interconnecting canals and defensive gates that still exist.

Policemen in the palace grounds.

THE IMPERIAL PALACE AND SURROUNDINGS

There are several entrances to the outer grounds of the palace which are open throughout the year: a popular approach is to head directly west from Tokyo Station along broad Gyoko-dori towards the east section of the inner defensive canal known as the Babasaki Moat (Babasaki-bori).

Wadakura Fountain Park

Address: Kyokyo-Gaien, Chiyoda-ku
Entrance Fee: free

Main Attractions
Niju Bridge
Imperial Palace East Garden
National Museum of Modern Art
Science Museum
Yasukuni Shrine
Hibiya Park
Tokyo Station
Kite Museum
National Film Archive of Japan

Map
Page 88

Transport: Tokyo or Otemachi

Crossing the Babasaki Moat, you'll pass the pretty **Wadakura Fountain Park ❶** (Wadakura Funsui Koen), built to celebrate the royal wedding of the Emperor and Empress in 1961 and refurbished on the occasion of their son's marriage in 1995; inside is a restaurant/café that's often used for weddings.

Further on are the gravel paths of the broad **Imperial Palace Plaza** (Kokyo-mae Hiroba) planted with some 2,000 Japanese black pine trees and lawns in 1899, and split from the inner palace grounds by another ring of moats. Across the water in the plaza's southwest corner leaps the **Niju Bridge ❷** (Niju-bashi), a two-tiered construction referred to as the 'Double Bridge'. Framed by willow trees, and the water that flows beneath it, stocked with orange carp and gliding swans, this is one of the most photographed of Tokyo's sights. The image is completed by massive stone ramparts and the graceful outline of the 17th-century **Fushimi Tower** (Fushimi Yagura), one of the few remaining original buildings in the complex.

The only times the general public are allowed beyond the bridge, further into the palace's inner grounds, are on 23 December (the emperor's birthday) and 2 January, when the Emperor and other key members of the Imperial family, standing on a balcony in front of the main palace building, wave to thousands of well-wishers. Tourists, however, can sign up for a free place on one of the two official daily tours into the inner sanctum – see www.kunaicho.go.jp for details.

On the tour you see that the current **Imperial Palace ❸** (Kokyo) is a 1968 ferro-concrete structure that embodies several traditional Japanese design elements – the exterior is all you will get to see of this state reception building that replaced older buildings damaged by fire in 1945. Separate from it are the offices of the **Imperial Household Agency** (Kunaicho), a body which exercises a very strict (some might say sinister) hand over everything to do with the royal family, from their personal appearances and conduct to press releases.

The grounds of the Imperial Palace.

A protective moat surrounds the grounds of the Imperial Palace.

The Imperial Palace jogging route is one of the most popular for runners in Tokyo. Start and finish a loop around the palace grounds at Sakurada-mon for a 5km run uninterrupted by traffic lights or crossings.

Manicured grounds of the Imperial Palace East Garden.

Ote Gate

In its heyday, the **Ote Gate** ❹ (Ote-mon) was the main entrance to Edo Castle. The present gate is an impressive 1967 replica of the original, which was destroyed by a bomb towards the end of World War II. Just inside the Ote-mon is the **Museum of the Imperial Collections** ❺ (Sannomaru Shozokan; www.kunai-cho.go.jp/e-event/sannomaru02.html; Tue–Thu and Sat–Sun Mar–mid-Apr and Sept–Oct 9am–4.15pm, mid-Apr–Aug until 4.45pm, Nov–Feb until 3.45pm; free), which displays a tiny fraction of the collection of 6,000 pieces of Japanese art owned by the Imperial family.

Imperial Palace East Garden

Ote Gate is one of three entrances to the **Imperial Palace East Garden** ❻ (Kokyo Higashi Gyoen; www.kuna-icho.go.jp/e-event/higashigyoen02.html; Tue–Thu and Sat–Sun Mar–mid-Apr and Sept–Oct 9am–4.30pm, mid-Apr–Aug until 5pm, Nov–Feb until 4pm; free), an immaculately kept ornamental Japanese garden replete with a pond, stone lanterns, a miniature waterfall, bridges and an authentic tea pavilion. The garden

was the site of Edo's original five-tiered keep, which burnt down in 1657. Only the keep's sturdy stone base survives but it's worth climbing to get a view of the surroundings including the mosaic-decorated **Peach Blossom Music Hall** (Toka Gagudo), built in celebration of the Empress Kojun's 60th birthday in 1963. One original feature of the old fortress is the **Shiomizaka** (or 'Tide-Viewing Slope') that once offered views of Tokyo Bay and Mount Fuji. Today's main prospect looks onto the business districts of Nihombashi and Otemachi.

Kitahane-bashi Gate (Kitahane-bashi-mon) ❼, the northern passage-way out of the Imperial Palace East Garden, leads into a central, stone-walled square and yet another gate, wickedly angled to ensnare any assailant who might be foolish enough to approach the castle.

National Museum of Modern Art

Address: 3-1 Kitanomaru Koen, Chiyoda-ku; www.momat.go.jp
Tel: 03-5777 8600
Opening Hours: Tue–Thu and Sun 10am–5pm, Fri and Sat until 8pm

Entrance Fee: charge
Transport: Takebashi

The lush and extensive grounds of **Kitanomaru Park** (Kitanomaru Koen; daily 24 hours; free), with trails through dense woodland, is home to several important cultural institutions including, on its southern edge the **National Museum of Modern Art ❽** (Kokuritsu Kindai Bijutsukan), which displays contemporary Japanese art from the Meiji Period to the present day. The 3,000 or more pieces in the collection, which also includes work by Western artists, are exhibited in rotation. Look for works by key Japanese artists here including Kishida Ryusei, Fujita Tsuguhara and Yoshihara Jiro. Outside is Gate, a sculpture by Noguchi Isamu made for the museum in 1969.

A little further west, the museum's superb annexe, the **Crafts Gallery** (Kogeikan; tel: 03-5777 8600; Tue–Sun 10am–5pm), is housed in a 1910 government-listed building, one of only a handful of Meiji-era brick structures left in Tokyo. The gallery exhibits a fine collection of lacquerware, bamboo, ceramics and textiles, and has occasional demonstrations by craftsmen.

Science Museum

Address: 2-1 Kitanomaru Koen, Chiyoda-ku; www.jsf.or.jp
Tel: 03-3212 8544
Opening Hours: daily 9.30am–4.50pm
Entrance Fee: charge
Transport: Takebashi

The Kogeikan (Crafts Gallery) annexe of the National Museum of Modern Art.

A short walk north from the National Art Museum, under a section of the Shoto Expressway, sticking to the paths of Kitanomaru Park (Kitanamaru koen), leads you to the **Science Museum ❾** (Kagaku Gijutsukan). Despite its unpromisingly austere exterior, the museum is both instructive and fun, especially

The palace grounds mark the spot where Ota Dokan built a fortified mansion in 1457 on a bluff rising from an inlet overlooking present-day Tokyo Bay. Edo's elevation to the world's largest city began when Ieyasu Tokugawa, the future shogun, chose the site as his new headquarters in 1590. Ieyasu's purpose was to create an unassailable stronghold, a military capital that would also reflect his own position as Japan's de facto ruler.

In the construction of Edo Castle, which took half a century, nothing was left to chance. The first line of defence involved the construction of a complex system of moats and canals integrating existing bodies of water to form a web that would entrap, or at least delay, the enemy. The water spirals were spanned by bridges guarded by fortified gates. By the time the castle was completed in 1640, it was the largest fort in the world comprising an astonishing 110 entry gates, 30 bridges, 21 watchtowers

and 28 armouries. Following the rules of Chinese geomancy, temples were also built in Ueno and Shiba to provide additional spiritual protection.

Fires, euphemistically referred to by the townspeople as 'the flowers of Edo', were a far greater problem to the city than armed rebellion. One of the most devastating, the infamous so-called 'Long-Sleeves Fire', occurred in 1657. The intensity of the heat not only destroyed most of the castle buildings, but also melted the shogun's gold reserves.

The Imperial Palace Plaza has also been witness to some fairly momentous scenes of recent history. Survivors of the Great Kanto Earthquake gathered here in 1923 and, in August 1945, several members of Japan's officer corps committed seppuku (ritual suicide) here, in order, it is said, to atone for their failure in World War II. In the 1950s and 1960s, student radicals and workers rallied at the plaza to take part in sometimes violent political demonstrations.

Admiring cherry blossoms from a row boat in Chidorigafuchi Park.

for children. Its four floors include space-age exhibits, working models, interactive displays and even a robot that gives lectures on electricity.

The octagonal **Nippon Budokan** ❿ (www.nipponbudokan.or.jp), which lies just northwest of the Science Museum along the same main pathway, was built in 1964 to stage the Olympic judo events, and selected for the same duties in 2020. Designed by Rokkaku Kijo, the roof of the building is designed to suggest overlapping mountains as seen in traditional screen paintings. Until the Tokyo Dome was built in 1986, the Nippon Budokan was the city's main rock venue. The Beatles performed at the Budokan in 1966 to scenes of mass hysteria. It is still used for concerts, exhibitions and tournaments of Japanese martial arts.

National Showa Memorial Museum

Address: 1-6-1 Kudan-minami, Chiyoda-ku; www.showakan.go.jp
Tel: 03-3222 2577
Opening Hours: Tue–Sun 10am–5.30pm
Entrance Fee: charge
Transport: Kudanshita

Exiting Kitanomaru Park by the **Tayasu Gate** (Tayasu-mon), one of the castle's finest gates, turn right and follow Yasukuni-dori towards the **National Showa Memorial Museum** ⓫ (Showa-kan) which houses exhibitions relating to Japan during World War II and the subsequent occupation. It's the first national museum to tackle Japan's war legacy and takes a predictably sanitised approach. Next door is the **Kudan Kaikan**, once a hall for

JAPAN'S WAR DEAD

Before an important battle, soldiers would sometimes exchange the words, 'Let us meet at Yasukuni', meaning the place where their spirits would be honoured. There are currently nearly 2.5 million souls enshrined at Yasukuni, including those of women and students who fought in the name of the Emperor in 13 different conflicts. This total also includes some Koreans and Taiwanese (Japan had occupied both countries before World War II).

The most controversial enshrinement was in 1978 when 14 convicted or suspected Class-A war criminals were added to Yasukuni's register, outraging Japan's neighbours who had suffered under Japan's colonial occupation. Emperor Hirohito was also not amused and refused to visit the shrine from that time until his death in 1998. Shrine officials have proved resistant, however, to calls to remove the war criminals from enshrinement, stating that all the soldiers' souls are combined at Yasukuni making individual removal impossible.

Every 15 August – the anniversary of Japan's defeat in World War II – the controversy erupts anew when a special ceremony is held at Yasukuni to mark the conflict's end. Japan's very vocal and heavily financed (yet minority) ultra-nationalist groups descend on the shrine en masse along with groups in opposition to them. What usually results is a highly charged, and at times bloody, day of confrontation. Japan's post-war constitution renounces both militarism and state-sponsored religion, so cabinet members who attend are asked whether they are there as private individuals or public figures. Prime Minister Koizumi Junichiro's public visit to the shrine in 2002 caused a diplomatic rift between China and Japan. Prime Minister Shinzo Abe reignited the issue when he visited Yasukuni in an official capacity as leader of the then opposition Liberal Democratic Party in October 2012, shortly after taking over as the party's leader. He did the same as Prime Minister in 2013 and the already frayed Japan-China relations became even more tense for a few weeks.

soldiers but now an events hall and hotel that hosts one of Tokyo's best roof top beer gardens every summer from May to September.

Yasukuni Shrine

Address: 3-1-1 Kudankita, Chiyoda-ku; www.yasukuni.or.jp
Tel: 03-3261 8326
Opening Hours: daily sunrise–sunset
Entrance Fee: free (museum charge)
Transport: Kudanshita or Ichigaya

Taking a left out of the **Tayasu Gate** (Tayasu-mon), then crossing Yasukuni-dori (Yasukuni Street) will lead you to the **Yasukuni Shrine** ⑫ (Yasukuni-jinja). Originally built in 1869 to commemorate the Imperial soldiers who had died in the civil war with the Togukawa's forces that engulfed Japan before the Meiji Restoration (see page 37), this controversial Shine shrine has since become the place where all of Japan's war dead are worshipped – including the 2 million who died in World War II. The original gate was requisitioned in 1943 as part of the war effort, and then melted to make armaments. To the shrine's rear you'll find a pretty ornamental garden with a teahouse and an adjacent sumo ring where bouts are held during the shrine's spring festival.

Yasukuni's fascinating museum **Yushukan** (tel: 03-3261 0998; www.yasukuni.or.jp; daily 9am–4.30pm) displays torn uniforms, fading photos and letters from soldiers, as well as a Zero fighter plane used in World War II. There's a deliberate absence of data on the horrors perpetrated by the Japanese military in Asia, resulting in the museum conveying a disturbingly one-sided impression of the war.

Chidorigafuchi Park

Leaving the shrine and returning to the Imperial Palace grounds you'll find **Chidorigafuchi Park** ⑬ (Chidorigafuchi Koen; daily 9am–5pm; free) between the eastern part of Uchibori-dori and the moat. The boathouse rents out rowing-boats which are an ideal way to view the many cherry trees that blossom along here during *hanami* season.

Further south along Uchibori-dori is the **National Theatre** (Kokuritsu Gekijo; tel: 03-3265 7411; www.ntj.jac.go.jp/english/access/facilities_01.html), a

Votive tablets on display at Yasukuni Shrine.

Marunouchi district by night.

is the **Prime Minister's Residence** (Shusho Kantei).

Hibiya Park

Continuing along Uchibori-dori, past **Sakurada Gate** (Sakurada-mon) – another gate leading to the Imperial Plaza – turn right into **Hibiya Park** ⑮ (Hibiya Koen; open 24 hours; free). This 16-hectare (41-acre) former parade ground was restyled as Japan's first Western-style park in 1903. It remains a curious mixture of Meiji-Period Japanese and European landscaping, with its original wisteria trellis, crane fountain and a Japanese garden, tucked into the southwest corner, complete with stone lanterns and a pond. At weekends events are often held here, including charity fun runs for Tokyo English Lifeline in May and Run for the Cure in late November.

Imperial Hotel

Across from the park on the corner of Hibiya-dori and Miyuki-dori stands the **Imperial Hotel** ⑯ (Teikoku

Modern architecture along Naka-dori, Marunouchi.

centre for traditional Japanese performing arts. The larger of its two auditoriums stages kabuki plays and gagaku recitals. Performances of bunraku puppet dramas and kyogen farces take place in the smaller hall.

National Diet Building

Address: 1-7-1 Nagatacho Chiyoda-ku; www.sangiin.go.jp
Tel: 03-5521 7445
Opening Hours: Mon–Fri 8am–5pm
Entrance Fee: free
Transport: Nagatacho

Two blocks south of the National Theatre, past the Supreme Court and National Diet Library, is the Japanese parliament's **National Diet Building** ⑭ (Kokkai Gijido) in the area known as Nagatacho. A plaza with fountains and gardens stands in front of the main edifice, which dates from 1937 and is split into the House of Councillors and House of Representatives. Free hour-long tours of the former are available when parliament isn't in session. The Diet is surrounded by an assortment of government offices including, to the south, a handsome modern construction that

Hoteru). The present building was completed in 1970, but there's been a Western-style hotel here since 1890. Its most famous incarnation is the Mayan-style building designed by Frank Lloyd Wright. It opened in 1923, on the day the Great Kanto earthquake struck Tokyo, yet managed to survive that tremor and the devastation of World War II. After Wright's decaying building was torn down in 1968, the front section was rebuilt in Meiji-Mura architectural park near Nagoya; the only part of the present Imperial to bear Wright's design is the Old Imperial Bar.

MARUNOUCHI AND SURROUNDINGS

Meaning 'Within the Castle Walls' Marunouchi – an area extending from the Imperial Plaza, down to Yurakucho (see page 102) and over to the old western facade of Tokyo Station where it meets the neighbouring business district of Otemachi – has long been identified with power and prestige. This was where Tokugawa Ieyasu instructed his senior retainers to build their mansions in the early 1600s. Concealed from view behind steep walls of their own, the defining features of the area's sprawling feudal villas were their gates, plain or ostentatious according to wealth and rank. With the fall of the shogunate in 1868, the walls and gates were torn down and, with the land eventually sold off, Marunouchi became the site of Japan's first Western-style office buildings.

Naka-dori

Over the decades Marunouchi's office buildings have gone through several incarnations. The last of the original red-brick buildings designed by Josiah Conder was torn down in 1968. In the late 1990s, Mitsubishi Estates commenced an ambitious plan to revive the area's aging stock of office buildings, at the same time adding high-end consumer shopping and entertainment facilities to rival nearby Ginza. Particularly benefitting from Marunouchi's revival has been **Naka-dori**, a chic thoroughfare dotted with public art that has been dubbed Tokyo's 'Rodeo Drive' for its abundance of luxury boutiques.

FACT

There are hundreds of cherry trees in Yasukuni's grounds, making this a prime spot for *hanami*, cherry-blossom viewing, in spring. Festivals to entertain the spirits of the dead are also held in the shrine grounds at the end of April and in mid-October.

Artists at work outside Tokyo Station.

Aside from being one of the main gateways into the city centre, Tokyo Station also has the dubious distinction of being the place where two prime ministers were assassinated in the 20th century.

Mitsubishi Ichigokan Museum

Address: 2-6-2 Marunouchi, Chiyoda-ku; www.mimt.jp
Tel: 03-5777 8600
Opening Hours: Tue–Thu and Sat–Sun 10am–6pm, Fri until 8pm
Entrance Fee: charge
Transport: Tokyo

An unexpected bonus has been the meticulous recreation of Conder's original office building which, with its brick facade and copper roof detailing, forms an elegant corner of the **Brick Square** commercial development. Inside, the **Mitsubishi Ichigokan Museum** ⓱ (Mitsubishi Ichigokan Bijutsukan) has changing exhibitions focusing on 18th- and 19th-century Japanese and European art as well as a café-bar (Café 1894) in the lofty space that was once a banking hall. Behind the museum is charming courtyard garden that is an oasis for the area's office workers.

Mitsubishi Estates

Among the buildings that Mitsubishi Estates has reconstructed and expanded is the **Marunouchi Building** ⓲ (www.marunouchi.com/marubiru).

Commonly known as the 'Maru-biru' this 36-storey office complex also has superb gourmet food stores, a shopping zone and all manner of restaurants. The upper levels offer sweeping views of the Imperial Palace grounds and beyond – ignoring the one-time ban on buildings over eight floors high in Marunouchi in deference to the privacy of the royal family.

Across the street on the same side, the **Shin Maru Building** (www.marunouchi.com/shinmaru) a 38-storey structure designed by the British architect Sir Michael Hopkins, offers a similar mix of shopping, dining and offices. Its opening in 2007 capped the first 10-year phase of Mitsubishi Estate's redevelopment plans for the area.

Tokyo Station

An outstanding survivor of Marunouchi's early 20th-century glory days is the **Tokyo Station** ⓳ (Tokyo-eki). With the extension of the railway from Shimbashi into the centre of the city and the completion of Tokyo Station in 1914, Marunouchi's future was assured. The station's red-brick, Queen Anne-style design, based on the Amsterdam Central Station, was

BIRTH OF A BUSINESS DISTRICT

In 1890, the Japanese government, needing to drum up funds to feed its growing military machine, persuaded the Iwasaki clan (founders of the giant trading firm Mitsubishi) to purchase 267,300 sq metres (319,688 sq ft) of land near the palace grounds for commercial development. The price for this land, plus sections of Yurakucho and Kanda, was ¥1.28 million to be paid in eight instalments.

Mitsubishi hired the English architect Josiah Conder to realise their vision of a Western-style business complex. Conder was one of the many 'foreign experts' the Japanese government had employed to introduce modern technology into their formerly feudal society. Doubts about earthquakes and Tokyo's sub-tropical summers were put aside as Conder's blueprint for Marunouchi materialised with the block of three-storey, red-brick neoclassical buildings known as Iccho Rondon, (One Block London), and the Mitsubishi Ichigokan. Conder went on to design several other key buildings in the city including Nikolai Cathedral in Ochanomizu and Rokumei-

kan reception hall in Hibiya (which was destroyed in 1940).

Although the European architecture eventually overcame the problems of its transplant, Paul Waley in his collection of narratives *Tokyo: City of Stories* said that it revealed 'a pronounced sense of unease. The buildings need carriages and trolleys and the bustle of late-Victorian and Edwardian London. Instead, all they have to look out on is a few rickshaws and the occasional disoriented passer-by.'

Most of Conder's buildings were replaced in the 1930s by larger, more modern structures and the last of the original Mitsubishi blocks was demolished in the late 1960s. As Japan's economy matured, Mitsubishi Estate, still the majority landowner in the immediate area, began to look to the past as a way of moving forward the development of the area, and in 2009 the meticulous resurrection of the original Mitsubishi Ichigokan was completed. It is now a museum and a monument to the birth of Japan's first modern office district.

Mitsukoshi department store's well-known label.

the work of Tatsuno Kingo, a former student of Josiah Conder. Along with the redevelopment of Marunouchi, the station, which handles 4,000 train arrivals daily, has undergone a massive reconstruction. Modern facilities and buildings on the eastern Yaesu side of the station have been completed, and the old red-brick entrance on the Marunouchi side has been restored to its original splendour, reopening in winter 2012 with a great deal of hype. The new facilities include the very plush Tokyo Station Hotel.

NIHOMBASHI

Heading over to Tokyo Station's east side via Eitai-dori, you'll soon hit **Nihombashi** ㉑, an area named after the bridge of the same name. Meaning 'Bridge of Japan' Togukawa Ieyasu had the original wooden, arched Nihombashi built here as a starting point and distance post for the five main roads that led out of the city. These included the Tokaido, the great 'Eastern Road' connecting Edo and Kyoto. The present bridge, a solid, elegant structure made of stone and metal, was completed in 1911; unfortunately it is overshadowed by the

raised Shuto Expressway. A bronze marker called the **Zero Kilometre Marker** (Tokyo-to Dorogenpyo) in the middle of the bridge continues to serve as a distance post for the city's national highways.

Mitsui Memorial Museum

Address: 2-1-1 Nihonbashi-Muromachi, Chuo-ku; www.mitsui-museum.jp
Tel: 03-5777 8600
Opening Hours: Tue–Sun 10am–5pm
Entrance Fee: charge
Transport: Mitsukoshimae

Walking north along Chuo-dori, past the original branch of department store **Mitsukoshi** is the **Mitsui Honkan Building** on the seventh floor of which is the **Mitsui Memorial Museum** ㉑ (Mitsui Bijutsukan). Here are featured beautiful items from the collection of the Mitsui family – exhibitions change five times a year but there's always a section showcasing tea ceremony utensils including a replica of the fine teahouse Jo'an.

FACT

Naka-dori is lined with boutiques selling both luxury Japanese and overseas brands, including Armani Collezioni, Comme des Garcons and Issey Miyake. For a full directory see www.marunouchi.com.

The Kite Museum brings colour to a business district.

Currency Museum

Address: 1-3-1 Nihonbashi-Hongokucho, Chuo-ku; www.imes.boj.or.jp/cm
Tel: 03-3277 3037
Opening Hours: Tue–Sun 9.30am–4.30pm
Entrance Fee: free
Transport: Mitsukoshimae

A block northwest of Mitsukoshi along Nichigin-dori, and directly behind Mitsui Honkan Building is the imposing **Bank of Japan** (Nippon Ginko; www.boj.or.jp). Built in 1898 on the former site of the shogun's gold, silver and copper mints, the bank represents the city's first Western-style construction designed by a Japanese architect and is said to be modelled after the Bank of England in London. An annexe houses the **Currency Museum** ㉒ (Kahei Hakubutsukan), displaying coinage from the Roman Period to the introduction of Chinese currency during the late Heian Period, as well as all the Japanese coins ever put into circulation.

Tokyo Stock Exchange

Address: 2-1 Nihombashi Kabutocho, Chuo-ku; www.jpx.co.jp/english
Tel: 03-3665 1881
Opening Hours: Mon–Fri 9am–4.30pm

Entrance Fee: free
Transport: Kayabacho or Nihombashi

Facing the Nihombashi River (Nihombashi-gawa), the enormous **Tokyo Stock Exchange** ㉓ (Tokyo Shoken Torihikijo) is located a few minutes' walk north of Kayabacho Station on the Tozai Line. When the exchange opened in Kabuto-cho in 1878, trading hours were determined by burning a length of rope. Business was conducted in a kneeling position above tatami mats, and messages were relayed by young boys positioned at street corners. When the rope burned down, the day's trading came to an end. In this computer age, such charming practices are long gone. If you want to learn how the exchange's business is conducted today make an advance reservation for one of the guided tours in English, held Monday to Friday at 1pm and 2pm, or try one of the trading simulation games held weekdays from 10am.

Kite Museum

Address: 5F Taimeiken, 1-12-10 Nihombashi, Chuo-ku; www.tako.gr.jp
Tel: 03-3271 2465
Opening Hours: Mon–Sat 11am–5pm
Entrance Fee: free
Transport: Nihombashi

Creating masterpieces at the Kite Museum.

A film poster at the National Film Archive of Japan showing a heavily tattooed woman.

West of the stock exchange, just out from the A4 Exit of Nihombashi Station – on the fifth floor above the restaurant Taimeiken – the **Kite Museum ㉔** (Tako-no-Hakubutsukan) is a splash of colour in this business district. Kite flying has a long tradition in Japan among children and adults, who stage jousting contests. The museum's collection exceeds 3,000 kites from around the world. Among the Japanese displays are kites shaped to resemble birds, squid and Mount Fuji. Others are like canvases, with paintings of samurai warriors, manga characters and ukiyo-e style woodblock images.

Bridgestone Museum of Art

Address: 1-10-1 Kyobashi, Chuo-ku; www.bridgestone-museum.gr.jp
Tel: 03-3563 0241
Opening Hours: closed for reconstruction until mid-2019
Entrance Fee: charge
Transport: Nihombashi

Returning to Chuo-dori and heading south past the department store

Takashimaya, on the corner of Yaesu-dori is the **Bridgestone Museum of Art ㉕** (Bridgestone Bijutsukan). Reopened in 2019 after a few years of extensive renovation works, its excellent collection comprises mainly the works of the Impressionists, but there are some works of early 20th-century painters and post-Meiji-period Japanese artists, as well as Greek and modern sculptures.

National Film Archive of Japan

Address: 3-7-6 Kyobashi, Chuo-ku; www.nfaj.go.jp
Tel: 03-3561 0823
Opening Hours: Tue–Sat 11am–6.30pm
Entrance Fee: charge
Transport: Takaracho or Kyobashi

Continue south along Chuo-dori then turn east at the next major intersection (above Kyobashi subway station) to reach the **National Film Archive of Japan ㉖** (Kokuritsu Eiga Aakaibu) set up to research and preserve Japanese archival footage and foreign films. There are almost 20,000 films in its collection. Two cinemas hold screenings throughout the year. Film buffs can enjoy its gallery of photos and posters and film-related design, as well as its library.

TIP

The Tokyo rush hour is not confined to a single hour in the morning and evening. On subway lines and routes like the Yamanote Line, which has one of the highest passenger capacities of any urban railway in the world, the evening crush can easily last from 5pm until 8 or 9pm.

Bridgestone Museum of Art.

Glittering Chuo-dori, Ginza.

YURAKUCHO, GINZA AND SHIODOME

Both elegance and exclusivity mark Ginza as a world-famous shopping destination. But there are also theatres, a traditional bathhouse, stunning contemporary architecture and lots of tiny art galleries.

During the Edo Period there was little to suggest the sartorial elegance and good taste the name Ginza now conjures up. Contiguous with the southern ribbon of the teeming, plebeian quarters of the townspeople, it occupied a rather undefined area between the feudal mansions of the Outer Lords and the newly reclaimed land of Tsukiji.

History of the area

Tokugawa Ieyasu (see page 34), established a silver mint (*gin-za*) here in 1612. The mint moved on to nearby Nihombashi in 1800, but the name stuck. Fire and steam rather than coinage were the two main elements in Ginza's rise. In 1872, Ginza and Tsukiji suffered the second of two almost consecutive fires. Nearly 3,000 homes were destroyed and the area virtually reduced to cinder. The governor of Tokyo decided to build a European-style quarter in Ginza, consisting of hundreds of fireproof red-brick buildings, arcades and tree-lined avenues.

The plan coincided nicely with the opening the same year of a train line from Yokohama to Shimbashi, a district adjacent to Ginza. The rail terminus at Shimbashi brought new life

An advertisement for a Jackie Chan movie in Ginza.

to Ginza, which suddenly found itself in the enviable position of being the main gateway into Tokyo.

The remodelling of Ginza took 10 years. By the time it was completed, its streets could boast a horse-drawn tram (soon replaced by an electric tram system), shops selling Western goods, theatres, European-style cafés, bakeries, beer halls, tearooms and the offices of several newspaper companies. By 1894 the district's most famous landmark, the Hattori Clock Tower (now part of Wako

Main Attractions
Idemitsu Museum of Arts
Tokyo International Forum
Ginza 4-chome crossing
Yamaha Ginza
Shiseido Gallery
Konparu-yu
Railway History Exhibition Hall
ADMT Advertising Museum Tokyo

Map
Page 102

department store), was already in place. The city's keen instinct for merchandising had found a new home. Many of the best-known businesses and shops that line Ginza today date from this time.

Despite its new reinforced buildings, Ginza was not immune to disaster – its brick buildings were laid to waste in the Great Kanto Earthquake of 1923. Undeterred, larger, more fortified buildings sprang up in the 1930s. Most, however, suffered a similar fate during the air raids of 1945. The Wako Building at Ginza Crossing, dating from 1932, is virtually all that remains of an older Ginza, with the exception of a few smaller prewar structures in some of the backstreets.

Facing stiff competition from trendy new retail complexes in Roppongi and Aoyama, not to mention from nearby Marunouchi, Ginza has had to up its game in recent years in order to maintain its position as the city's most exclusive shopping district.

An excellent place to sample different brands of sake and learn about the brewing process is the Japan Sake and Shochu Information Center. Located at Nishi-Shimbashi (tel: 03-3519 2091; www.japansake. or.jp), it is open from Mon to Fri 10am–6pm.

It has succeeded with a mixture of architectural upgrading of older establishments such as Mikimoto, Shiseido and Chanel – mainstays of its core clientele of well-heeled older women – as well as providing a platform for more modern brand names such as Muji, Apple and Uniqlo.

YURAKUCHO

Idemitsu Museum of Arts

Address: 9F Teigeki Building, 3-1-1 Marunouchi, Chiyoda-ku; http://idemitsu-museum.or.jp/en
Tel: 03-3213 9402
Opening Hours: Tue–Thu, Sat–Sun 10am–5pm, Fri until 7pm
Entrance Fee: charge
Transport: Yurakucho or Hibiya

There are several possible starting points from which to explore Ginza and its environs. One of the easiest is from the JR Yurakucho Station or the Yurakucho Line subway. This area is named after a daimyo (powerful

Yurakucho, Ginza and Shiodome

Idemitsu Bijutsukan (Idemitsu Museum of Art)
Teikoku Gekijō (Imperial Theatre)
Tokyo Kokusai Forum (Tokyo International Forum)
Yūrakuchō
Hibiya
YURAKUCHO
Kyōbashi
YAESU
Takarachō
Bridgestone Bijutsukan (Bridgestone Museum of Art)
Tokyo Kōtsū Kaikan
Mikimoto Ginza 2
Marronnier Gate Ginza 2 & 3
Yūrakuchō Mullion
GINZA
Chanel
Ginza-itchōme
De Beers Ginza
Antique Mall Ginza
Teikoku Hoteru (Imperial Hotel)
Ginza Sony Park
Wako Building
Bvlgari
Louis Vuitton
Matsuya Ginza Dep. Store
CHŪO-KU
SHINTOMI
Maison Hermès
Ginza 4-chome Crossing
Mitsukoshi Department Store
Ginza Nōh-Gakudō
Nissan Crossing
Magazine House
Uniqlo
Ginza Six Department Store
Higashi-ginza
Kabuki-za
Ginza Graphic Gallery
Yamaha Hall
Yamaha Ginza
Konparu-yu (Bathhouse)
Shiseido Gallery
Nicolas G. Hayek Center
Shōchiku Kaikan
Tsukiji
Tokyo Gallery + BTAP
Shimbashi
Shimbashi (Yurakumore Station)
Shimbashi-Embujō
Kokuritsu Gan Center (National Cancer Centre)
Tsukiji Hongan-ji
Railway History Exhibition Hall
TSUKIJI
SHIODOME
ADMT Advertising Museum Tokyo
Satura-dōri
Yumago-dōri
Marronnier-dōri
Matsuya-dōri
Chūo-dōri
Namiki-dōri
Harumi-dōri
Showa-dōri
Harumi-dōri
Hanatsubaki-dōri
Shin-Ohashi-dōri
0   500 m
0   500 yds

land-owning lord) who established his estate here in the 17th century. On the west side of the station, and across Naka-dori, your first port of call should be the outstanding **Idemitsu Museum of Arts** ❶ (Idemitsu Bijutsukan), on the ninth floor of the Teigeki Building. Its collection, one of the finest showcases for Asian art in the city, reflects the eclectic but discerning tastes of its wealthy founder, petroleum industrialist Idemitsu Sazo.

Its main room features an impressive collection of Chinese ceramics. There are fine Japanese pieces here too, including examples of Kakiemon, Imari, Kutani and Seto wares. Ancient pottery shards from all over the world crowd the showcases of a room with a magnificent view of the Imperial Palace. There are also gold-painted screens, Zen calligraphy and ukiyo-e prints.

Tokyo International Forum

Address: 3-5-1 Marunouchi, Chiyoda-ku; www.t-i-forum.co.jp
Tel: 03-5221 9000
Opening Hours: daily 7am–11pm
Entrance Fee: free

Transport: Yurakucho

Ginza by night.

YAKITORI EATERIES

Between Yurakucho and Shimbashi you'll find a number of cubbyhole restaurants and stalls located directly under the raised railway tracks. These are the last remnants of the American Occupation years when the area played host to a lively, downtown throng of street markets, small workshops, and pavement beer and sake stalls lit up with roadside lanterns. A glimmer of those days remains in Yurakucho's no-frills yakitori (charcoal-broiled skewers of chicken slathered with a sweet sauce) joints housed in cave-like spaces beneath rumbling trains. There are few more appetising and atmospheric places to eat yakitori than here, among the lively, alcohol-stimulated babble of salarymen and office ladies.

Two blocks east of the Idemitsu Museum of Arts, pressed against the tracks of the Yamanote Line, an architectural vision unlike any other you are likely to have seen rises in the spectacular form of the **Tokyo International Forum** ❷ (Tokyo Kokusai Forum). In a tough international competition, New York-based architect Rafael Vinoly won the contract to design this exhibition space divided into two enormous, interconnecting buildings. The right-side contours of the east building, the forum's Glass Hall, follow the curving tracks of the elevated JR train lines.

Completed in 1996, this postmodernist masterpiece includes a conference, concert, dance and theatre space. The visual highlight of the complex is its futuristic 60-metre (196ft) -high glass atrium, with its sweeping skywalks, curved walls and immense roof. For the best experience of the space take the lift up to the seventh floor and then descend by the stairs. The open-air plaza in the middle of the forum is the venue for the Oedo Antique Market, while in the basement is the excellently presented **Mitsuo Aida Museum** (www.mitsuo.co.jp/museum/foreign; Tue–Sun 10am–5.30pm) with interesting information about the poet and calligrapher.

Tokyo Kotsu Kaikan

Heading south from the Tokyo International Forum and walking back under the railway tracks brings you to the **Tokyo Kotsu Kaikan** ❸, a building topped by a revolving restaurant. Lower down in the complex you'll find several shops that specialise in products from different prefectures in Japan; for example, there are ones that sell goods made in Hokkaido and Okinawa. Nearby, fronting Harumi-dori, is the 14-storey **Yurakucho Center Building** (Yurakucho Mullion), a cinema and theatre complex that also includes the department store **Hankyu**.

GINZA

Harumi-dori heads east into the heart of Ginza. At the main intersection with Sotobori-dori was – until 2017 – one of the area's main landmarks: the **Sony Building**. The area is currently undergoing a major transformation, and the iconic main building has been demolished. For now the space serves as a

The plush Matsuya department store in Ginza.

communal area, known as the **Ginza Sony Park**; below the ground, the 'lower park' houses lab and experiment facilities. In 2022, the Ginza Sony Park Project will be completed with the construction of the new Sony building, which will make up the 'upper park'.

Nearby is **Maison Hermès** (5-4-1 Ginza, Chuo-ku; tel: 03-3289 6811; Mon–Sat 11am–8pm, Sun until 7pm). The Japan HQ of the French luxury fashion group occupies a five-storey block built from glass bricks, designed by Renzo Piano. There's a rooftop garden, a private cinema and a gallery – one of the many small art spaces you'll find tucked away in Ginza, though undoubtedly the most beautiful, especially late in the day, when Ginza's evening neon is refracted through distinctive floor-to-ceiling glass panels.

Ginza 4-chome crossing

Two of the area's best-known retail landmarks stand on the corner of the **Ginza 4-chome crossing** ❹ (often just called 'Ginza Crossing') where Harumi-dori meets Chuo-dori – Wako and Mitsukoshi department stores. A little further on the left after Wako

Building, is the famous jewellery shop **Mikimoto**, which underwent a major remodelling in 2017. Chuo-dori, from 1-chome to 8-chome, is closed to traffic on Saturday 2pm to 6pm and Sunday, noon to 5pm, when it becomes a pleasant pedestrian zone, with café tables and umbrellas placed along its stretch, where you can enjoy a traditional *Gin-bura* (Ginza stroll), a tradition that goes back to the district's early days as an experiment in continental shopping and leisure.

Modern architecture

Heading north along Chuo-dori you'll come to **Chanel** ❺ (3-5-3 Ginza, Chuo-ku; tel: 03-5159 5555; www.chanel-ginza.com). The entire facade of the 10-storey tower is a giant LED screen that looks its best at night. Inside, apart from clothes, is an exhibition hall and Beige, one of the several Tokyo operations of star French chef Alain Ducasse. Next down the street from the Chanel building is the striking golden-brown flagship store of Cartier, and directly across Chuo-dori are the Matsuya department store (www.matsuya.com)

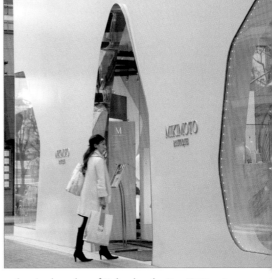

One of Mikimoto's stores in Ginza.

and major branches of **Bvlgari** and **Louis Vuitton**.

Turn the corner at Chanel to view a couple more striking pieces of contemporary architecture along Marronnier-dori. The first is the gracefully curvy **De Beers Ginza** ❻ (2-5-11 Ginza, Chuo-ku; tel: 03-5524 6055; daily 11.30am–7.30pm), a steel-clad showroom for the diamond merchant. Further along is the 10-storey **Mikimoto Ginza 2** ❼ (2-4-12 Ginza, Chuo-ku; tel: 03-3562 3130; daily 11am–7pm), designed by the renowned architect Toyo Ito and renovated in 2017. Its jewel-box-inspired architecture features a pinkish facade perforated by irregular-shaped windows. Besides pearls, the store sells cosmetics and high quality sweets.

Yamaha Ginza

Address: 7-9-14 Ginza, Chuo-ku
Tel: 03-3572 3171
Opening Hours: daily 11am–7.30pm
Entrance Fee: free
Transport: Shimbashi

Walking in the opposite direction along Chuo-dori from the Ginza

KABUKI THEATRES

The kabuki theatre Kabuki-za on the corner of Harumi-dori and Showa-dori was one of Ginza's, if not Tokyo's, most famous and photographed structures, until it closed in 2010. Thankfully, the modern replacement followed its forebear's Baroque revivalist architectural lines, and hosted its first shows in 2013.

Highly stylised kabuki melodramas (see page 62) combine art and high jinks in a programme of dance, sword fighting, romantic episodes and tragedy. Matinée and evening performances are staged twice a day, and at Kabuki-za English-language audio guides are available to help you make sense of proceedings. If a whole play seems too daunting, buy tickets for a single act. The nearby Shimbashi Embujo theatre also stages kabuki.

Wako Building is a landmark feature at the Ginza 4-chome intersection.

Opposite Yamaha Ginza is the **Shiseido Gallery** , located in the basement of Shiseido, the famous cosmetics boutique. The gallery which is one of Ginza's longest running, (it opened in 1919), features experimental art by mainly young Japanese and foreign artists.

Other notable galleries in the area include **Ginza Graphic Gallery** (7-7-2 Ginza, Chuo-ku; tel: 03-3571 5206; www.dnp.co.jp/gallery; Mon–Sat 11am–7pm; free), Tokyo's only space specialising in graphic art; and **Tokyo Gallery + BTAP** (7F, 8-10-5 Ginza; tel: 03-3571 1808; www.tokyo-gallery.com; Tue–Fri 11am–7pm, Sat until 5pm; free) specialising in Japanese, Chinese and Korean contemporary art.

4-chome crossing will take you past the **Nissan Crossing** car showroom, which reopened in a brand new building in 2016, on the left and flagship store of fast fashion retailer **Uniqlo** on the right. Further down the street, past **Ginza Six** – the largest department store in Ginza, inaugurated in 2017, with 241 shops, restaurants and even a Noh theatre in the basement – are a couple more of Ginza's best modern structures. **Yamaha Ginza** (7-9-14 Ginza, Chuo-ku) also occupies a dazzling building, which is home to a professional concert hall, as well as a showroom rammed with keyboards, guitars and other instruments. Next door is the equally impressive **Nicolas G. Hayek Center** (7-9-14 Ginza, Chuo-ku; Mon–Sat 11am–8pm, Sun until 7pm), designed by Shigeru Ban. It's home to seven boutiques of the watchmaker Swatch.

Shiseido Gallery

Address: B1F, 8-8-3 Ginza, Chuo-ku; www.shiseidogroup.com/gallery
Tel: 03-3572 3901
Opening Hours: Tue–Sat 11am–7pm, Sun until 6pm
Entrance Fee: free
Transport: Shimbashi

Konparu-yu

Address: 8-7-5 Ginza, Chuo-ku
Tel: 03-3571 5469
Opening Hours: Mon–Sat 2–10pm
Entrance Fee: charge
Transport: Shimbashi

The traditional communal bathhouse **Konparu-yu** has been located on the small street behind Shiseido since 1863. Most Tokyo neighbourhoods

JAPANESE BATHHOUSES

In the 8th century, some of the larger temples in Nara had baths built for monks and local residents. The connection between cleanliness and godliness may explain why many traditional public baths resemble temples. Edo's first public bath was built in 1591. A modest entrance fee of one *sen* was charged; public baths were henceforth called *sento*, meaning 'money water'. Mixed bathing was common and baths were not only centres for social intercourse but also sexual license. Although the number of public baths left in the Tokyo area is dwindling you'll still find one in many neighbourhoods, particularly in the old *shitamachi* districts to the north and east of the city such as Asakusa, Ueno and Yanaka.

TIP

For full listings of the many small commercial art galleries in Ginza and other areas of Tokyo check the website of Tokyo Art Beat (www.tokyoartbeat.com). Note most galleries are closed on Monday.

had *sento* (public baths) until the 1970s; although most families have private baths these days, trips to the sento are still a highly popular local pastime, and you'll find them across Tokyo. A Shinto altar sits in the rafters above the men's and women's sections, which have two baths apiece – one marked 'tepid', the other 'very hot'. For ¥460 you can soak in both until prune-like.

SHIODOME

Railway History Exhibition Hall

Address: 1-5-3 Higashi-Shimbashi, Minato-ku; www.ejrcf.or.jp/shinbashi
Tel: 03-3572 1872
Opening Hours: Tue–Sun 10am–5pm
Entrance Fee: free
Transport: Shimbashi

The raised Tokyo Expressway separates Ginza from Shimbashi and the Shiodome City Centre complex, both to the south. Shiodome's clutch of shiny new skyscrapers stand where the original Shimbashi Station was located in 1872. A copy of that stone building now houses the **Railway**

History Exhibition Hall ⓫. Inside you can see foundations of the original building and get an idea of what Shimbashi looked like back in its late 19th-century heyday as the birthplace of Japan's railway system.

ADMT Advertising Museum Tokyo

Address: Caretta Shiodome, 1-8-2 Higashi-Shimbashi, Minato-ku; www. admt.jp
Tel: 03-6218 2500
Opening Hours: Tue–Fri 11am–6.30pm, Sat until 4.30pm
Entrance Fee: free
Transport: Shiodome

Among the many big corporations that have their HQs in Shiodome is advertising giant Dentsu, who occupy much of the Caretta Shiodome building. In the basement you'll find the **ADMT Advertising Museum Tokyo** ⓬, which provides wonderful glimpses into Japanese commercial art. Starting with woodblock flyers from the Edo Period, moving to Art Deco, Meiji and Taisho Period creations, the exhibits bring you right up to date with the best of TV advertising.

TIP

Bathhouse etiquette dictates that everyone should thoroughly soap and rinse themselves before entering the shared bath, which is for soaking only.

The Kabuki-za Theatre.

Creative advertising near Ikebukuro Station.

IKEBUKURO

Sightseeing options of a more eclectic nature can be found in these northern districts of Tokyo, including two giant department stores, a famous cemetery, several beautiful gardens and a Catholic cathedral.

One of the premier shopping and entertainment centres along the Yamanote Line, Ikebukuro was a relative latecomer to the Tokyo scene. While other sub-cities such as Shinjuku and Shibuya were rapidly developing in the latter part of the 19th century, Ikebukuro, literally meaning 'pond bag', was an unfashionable neighbourhood favoured by struggling writers and artists. But the coming of the railway in 1903 started to change all that.

The final phase in Ikebukuro's transformation from agricultural hamlet to one of Tokyo's main sub-cities, came about through the sibling rivalry of two half-brothers, Yasujiro Tsutsumi and Kaichiro Nezu, respective heads of the Seibu and Tobu commercial groups. Their first incisions into the area, the Seibu and Tobu train lines, were crowned with two opulent department stores of the same name. Seibu now dominates the east side, with a building that runs like a firewall along the edge of the station, while Tobu defends its interests along the western portion of the tracks.

NISHI-IKEBUKURO

Exit on the west side of Ikebukuro Station – the Tobu side. Navigate south to the well-signposted Metropolitan Plaza building to get your bearings.

Tokyo Metropolitan Theatre

Address: 1-8-1 Nishi-Ikebukuro, Toshima-ku; www.geigeki.jp
Tel: 03-5391 2111
Opening Hours: daily 9am–10pm
Transport: Ikebukuro

Two blocks west of Metropolitan Plaza, **Tokyo Metropolitan Theatre ❶** (Tokyo Geijutsu Gekijo) is a concert, theatre and exhibition venue. The main attraction of the building is its giant escalator, which carries visitors beneath a 28-metre (90ft) glass atrium

Statues at Gokoku-ji Temple.

TIP

Ikebukuro Station is a veritable labyrinth with five overhead train tracks and subway lines feeding into it. To add to the confusion, there are over 40 exits. If stuck, use one of the many maps dotted around the station; alternatively, head up the first exit at hand, and then use the department stores and other cardinal buildings to orient yourself.

up to hallway with a colourful domed ceiling painted by Koji Kinutani.

Ikebukuro Bosaikan

Address: 2-37-8 Nishi-Ikebukuro, Toshima-ku; www.tfd.metro.tokyo.jp/hp-ikbskan
Tel: 03-3590 6565
Opening Hours: Wed–Mon 9am–5pm
Entrance Fee: free
Transport: Ikebukuro

From Tokyo Metropolitan Theatre follow Gekijo-dori south to the corner where you'll see the Ikebukuro Fire Station. Inside you'll find the **Ikebukuro Bosaikan ②**, an earthquake simulation centre. It is not the most obvious sight that springs to mind on a trip, but in a city like Tokyo, earthquakes are an ever-present possibility. The experience of being in a room during an earthquake of magnitude six is decidedly weird, as is escaping from the smoke maze that simulates

fleeing a burning building. You can also play with fire extinguishers.

Jiyu Gakuen Myonichikan ③

Address: 2-31-3 Nishi-Ikebukuro, Toshima-ku; www.jiyu.jp
Tel: 03-3971 7535
Opening Hours: Tue–Sun 10am–4pm
Entrance Fee: charge
Transport: Ikebukuro

Follow signs on the residential streets behind the Bosaikan to discover the only Frank Lloyd Wright-designed building still standing in Tokyo. Myonichikan means 'House of Tomorrow' and the American architect was assisted by Endo Arata on the project, which originally housed the Jiyu Gakuen (meaning 'School of Freedom') and opened in 1921. Appreciate the low-slung building's interior while sipping tea in its central hall. Weddings are often held here and at the chapel across the road on weekends.

Ikebukuro

HIGASHI-IKEBUKURO

Returning to the main road, turn right and head for the tunnel beneath the railway tracks, emerging on Meiji-dori. You're now in Higashi-Ikebukuro (East Ikebukuro). The broad avenue Green Odori runs east from the main exit of Ikebukuro Station. Branch off along the mainly pedestrian shopping street Sunshine 60-dori leading past several cinemas and a large branch of the handicrafts store Tokyu Hands.

Nekorobi

Address: 1-28-28 Higashi-Ikebukuro, Toshima-ku
Tel: 03-3980 6111
Opening Hours: daily 11am–10pm
Entrance Fee: charge
Transport: Ikebukuro

East of Ikebukuro station, on the third level of a nondescript building, you'll find one of Tokyo's crazes – a cat café! Though recently superseded by cafés filled with snakes, owls and hamsters, the feline variety is usually far better for the welfare of its animals. At **Nekorobi** ❹, you pay a charge for a one-hour stay, including unlimited coffee, tea and soft drinks, which you can enjoy while petting several dozen pedigree kitties.

Otome Road

Just beyond the raised expressway west of the Sunshine 60 building is **Otome Road** ❺, where you won't fail to notice a rash of shops selling anime and manga products. There's no official sign, but the area has been dubbed Otome Road (Maiden Road) after the legions of female fans who gather here to shop for products that feature their favourite cartoon characters. On a much smaller scale, it's the girls' equivalent of male otaku paradise, Akihabara (see page 187). One of the main establishments here is the Animate store, the largest retailer of anime, games and manga in Japan. Another popular shop is Mandarake,

Inside Sunshine City.

one of the biggest Tokyo vendors of used anime and manga products.

Sunshine City

Sunshine City ❻ (www.sunshinecity. co.jp), a complex of four buildings, is another Tokyo institution. Built in 1978, this self-styled 'city within a city' looks dated in comparison with newer developments such as Roppongi Hills and Tokyo Midtown. Nevertheless, its attractions could easily fill up a day's sightseeing.

The first building in the set is Sunshine 60. One of the world's fastest elevators will carry you up to the 60th floor of the tower where there is an observation gallery with a sweeping view of Tokyo: suburbs vanishing into infinity, the neon towers of Shinjuku and, on a clear day, the distant outline of Mount Fuji.

The Sunshine City Prince Hotel occupies the second building, and the World Import Mart, the third. On the 10th floor of the latter are a large

FACT

At the Swallowtail Butler's Cafe in Ikebukuro girls can enjoy being treated like ladies and are waited upon by young men dressed as butlers.

planetarium (daily 11am–8pm) and an aquarium (daily Apr–Oct 10am–8pm, Nov–Mar 10am–6pm).

Ancient Orient Museum

Address: 7F Bunka Kaikan, Sunshine City, 3-1-4 Higashi-Ikebukuro, Toshima-ku; http://aom-tokyo.com
Tel: 03-3989 3331
Opening Hours: daily 10am–5pm
Entrance Fee: charge
Transport: Ikebukuro

On the seventh floor of Sunshine City's Bunka Kaikan section, the **Ancient Orient Museum** ❼ (Kodai Orient Hakubutsukan) is an archaeological museum with a fine collection of artefacts from the Indian subcontinent and the Middle East. These include objects excavated and retrieved by Japanese teams before a dam was built on the Euphrates River in the 1970s.

If you have kids to entertain, or are looking for bizarre pop cultural and culinary distractions, you might also want to visit **Namco Namjatown** (tel: 03-5950 0765; www.namja.jp; daily 10am–10pm) a noisy, inventively

decorated indoor theme park notable mainly for its **Ikebukuro Gyoza Stadium** offering dumplings from chefs around Japan.

Zoshigaya Cemetery

Exit Sunshine City at its southeastern corner and continue south for about five minutes through the side streets towards the raised expressway and Higashi-Ikebukuro subway station, also a stop on the Toden Arakawa tram line. You can hop on the tram here for one stop to Zoshigaya-mae or continue walking for another two minutes to reach **Zoshigaya Cemetery** ❽ (Zoshigaya Reien).

The cemetery's tree-lined paths and avenues of cherry trees lead you to the resting grounds of several well-known literary figures, including the novelists Natsume Soseki and Lafcadio Hearn and one of Tokyo's finest chroniclers, Nagai Kafu. The inscription on the headstone of this self-effacing novelist modestly reads: 'The Grave of Kafu the Scribbler'. Pick up a map (in Japanese) from the Funeral Hall to locate their graves.

Gokoku-ji Temple.

Zoshigaya Missionary Museum

Address: 1-25-5 Zoshigaya, Toshima-ku
Tel: 03-3985 4081
Opening Hours: Tue–Sun 10am–4.30pm
Entrance Fee: free
Transport: Higashi-Ikebukuro

A short walk south of the cemetery in a quiet residential street is the little-visited but charming **Zoshigaya Missionary Museum** ❾ (Zoshigaya Kyu-Senkyoshikan), a lovingly preserved American colonial-style house built in 1907 by an American missionary, John Moody McCaleb. The interior has been kept pretty much as it was during the 50 years he spent living in Japan.

Gokoku-ji ❿

Walking east from the cemetery, under the raised expressway, will bring you to a gate opening into another cemetery in the grounds of

this well-preserved temple complex (tel: 03-3941 0764; www.gokokuji.or.jp). Established by the fifth Shogun Tokugawa Tsunayoshi in 1681, it has been designated an Important Cultural Property. The Emperor Meiji (1852–1912) is buried here, as are several of his children. Exit the temple by its magnificent Nio-mon Gate housing two fierce-looking statues placed at either side to ward off evil spirits. The entrance to Gokoku-ji subway station is also here.

Feline friend at Namco Namjatown theme park in Sunshine City.

MEJIRODAI

St Mary's Cathedral

Address: 3-15-16 Sekiguchi, Bunkyo-ku; www.tokyo.catholic.jp
Tel: 03-3943 2301
Opening Hours: daily 9am–5pm
Entrance Fee: free
Transport: Edogawabashi

About 10 minutes south on foot from Gokoku-ji, through the prosperous residential back streets of Mejirodai, is **St Mary's Cathedral** ⓫ (Tokyo Katedoraru Sei Maria Daiseido) with its towering steel-clad bell tower. Designed by Kenzo Tange in 1964, the seat of Tokyo's Roman Catholic church – like the architect's Olympic stadium in Yoyogi (see page 137) – still appears utterly modern. The interior is dominated by a giant pipe organ, the largest of its kind in Japan, on which concerts are occasionally given.

Chinzan-so

Opposite the cathedral, a wedding hall and the **Hotel Chinzan-so** ⓬ share the view across these lovely gardens (https://hotel-chinzanso-tokyo.jp/garden/; daily 9am–8pm; free), whose name means 'House of Camellias'. Designed in the late 19th century, the 66,000 sq metres/yds of gardens include a 1,000-year-old pagoda that originally hails from a temple in Hiroshima prefecture, ancient stone lanterns and monuments, and several

St Mary's Cathedral (Katedoraru Sei Maria Daiseido) is located in the Sekiguchi district.

fine traditional restaurants including **Mucha-an** and **Kinsui**.

KOMAGOME AND AROUND

East of Ikebukuro, the Yamanote Line takes you to **Komagome** ⓭ which has two excellent gardens. **Rikugien** (6-16-3 Hon-komagome, Bunkyo-ku; http://teien.tokyo-park.or.jp/en/rikugien; daily 9am–5pm), the closest to the station, was created in 1702 by feudal lord Yoshiyasu Yanagisawa and is a prime example of an Edo-era stroll garden with the landscaping of hills and ponds inspired by the verses of Waka poetry. The garden is especially attractive in autumn and when the cherry blossoms briefly bloom in early spring.

The other sight of note is **Kyu Furukawa Garden** (Kyu Furukawa Teien; 1-27-39 Nishigahara, Kita-ku; http://teien.tokyo-park.or.jp/en/kyu-furu-kawa; daily 9am–5pm), a 10-minute walk north of the station. The garden and its main building, a charcoal-grey stone residence resembling a Scottish manor house and completed in 1917, are the work of British architect Josiah Conder. There's a tea-house in the garden where you can sip matcha (powdered green tea). The garden is known for its display of azaleas in April.

Koishikawa Botanical Gardens ⓮

Address: 3-7-1 Hakusan, Bunkyo-ku; www.bg.s.u-tokyo.ac.jp/koishikawa
Tel: 03-3814 0139
Opening Hours: Tue–Sun 9am–4.30pm
Entrance Fee: charge
Transport: Hakusan

Nature lovers and botanists will also want to check out these leafy gardens belonging to Tokyo University's Graduate School of Science. This 161,588-sq-metre (193,258-sq-yd) compound, home to 4,000 different living species, is Japan's oldest botanical garden, originally having been established as a medicinal herb garden in 1684 by the Tokugawa Shogunate. While strolling the grounds look for 'Newton no Ringo' – an apple tree grown from a cutting from the very same one Isaac Newton sat under when the apocryphal apple fell.

THE CHIN CHIN DENSHA

Less than a century ago Tokyo was criss-crossed by tramlines. Practically all of them have long since been ripped up to be built or paved over. The sole remaining central service is the Sakura Line, running between Waseda and Minowa-bashi. It's affectionately known as the *chin chin densha*, meaning 'ding, ding train' after the bell that the driver sounds on leaving each station.

Tickets cost ¥170 regardless of how far you travel on the line: the stretch between Higashi-Ikebukuro and Shin-Koshinzuka Station, next to Nishi-Sug-amo Station on the Toei Mita Line will give you a taste of what public transport in Tokyo was once like.

Cherry blossoms in Zoshigaya Cemetery.

Beautiful colours at Koishkawa Botanical Gardens.

Shinjuku is home to a 12-metre (40ft) Godzilla head.

SHINJUKU

Over 3.5 million people pass through Shinjuku each day. This unrivalled density makes it a microcosm of all that is Tokyo: soaring high-rises, massive malls, tiny shops, classy boutiques and a maze of entertainment venues.

With no castle, river or temple to found itself on, Shinjuku came into existence because of its position at the junction of two key arteries leading into the city from the west. It even had to invent its own name. Shinjuku simply means 'New Lodgings', a reference to the post station that was built on the more important of the two routes, the Koshu Kaido, to allow weary horses and travellers to rest overnight before completing the last leg of their journey in Edo.

The facility, proposed by five brothel owners from Edo's thriving pleasure quarters, was little more than a pretence to tap the captive market of travellers. Inns and shops soon lined the streets of Naito Shinjuku, as it was called. Its main attractions were the teahouses employing dozens of 'rice-serving girls', whose function was more carnal than culinary. The district was closed down after an incident at one teahouse involving a relative of the shogun, but reopened in 1772. Within a decade, over 50 inns and teahouses had sprung up.

Freight trains started to roll into Shinjuku Station in 1885, followed by passenger trains and a tram system. The major factor in Shinjuku's rise to urban pre-eminence, however,

occurred with the Great Kanto Earthquake of 1923. While most of the old city centre was laid to waste, Shinjuku largely emerged unscathed. Huge numbers of residents moved in and, soon, department stores like Mitsukoshi and Isetan opened new branches here, followed by theatres, cafés and artists' studios. By the early 1930s, with writers, painters and students in situ, Shinjuku had become Tokyo's bohemian quarter.

The area's commercial importance and high civilian population made

Main Attractions
Tokyo Metropolitan Government Office
Shinjuku Central Park
Sompo Japan Museum of Art
Mode Gakuen Cocoon Tower
Omoide Yokocho
Shinjuku Gyoen
Hanazono-jinja
Golden gai
Kabuki-cho

Map
Page 118

The bright lights of lively Shinjuku.

Vending machines are a ubiquitous feature of Tokyo life. They sell everything from food and beverages to flowers and film tickets. There are an estimated 5 million nationwide.

subways make Shinjuku Station the busiest in the world.

Shinjuku today likes to style itself as 'the city of the future'. Like so many other self-designations in Tokyo, this is only half-true, applicable in this case to just one side of the mini-city – its western interface, Nishi-Shinjuku, where the Keio and Odakyu department stores face the locus of skyscrapers that define this area.

NISHI-SHINJUKU

Tokyo Metropolitan Government Office ❶

Address: 2-8-1 Nishi-Shinjuku;
www.metro.tokyo.jp
Tel: 03-5321 1111
Opening Hours: daily
9.30am–10.30pm
Entrance Fee: free
Transport: Tochomae

Nishi-Shinjuku's most conspicuous structure is the capital's City Hall (Tocho). Its twin 48-storey towers are

it an inevitable target for American bombing missions, the most terrifying of which occurred on 25 May 1945, when air raids levelled the entire district, leaving only one building standing, the Isetan department store. The area quickly resurrected itself, however. The first skyscraper to go up in this part of Tokyo was the Keio Plaza Hotel in 1971. Since then many have followed, including the dazzling Mode Gakuen Cocoon Tower. Multiple railway lines and

Shinjuku

the work of Kenzo Tange, who designed the original metropolitan offices in Yurakucho in 1957. The observation galleries (North Observatory daily 9.30am–10.30pm, South Observatory daily 9.30am–5.30pm; free) on the 45th floors of both towers afford superlative views across the city and, on fine days, even Mount Fuji.

South of the Tocho, along Tocho-dori, the highlight of the 30-storey **NS Building** ❷ is its hollowed-out interior and a roof made from 6,000 pieces of glass. With a glass elevator to match, the views as you ascend the exterior of the building are spectacular. An observatory on the 29th floor, and restaurants there, afford more good views.

Shinjuku Central Park

West Shinjuku has tended to develop vertically, leaving plenty of intermittent space between tower blocks in which to stroll. Adding to that sense of space is **Shinjuku Central Park** ❸ (Shinjuku Chuo Koen; daily 24 hours; free), with its pleasant pathways, trees and hillocks – it has also been adopted by some of the area's homeless as a place to live.

Tucked into the northwest corner of the park is **Kumano-jinja**, a small shrine founded in the 15th century. The shrine, which once stood at the centre of a geisha district, seems cowed by the wall of skyscrapers that rise on its eastern flank.

Bunka Gakuen Costume Museum

Address: 3-22-7 Yoyogi, Shibuya-ku; http://museum.bunka.ac.jp
Tel: 03-3299 2387
Opening Hours: Mon–Sat 10am–4.30pm
Entrance Fee: charge
Transport: Shinjuku

Walking southeast and crossing the broad avenue Koshu Kaido that brought Shinjuku into existence brings you to the **Bunka Women's University**, with its prestigious

Tokyo Metropolitan Government Office building, or Tocho.

fashion school, and the **Bunka Gakuen Costume Museum** ❹ (Bunka Gakuen Fukushoku Hakubutsukan). The complete collection is too large to show at one time, but its partial displays are always interesting, particularly its Edo Period clothing. Exhibits range from *kosode* dresses and *noh* drama costumes to tribal wear from overseas and the cream of modern design.

Shinjuku Park Tower

A little west of the museum, back on the other side of Koshu Kaido, the hand of Kenzo Tange surfaces again in the 52-storey **Shinjuku Park Tower** ❺ (www.shinjukuparktower.com). Six floors are set aside for the shops and showrooms of the **Living Design Centre Ozone** (www.ozone.co.jp; Thu–Tue 10.30am–7pm; free), which has exhibitions relating to modern interior design, much of it eco-conscious.

Occupying the top 14 floors is the luxury **Park Hyatt Tokyo.** The bamboo garden on the 41st floor that forms the centrepiece of Peak Lounge, with its superb views, is one of the most sophisticated spots in the city to take high tea. Park Hyatt Tokyo was where Sofia

Coppola's award-winning film *Lost in Translation* was set: the 52nd-floor New York Bar was an on-screen watering hole of Bill Murray's character.

NTT InterCommunication Center

Address: 4F Tokyo Opera City Tower, 3-20-2 Nishi-Shinjuku, Shinjuku-ku; www.ntticc.or.jp
Tel: 0120 144 199
Opening Hours: Tue–Sun 11am–6pm
Entrance Fee: charge
Transport: Hatsudai

Southwest of Shinjuku Park Tower, **Tokyo Opera City** (www.operacity.jp/en) is a 54-floor complex of shops, offices and restaurants. There's an art gallery (Tue–Sun 11am–7pm) here with a focus on emerging Japanese artists, and a concert hall, but you're likely to find the most interesting part of the complex to be the **NTT InterCommunication Center** ⑥ on the fourth floor. This interactive high-tech exhibition space also has an electronic library and internet café. Also part of the complex is the **New National Theatre** (Shin Kokuritsu Gekijo).

Shinjuku Sumitomo Building

Back on Chuo-dori – the street that runs from Shinjuku's west exit to the Tokyo Metropolitan Government Office – is a cluster of older buildings, many of them with observation floors that allow free entry and/or restaurants that provide panoramic views. A good example is the six-sided 52-storey **Shinjuku Sumitomo Building** ⑦ constructed around an open well. Light floods down to the lobby through a massive glass roof.

Sompo Japan Museum of Art

Address: 42F Sompo Japan Building, 1-26-1 Nishi-Shinjuku; www.sjnk-museum.org
Tel: 03-5405 8686
Opening Hours: Tue–Sun 10am–6pm
Entrance Fee: charge
Transport: Shinjuku

Behind the Center Building is the **Sompo Japan Building** where, on the 42nd floor, you'll find the **Sompo Japan Museum of Art** ⑧ (Sompo

The commercial side of Shinjuku has a thriving nightlife.

Kumano-jinga shrine in Shinjuku Central Park.

Bijutsukan) displaying works by several Japanese artists. The core of the exhibition is the collection of works by Seiji Togo (1897–1978), a skilful painter who specialised in portraits of young women. The highlight of the museum, however, is Van Gogh's *Sunflowers*, which was bought for a whopping ¥6 billion (US$40 million) during the free-spending bubble economy years. There is also one work apiece by Cezanne, Gauguin and Renoir.

Mode Gakuen Cocoon Tower

The ultra-contemporary crosshatched **Mode Gakuen Cocoon Tower** ❾ was added to Nishi-Shinjuku's collection of skyscrapers in 2008. Designed by Tange Associates, and occupied by a fashion and computer studies school, this 50-storey glass stunner has a large bookshop **Book 1st** (www.book1st.net) in its basement including the Tokyo Magazine Centre with some 5,000 titles from around the world.

Omoide Yokocho

Hard up against the thick band of tracks heading north out of Shinjuku Station you'll find a remnant of the old Shinjuku before giant neon-clad buildings became the norm. This cramped, run-down, four-block neighbourhood is officially called **Omoide Yokocho** ❿. However it's also popularly known as Shomben Yokocho (Piss Alley), a reference to the time when there were no toilets here and patrons would urinate in the alley (there are toilets these days). Hung with red lanterns and packed with more than 60 friendly hole-in-the-wall restaurants and bars, it's a great place to return in the evening for inexpensive yakitori (grilled chicken), ramen, *yakiniku* (barbecued meat) and beers. On the southwest corner of you'll find the appealing **Tajimaya Coffee House.**

HIGASHI-SHINJUKU

The east exit of the station, incorporating the fashion shopping

TIP

The epicentre of Tokyo's gay scene is Shinjuku ni-chome, near Shinjuku Sanchome Station. There's not much going on during the day but come sundown around 300 gay bars, clubs and restaurants open for business.

complex called **Lumine Est**, comes out onto a small plaza in front of the landmark **Studio Alta** ⓫, several floors of youthful designer clothing with a huge, signature video screen, one of Tokyo's best-known rendezvous points. The Alta sits at the head of **Shinjuku-dori**, the area's main commercial thoroughfare along which you'll find department stores such as Marui and the venerable **Isetan** ⓬, as well as **Bicqlo**, a joint venture megastore launched in 2012 combining goods from home electronics giant Bic Camera and budget fashion retailer Uniqlo.

Two small blocks east of Isetan, north of the main road, look out for the rows of coloured lanterns that decorate the outside of **Suehiro-tei** (3-6-12 Shinjuku, Shinjuku-ku; tel: 03-3351 2974) a small wooden theatre. It's one of the few stages left in Tokyo dedicated to *rakugo*, a form of traditional storytelling in which the narrator addresses the audience in a seated position, as well as *manzai*; comic performances by a pair of actors.

Shinjuku Gyoen

Address: Naito-machi, Shinjuku-ku; www.env.go.jp/garden/shinjukugyoen/english/index.html
Tel: 03-3350 0151
Opening Hours: Tue–Sun 9am–4.30pm
Entrance Fee: charge
Transport: Shinjuku-Gyoen-Mae

From Shinjuku-dori head back towards Koshu Kaido to find the main entrance of **Shinjuku Gyoen** ⓭. The lovely 60-hectare (150-acre) grounds, once part of the estate of the daimyo (feudal lord) Naito during the Edo Period, were opened to the public in 1949.

The park is divided into three sections: a northern section containing a garden in the formal French manner; a landscaped English garden at the centre; and a traditional Japanese garden, with winding paths, arched bridges, stone lanterns and artificial hills, in the southern section. Look out for the **Taiwan-kaku Pavilion**, a Chinese-style gazebo built to commemorate the wedding of the Emperor Hirohito in 1927. The park's old botanical

Bustling Chuo-dori.

TOKYO'S 'KOREATOWN'

The narrow roads or alleys that run north from Kabuki-cho lead to lively Okubo-dori. From here up to and around the overland train stations Shin Okubo and Okubo, the prevalence of Korean script on hotel, shop and restaurant signs is noticeable. This is Tokyo's Koreatown, a place where locals flock when they want to sample the most authentic and spicy Korean cuisine as well as buy the latest music from Korean pop singers (K-Pop) or a DVD of one of the hugely popular South Korean TV soap operas. There are around 100,000 Koreans living in Tokyo, but the area has become popular with other Asian immigrants, too, so you'll also find several good Thai, Filipino and Chinese restaurants here.

greenhouse contains some splendid subtropical plants.

Shinjuku Historical Museum

Address: 22 Saneicho, Shinjuku-ku
Tel: 03-3359 2131
Opening Hours: Tue–Sun 9.30am–5.30pm
Entrance Fee: charge
Transport: Yotsuya-Sanchome

A fair distance northeast of the garden, signposted from Yotsuya-Sanchome Station, is the small but stimulating **Shinjuku Historical Museum ⓮** (Shinjuku Rekishi Haku-butsukan), which provides insights into what the district must have looked like in its days as a post town.

Jokaku-ji ⓯

A little north of Shinjuku Garden, next to **Shinjuku Ni-chome**, the enclave of gay and lesbian bars is this easily passed, unexceptional-looking temple. Closer scrutiny reveals a tombstone, placed here in 1860 by innkeepers from the brothel district, marking the spot of a communal grave where prostitutes who died

were unceremoniously disposed of without the usual burial rites. The place is a sober reminder of the unglamorous existence of Shinjuku's 'rice serving girls'.

Hanazono-jinja

Address: 5-17-3 Shinjuku, Shinjuku-ku
Tel: 03-3209 5265
Opening Hours: daily sunrise–sunset
Entrance Fee: free
Transport: Shinjuku-Sanchome Station

Retrace your steps to Isetan, walk along its eastern flank down Meiji-dori, until you reach the wide boulevard called Yasukuni-dori. Cross it and turn left. Immediately on your right you will see the narrow entrance to the **Hanazono-jinja ⓰**, an oasis of calm at the edge of one of Tokyo's raunchiest entertainment and red-light areas. The shrine dates back to the 6th century, but the current concrete and granite structure is more recent. One of the ubiquitous Inari fox shrines (Inari being a major fox deity and also messenger to Ebisu, the god of business and commerce),

TIP

Shinjuku Gyoen is worth visiting in any season but it's particularly beautiful in April when acres of cherry blossom trees are in full bloom, or in late October when the autumn leaves are the attraction. Displays of chrysanthemums, the imperial flowers, are held during the first two weeks of November.

Exploring Shinjuku at night.

Shinjuku Gyoen.

A typical eatery in the Shinjuku area.

market is held in the shrine grounds every Sunday.

Golden Gai

Shinjuku has a relationship with alcohol not unlike like that of Venice with water: it's built on it. Right next door to the shrine, forming a warren of narrow alleys with a grid of tiny, two-storey bars, is **Golden Gai** ⑰, an endearing retro crevice of Tokyo saved, for the time being, from the clutches of the speculator. Each of the some 200 bars in this area has a different clientele – some attract just writers, others mostly photographers, and so on – and most have a cover charge, to dissuade non-regulars, of anything from ¥1,000 to ¥4,000; it's one of the most atmospheric night-life areas of Tokyo and worth looking at even if you're not planning to drink.

Kabuki-cho

Follow Shiki-no-michi (Four Seasons Pathway), the attractive

Hanazono is popular with local shop-keepers who come here to pray for success in business. The vermillion and gold interior of the main hall is impressive. Stone lamps and spot-lights come on at night, creating an enchanting atmosphere. A lively flea

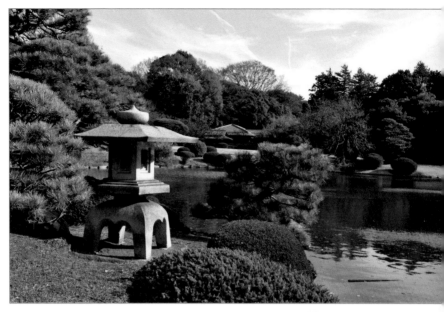

pedestrian route that skirts the east side of Golden Gai, to emerge just a few steps to the right of Kuyakusho-dori, and the heart of **Kabuki-cho** ⓲. Relatively tame-looking by day, Kabuki-cho undergoes a transformation at twilight, when the area's seedy hostess bars, strip joints, porno fleapits, peepshows and brothels (innocuously named 'Soaplands') spark into neon-lit action. All these red-light establishments share the streets with numerous reputable bars, restaurants and small music venues.

Kabuki-cho is so called because, after World War II, it was proposed that a kabuki theatre be built here. That plan never came to pass but this raunchy area of Shinjuku kept the classier-sounding name.

Shinjuku Toho Building

The area's former lynchpin, the Koma Theatre and neighbouring Toho Kaikan building, closed in 2008. Replacing them is the

Shinjuku Toho Building ⓳, opened in 2015, housing the 12-screen Toho Cinema Shinjuku, several restaurants, amusement shops and the Gracery Hotel.

A 12-metre (40ft) **Godzilla head**, towering 52 metres (170ft) above ground level, was installed on the outdoor terrace of the complex and has become a popular ambassador of the area. The brightest star in Japanese film history, with 32 films to its credit (plus three Hollywood ones), the monster occasionally lights up and roars, much to the amusement of passers-by. The huge 970-room Gracery Hotel even boasts Godzilla View Rooms, commanding a view of the monster's head. Following a close encounter with Godzilla, you can either head back a few blocks south across Yasakuni-dori to Shinjuku Station, or north to the neighbouring **Hyakunincho** area, where you'll find a collection of Southeast Asian restaurants, and on to Shinjuku's **Koreatown**.

The steamier side of things in Kabukicho district.

TIP

In Kabuki-cho men may get approached by touts, often from West Africa, offering 'great deals' on drinks and girls. Avoid the kind of places they advertise and the area is perfectly safe to explore and drink in.

Dior store on Omotesando Street.

AOYAMA AND OMOTESANDO

Fashionistas should make a beeline to Aoyama and, in particular, the luxury shopping boulevard Omotesando, lined with zelkova trees and an amazing collection of modern architecture.

oyama is centred on the main axes of Aoyama-dori and Omotesando-dori. Tokyoites like to think of gently sloping **Omotesando-dori** as the capital's Champs Elysées, a boulevard whose chic designer label establishments carry a hallmark of quality. However, the boulevard was originally created as the frontal approach to the important shrine Meiji-jingu (see page 129). More recently it has also become known for its impressive stash of contemporary-designed buildings. This chapter covers the sights along and around Omotesando up to Meiji-dori; sights further west of here are covered in the chapter Harajuku and Shibuya (see page 135).

AOYAMA

Although there is little to remind you of Tokyo's past in Aoyama, where designer quarters, cosmopolitan tastes and sophistication reign today, the area was once home to lush rice paddies, hunting grounds and sprawling feudal estates. A close advisor of the shogun Tokugawa Ieyasu, Aoyama Tadanari, was given land here in 1590, the year Edo became the nation's martial capital.

Aoyama Cemetery

In the years after the Meiji Restoration, these estates were turned into military parade grounds and cemeteries. **Aoyama Cemetery** ❶ (Aoyama Reien) was one of Tokyo's four largest burial grounds, created by the government after it had abandoned a rather quirky scheme to plant the area with mulberry trees in the hope of cultivating raw silk to export in exchange for foreign currency.

The area's arboreal dreams resurfaced, however, when hundreds of

The busy shopping area of Omotesando.

attractive cherry trees were planted later. The plaintive setting of the cemetery is perfect for the evanescence the cherry blossoms symbolise. Well over 100,000 people are buried here, including many of Tokyo's eminent political and military leaders, writers, a few notable foreigners and the owner of ever-faithful dog Hachiko (see page 140). The cemetery can be approached from several directions but one of the easiest is to alight at the subway at Gaienmae Station from where it's just a few minutes' walk south.

Baiso-in

Address: 2-24-8 Minami-Aoyama, Minato-ku
Tel: 03-3404 8447
Opening Hours: 9am–5pm
Entrance Fee: free
Transport: Gaienmae

Many people choose to have a Buddhist funeral in Japan, so it's common to find temples clustered around cemeteries. From Aoyama-dori, a corridor of lofty bamboo plants leads to **Baiso-in ❷**, founded in 1643 as a family temple of the Aoyama clan. It is the 24th point on the Great 33 Kannon pilgrimage of temples in Tokyo and is also known for its Gujo-odori dance festival, which is held every June.

What is most unusual about the temple is its thoroughly modern main building, designed by Kengo Kuma, a famous local architect who is responsible for several other projects in the area. The coolly beautiful structure features plenty of glass shaded by steel louvres.

Meiji Memorial Picture Gallery

Address: 1-1 Kasumigaokamachi, Shinjuku-ku; www.meijijingugaien.jp/english/seitoku-gallery.html
Tel: 03-3401 5179
Opening Hours: daily 9am–5pm
Entrance Fee: charge
Transport: Kokuritsu-Kyogijo

Aoyama and Omotesando

Heading northeast from Baison-in along Aoyama-dori, Icho-Namiki, better known as **Gingko Tree Avenue**, is on the left, equidistant between Gaienmae and Aoyama-Itchome metro stations. The trees are at their best in October when their leaves turn gold and yellow.

The avenue leads straight to the **Meiji Shrine Outer Gardens** (Meiji-Jingu Gaien), home to several sporting stadia, tennis courts, and baseball and golf practice ranges. The highlight, however, is the **Meiji Memorial Picture Gallery ❸** (Seitoku Kinen Kaigakan), built in 1926 to commemorate the life and achievements of the Meiji Emperor. Solemn looking on the outside, its interior is more impressive, with a domed ceiling and an imposing stairwell made of marble from Gifu prefecture. Its 80 Japanese- and Western-style works have detailed explanations in English. The gallery can also be approached from the north from either the overground station Sendagaya or the subway station Kokuritsu-Kyogijo, in which case you'll pass both the **Tokyo Gymnasium** and the site where the **National Olympic Stadium** is being developed for the 2020 Olympic Games.

Watari-um Museum

Address: 3-7-6 Jingumae, Shibuya-ku
Tel: 03-3402 3001
Opening Hours: Tue and Thu–Sun 11am–7pm, Wed until 9pm
Entrance Fee: charge
Transport: Gaienmae

Heading back west in the direction of Gaienmae Station, where Aoyama-dori crosses Gaien-Nishi-dori, turn right.

On the left side is the exposed concrete and black granite striped **Watari-um Museum ❹** (Watari-um Bijutsukan), an ultra-modern art space designed by Swiss architect Mario Botta. It features the work of some of today's best Japanese and international avant-garde artists. Also in the building is a chilled-out café and the excellent art bookshop **On Sundays.** Watch out when crossing Gaien Nishi-dori – it's also rather disconcertingly known as 'Killer-dori' on account of

Aoyama Cemetery.

the huge number of traffic accidents that have occurred along it.

Spiral Building

Address: 5-6-23 Minami-Aoyama, Shibuya-ku; www.spiral.co.jp
Tel: 03-3498 1171
Opening Hours: daily 8am–11pm
Entrance Fee: free
Transport: Omotesando

Return south to Aoyama-dori and continue west, past Omotesando, to discover the contemporary lines of the striking **Spiral Building** ❺. Owned by the lingerie company Wacoal, the building incorporates a gallery, theatre, gift shop and café. The building is the work of leading architect Fumihiko Maki and its centrepiece is a spiral ramp, a structure that floats and curves upwards to the next floor around the exhibition space below.

Of late, Spiral Hall has been given some competition in the architectural showstopper stakes by the

AO Building, designed by Sakura Associates, which stands on the opposite side of the street. The glass tower, which looks spectacular when lit up at night, houses many top fashion boutiques, restaurants and, in the basement, the supermarket Kinokuniya whose original building once stood on this spot.

United Nations University

Just along from the AO Building is the **United Nations University** ❻ (Kokuren Daigaku; www.unu.edu), a development and coordination centre for the world peace organisation. Kenzo Tange, who won the Pritzker prize in 1987 – the equivalent of the Oscar in the architectural world – designed this UN facility. It's a symmetrical building with a solid main axis, said to represent well-intended authority. Every weekend one of Tokyo's best farmer's markets is held here.

hpgrp Gallery Tokyo

The **hpgrp Gallery Tokyo** ❼ (http://hpgrpgallery.com; Tue–Sun noon–8pm; free), close to the Spiral building, is an interesting gallery presenting only the highest quality works of art. Every month, the venue hosts a new exhibition by a carefully selected young and

Modern design on Minami-Aoyama.

inic Minami Aoyama

talented artist. The gallery also has an excellent branch in New York.

Taro Okamoto Memorial Museum

Address: 6-1-19 Minami-Aoyama, Minato-ku; www.taro-okamoto.or.jp
Tel: 03-3406 0801
Opening Hours: Wed–Mon 10am–6pm
Entrance Fee: charge
Transport: Omotesando

You'll find numerous works by one of Japan's most prolific and zaniest artists, Taro Okamoto, at the **Taro Okamoto Memorial Museum ❽** (Okamoto Taro Kinenkan), a small museum created out of an old studio, a short walk back towards Omotesando. To find it hang a right on **Kotto-dori**, also known as 'Antique Street', for its proliferation of antiques shops and art dealers, then duck into the backstreets near where you see the famous jazz club Blue Note Tokyo.

Nezu Museum

Address: 6-5-1 Minami-Aoyama, Minato-ku; www.nezu-muse.or.jp
Tel: 03-3400 2536
Opening Hours: Tue–Sun 10am–5pm

Entrance Fee: charge
Transport: Omotesando

Further along the Kotto-dori, down the same side street as Blue Note Tokyo, is the excellent **Nezu Museum ❾** (Nezu Bijutsukan). In a beautiful building designed by Kengo Kuma, it houses the collection of Meiji-era politician and railway tycoon Kaichiro Nezu.

The museum's collection boasts more than 7,000 pieces and among the permanent displays are fine examples of Chinese bronzes, ceramic and lacquerware, calligraphy, textiles and Chinese and Japanese paintings. Several exceedingly rare objects are registered as National Treasures. Among these is a screen painting by Ogata Korin called *Irises*, which is displayed for a month each year at the end of April when the museum is very busy.

As much as the art, the highlight of the museum is its lovely garden in a densely wooded and hilly landscape with a small iris pond and a number of traditional teahouses. None of these are open to the public, but in his renovation of the property, Kuma added a modern café that provides a wonderful view of the gardens and is a lovely spot for lunch or tea.

Delicate screen painting of purple irises by Ogata Korin (1658–1716) on display at the Nezu Museum.

Shoppers outside the Hermès store.

Funky Cat Street in Omotesando offers more affordable shopping options.

Omotesando Hills received a mixed reception when it opened.

OMOTESANDO

From the Nezu Museum, turn left into the start of Aoyama's principal shopping destination: Omotesando.

Architectural statements

On the left is the striking mass of concrete, glass and aluminium panels that make up **Collezione** ⑩, a 1989 work by well-known architect Tadao Ando. Completely self-taught, the Osaka-born Ando was a boxer before turning to creating buildings. The inspiration for this 'strata architecture' as Ando calls it, came from a visit to an Indian well where, descending to the water's edge, 'the eyes perceive gradations of light and the skin experiences a reduction in temperature.'

Even more arresting is **Prada Aoyama** ⑪, further along on the same side. A diamond-shaped, steel latticework wraps around the building, creating the effect of a three-sided column of bubble wrap. The design is the work of Swiss architecture firm Herzog & de Meuron, who are reported to have said, 'We could only do this building here in Japan.' Across the street from Prada, and nowhere near as impressive on the eye on the outside, is the **Tessenkai Noh Theatre** ⑫. Inside, however, the theatre's stark wooden stage, which is accented by ornately painted backdrops, is a thing of beauty.

Heading across Aoyama-dori, into the heart of Omotesando, the roll call of modern architectural masters reaches fever pitch. First on the right is **ONE Omotesando** ⑬ where Kengo Kuma's trademark steel louvres are again in evidence on a building that houses several boutiques.

On the opposite side of the zelkova-lined avenue, the branches of the trees are the clear inspiration for the bands of concrete and angled panes of glass wrapping the facade of shoe boutique **Tod's** ⑭, the work of architect Toyo Ito. On the next block along is **Louis Vuitton Omotesando** ⑮, the flagship store of the luxury brand. It was designed by Jun Aoki to resemble a series of stacked ornamental boxes, and looks as if a giant has left his Vuitton luggage piled up on the sidewalk.

Omotesando Hills

From the exterior, **Omotesando Hills** ⑯ – another Tadao Ando design – appears a relatively modest, low-key structure. But this is deceptive since the luxury shopping mall and apartment complex is best viewed from inside where the space opens up to reveal a 12-storey building with a huge atrium, half of which is buried underground. Ando's complex replaced the ivy-covered Dojunkai Apartments dating from 1927 which were much loved and missed: the architect paid homage to them by recreating a small section of the apartments and incorporating it into his design (at the far south end of the complex).

Opposite Omotesando Hills are several other shops you'll most likely want to check out including the antiques and souvenir shops **Oriental Bazaar** and **Fuji Torii**, and the toyshop **Kiddyland**.

Cat Street

Kiddyland is on corner of the junction with Kyu Shibuya-gawa, a sinewy retail promenade that follows the path of the cemented-over Shibuya River. It's more popularly known as **Cat Street** ⓱ and provides a funkier, more youthful and affordable counterpoint to the high gloss, luxury-brand shopping experience of Omotesando. You'll see queues of customers – mainly young local girls – waiting to get into certain establishments, most commonly serving crepes, waffles or bubble tea. Heading south the street shadows Meiji-dori, which it eventually joins to bring you to Shibuya Station.

Design Festa Gallery

Address: 3-20-2 Jingumae, Shibuya-ku; www.designfestagallery.com
Tel: 03-3479 1442
Opening Hours: daily 11am–8pm
Entrance Fee: free
Transport: Meiji-Jingumae

Follow Cat Street northeast from Omotesando to the point where there's a fork in the road, then take the left-hand lane to reach one of the entrances to the **Design Festa Gallery** ⓲, an anarchic explosion of contemporary art galleries that have taken over several old houses and an apartment block. The art here reaches beyond the exhibition spaces to engulf every part of the complex, from the paint-bombed toilets and graffiti-covered bins to the friendly

café-bar and *okonomiyaki* restaurant Sakuratei. It's great fun to explore this ever-interesting complex, which has grown out of a twice-yearly design event of the same name that takes place at Tokyo Big Sight on Odaiba (see page 209).

The Iceberg

There's one more contemporary structure worth seeing before moving on from this area. From the junction of Omotesando and Meiji-dori, head south until you reach, on the left, the Audi Forum. This showroom for the German car manufacturer is housed in a building known, for obvious reasons, as **The Iceberg** ⓳. Designed by British-born, Tokyo-based architect Benjamin Warner, this multifaceted glass tower looks as if it has floated to Tokyo from the Antarctic.

TIP
There's no need to get up early to go shopping. Most boutiques in Aoyama and along Omotesando don't open until at least 11am and close around 8pm.

Brightly painted signs direct visitors towards an exhibition at the Design Festa Gallery.

HARAJUKU AND SHIBUYA

While Harajuku, home of the stately Meiji Shrine, has a few time-honoured reminders of the past, Shibuya is firmly wedged in the present, partying (and shopping) with youthful vigour.

Harajuku has become well known beyond Tokyo as a byword for youthful style. On any day of the week you need only linger around the station – take your pick from either the Takeshita-dori end or by the top of Omotesando – to see many a prime example of the so-called 'Harajuku Girls': women whose fearless fashion sense results in looks ranging from *kawaii* (super cute) Victorian doll meets punk rock princess to the edgier Goth-loli (standing for Gothic Lolita) glamazon.

Back in the 11th century, Harajuku was a post station on the Kamakura Kaido, the road to the wild northern provinces. Hara, in fact, means 'field', juku, a 'place of lodging'. Beyond the area's multitude of cafés there are hardly any places for travellers to rest these days but even so, among Harajuku's swirl of boutiques and fashion houses and other contemporary implants, are reminders of an older city in the roadside shrines and cultural museums.

Ukiyo-e Ota Memorial Museum of Art

Address: 1-10-10 Jingumae, Shibuya-ku; www.ukiyoe-ota-muse.jp
Tel: 03-3403 0880
Opening Hours: Tue–Sun 10.30am–5.30pm

Entrance Fee: charge
Transport: Harajuku

A short stroll from the intersection of Meiji-dori and Omotesando-dori, just behind the boutique complex Laforet is the **Ukiyo-e Ota Memorial Museum of Art ❶** (Ukiyo-e Ota Kinen Bijutsukan) with what is arguably the city's finest collection of Edo Period *ukiyo-e* woodblock prints, over 12,000 works in all, including extremely rare prints by artists such as Utamaru, Sharaku and Hiroshige.

Fancy dress shop in Harajuku.

Eye-catching sign on Takeshita-dori.

Visitors have to remove their shoes before entering the museum.

Takeshita-dori

A short walk northeast from the museum, the atmosphere couldn't be more different on **Takeshita-dori** ❷, a pedestrian street that runs between Meiji-dori and Harajuku Station. Cheap fashion, accessories, cuddly toys, 'idol goods' and fast food restaurants lure teenagers for a taste of distilled subcultural kitsch. It can get very busy along this shopping strip, particularly at weekends when the street is as packed as a Tokyo train at rush hour.

Togo-jinja

Address: 1-5-3 Jingumae, Shibuya-ku
Tel: 03-3403 3591
Opening Hours: daily 6am–6pm
Entrance Fee: free
Transport: Harajuku

Behind Takeshita-dori, but light years away in spirit, are the peaceful grounds of the **Togo-jinja** ❸, a shrine dedicated to Admiral Heihachiro Togo, whose ships defeated the Russian fleet in the Tsushima Straits during the 1904–5 Russo-Japanese War. The original building was destroyed in a World War II air raid, but was rebuilt along with the Togo Memorial Hall and a treasury.

Harajuku and Shibuya

Meiji-jingu and gardens

Exiting west out of Takeshita-dori, the mock-Tudor facade of **Harajuku Station** (Harajuku-eki) comes into view as you climb the hill. Designed in 1924, it is one of the few Tokyo stations to have survived intact from that era. The station abuts one of Tokyo's major sights, the Imperial shrine **Meiji-jingu ❹**. To reach the main entrance to the shrine, you have to pass across an open plaza above the railway tracks, a popular spot on weekends for cosplay-dressed kids, buskers and other street performers, and then through the **Ichi-no-torii**, a massive gate made from 1,700-year-old cypress trees taken from Mount Alishan in Taiwan.

The shrine, opened in 1920 and dedicated to the memory of the Meiji Emperor and his wife, Empress Shoken, is tucked in the centre of **Meiji Shrine Inner Gardens** (Meiji-Jingu Gyoen), an expanse of dense forest of over 125,000 trees and shrubs brought from all over Japan. The park's famous **Iris Garden** (Jingu Naien; daily Mar–Oct 9am–4.30pm, Nov–Feb until 5pm), where over 100 varieties come into bloom in mid-June, was designed by the Meiji Emperor for his wife. The benches by the garden's carp-filled pond are some of the most peaceful places in central Tokyo.

The shrine itself, about 1km (half a mile) from the entrance, is a sublimely beautiful example of Shinto architecture, with its plain cypress pillars, sweeping copper roof and a white gravel forecourt. The original buildings burnt down in an air raid; what you see today is a perfect 1958 reconstruction. The compound, with its shrine maidens in white kimonos and orange tunics, plays host to lively events including formal Japanese weddings.

Meiji-jingu Treasure Museum

Located in the northern section of the park, the **Meiji-jingu Treasure Museum ❺** (Homotsuden Honkan),

in a building dating from 1921, displays a rather modest collection of sacred objects, garments and personal effects of the Imperial family. There's also a modern annex (Homotsu-Tenjishitsu) with a further display hall in a modern building near the main entrance to the shrine. Be aware that this museum is currently closed for reconstruction until further notice – please check before you visit.

Yoyogi Village

Address: 1-28-9 Yoyogi, Shibuya-ku; www.yoyogi-village.jp
Tel: 03-5302 2073
Opening Hours: daily 10am–7pm (cafés and bar open much later)
Entrance Fee: free
Transport: Yoyogi

A five-minute walk northeast of the Treasure Museum is this very hip eco-friendly 'village' of stores in **Yoyogi ❻**. Opened in 2011, the two-storey complex was put together by the producer of Japanese pop-rock band Mr. Children in collaboration with trend-conscious company Kurkku, who run an organic café and shop in Omotesando. As well as half a dozen or so shops, the Village is home to a chilled out café, an organic Italian restaurant, a spa and very trendy bar that attracts a good line-up of local DJs.

Yoyogi Park

Fringing the southwestern borders of the Meiji-jingu Inner Gardens is another generous swathe of green,

Detail of Meiji-jingu Shrine.

Wooden votive tablets outside the Meiji-jingu Shrine in Harajuku.

Rockabilly fans in Yoyogi Park.

Yoyogi Park ❼ (Yoyogi Koen).

American military personnel and their families were billeted here for several years after the war when the area was known as Washington Heights. The land was handed back to the Japanese government and turned into a village for athletes attending the Tokyo Olympics in 1964.

Ever since then the park has been a favourite gathering place for Tokyo's rockabilly devotees, particularly on weekends and holidays when quiff-haired, leather-jacket boys and hoop-skirted and bobby sock-clad girls can be found twisting to Elvis and the music of other rock legends. There's often free entertainment at weekends in the centre of the park from musicians, mime artists and other street performers. **Earthday Market** (www.earthdaymarket.com), selling organic food and drink and other eco-friendly products, is also held here one Sunday each month.

Opposite Harajuku Station and the main entrance to Yoyogi Park is **Yoyogi National Stadium** ❽ (Kokuritsu Yoyogi Kyogijo). Used for the 1964 Olympic Games' swimming and diving events, Kenzo Tange's highly original design looks remarkably contemporary even today. The smaller No. 2 Gymnasium, also part of the complex, houses a basketball court. The venue was selected to host handball competitions during the 2020 Summer Olympic Games.

SHIBUYA

During the late Edo Period, Shibuya sat on the western outskirts of the city, marking the transition from urban to rural. It is difficult to imagine that, only a century ago, this stridently trendy district, with its love hotels and consumer implants, was a place of tea plantations and rice mills.

NHK Studio Park

Address: 2-2-1 Jinnan, Shibuya-ku; www.nhk.or.jp/studiopark

Tel: 03-3485 8034
Opening Hours: daily 10am–6pm (closed 4th Mon of month)
Entrance Fee: charge
Transport: Shibuya

Next to the sports stadia is the **NHK Broadcasting Centre** ❾, the national television and radio headquarters, which has its main entrance on Inokashira-dori. Tours (only in Japanese) of its **Studio Park** complex, with its entrance near Koen-dori, offer the chance to see programmes as they are filmed, play around with broadcasting technology and become acquainted with NHK's big mouthed mascot Domo-kun.

Gallery X by Parco

Address: 13-17 Udagawacho, Shibuya-ku; www.art.parco.jp
Tel: 03-6712 7505
Opening Hours: daily 11am–8pm
Entrance Fee: charges for some exhibitions
Transport: Shibuya

Located within "Part 1" of the Parco fashion department store, **Gallery X by Parco** is always worth taking a look at. Dedicated to the generation and promotion of contemporary art

Young shoppers in the Shibuya district.

and culture in Tokyo, the exhibitions focus on accessible pop-cultural themes and art, and are well matched to the store's youthful consumers.

Shibuya Station

Both Meiji-dori and Koen-dori lead south down towards the human congestion of **Shibuya Station** ⑩ (Shibuya-eki). Along with the exodus of people who moved into the western suburbs after the 1923 Kanto Earthquake, Shibuya-eki played a significant role in the growth of the area. What really put the district on the map were the choice of Shibuya as the site for the terminals for the Inokashira and Toyoko lines, and the incorporation of the Ginza and Hanzomon subway lines.

More recently they have been joined by the Fukutoshin subway line in an underground terminal designed by Tadao Ando – the plan is for this to eventually link up with the Tokyu Toyoko Line that runs to Yokohama (see page 216). Above ground to the east of the station, **Shibuya Hikarie**, a 34-storey tower containing shops, restaurants, offices and cultural facilities including a 2,000-seat theatre, modernised the area even further when it opened in 2012.

The plaza in front of the station's northwest exit – better known as the Hachiko exit (see page 140) – is the site of one of the city's most otherworldly concentrations of neon advertisements, giant video screens and illuminated glass.

Shibuya Hikarie

Address: 2-21-1 Shibuya, Shibuya-ku; www.hikarie.jp
Tel: 03-5468 5892
Opening Hours: daily 10am–9pm (restaurants until 11pm)
Entrance Fee: free
Transport: Shibuya
The 34-storey **Shibuya Hikarie** ⑪ is a commercial complex connected to the east side of Shibuya Station – the area's answer to developments like

Roppongi Hills and Tokyo Midtown. From the basement up to the fifth floor, Hikarie is home to the ultra-fashionable **ShinQs department store**, which combines deli and food floors, fashion, cosmetics and life-style goods. Above that are restaurant floors and a **five-floor theatre**, as well as a hipster-attracting '**creative space**' on the eighth floor that brings together a café, museum, gallery and travel store. The rest of the glistening complex is comprised of offices.

Myth of Tomorrow

Look up from the Hachiko statue and you'll see a pedestrian corridor bridging across from the Tokyu Toyoko department store to the terminus for the Keio-Inokashira Line (which you can hop on later to visit the Japan Folk Crafts Museum, see page 141). In this corridor is the giant 14-panel painting *Myth of Tomorrow* ⑫ (*Asu no Shinwa*) by Okamoto Taro (1911–1996), a powerful Guernica-like mural of the atomic bomb explosion. Originally created in the late 1960s for a luxury hotel in Mexico, the monumental work was rediscovered in 2003 and took five years to be restored and find its new home in the station. For more about Okamoto see page 130.

Bunkamura sign in Shibuya.

Hanging out in Tokyo.

This bronze statue of Hachiko near Shibuya Station makes for a popular meeting place.

of **Dogenzaka** ⑬ gets its name from a 13th-century highwayman, Owada Dogen, who attacked travellers here as they passed up the slope towards the mountains.

The narrow backstreets that snake around the slope, offering short-stay rooms in dozens of whimsically designed buildings, have given rise to its nickname: 'Love Hotel Hill' (see page 146). Dogenzaka's nightlife does not revolve exclusively around discreet carnality. This tiny but enthralling area, with cosy restaurants – some offering dishes regarded as sexually fortifying, such as grilled eel – old coffee shops and corner shrines, has a lively music night scene with rock venues like O-East and its counterpart O-West, and nightclubs such as Womb and Club Asia.

Dogenzaka

Immediately west of Shibuya Station's Hachiko exit, the **109 Building** – a striking silver capsule resembling a silo and housing a fashion emporium that embodies the trends and culture of the teenage girls who play a leading role in Japanese consumer culture – forms a wedge between Bunkamura-dori and Dogenzaka-dori, the slope that splits off to the left. The hilly area

Bunkamura Museum of Art

Address: 2-24-1 Dogenzaka, Shibuya-ku; www.bunkamura.co.jp
Tel: 03-3477 9111
Opening Hours: Sun–Thu 10am–6pm, Fri–Sat until 9pm
Entrance Fee: charge
Transport: Shibuya

To the north of Dogenzaka, at the end of Bunkamura-dori, is the main branch of department store **Tokyu** and the attached Bunkamura culture centre – its 2,150-seat Orchard Hall is home to the Tokyo Philharmonic. The name of this multi-complex art centre means 'Culture Village' in Japanese and it houses galleries, shops, boutiques, a cinema and the **Bunkamura Museum of Art** ⑭ (Bunkamura Bijutsukan), well regarded for its displays of modern art by Japanese and foreign artists. In the **Bunkamura Gallery** (free) to the left of the main lobby, exhibitions of photography, painting and contemporary art installations are regularly held.

Shoto Museum of Art

Address: 2-14-14 Shoto, Shibuya-ku; www.shoto-museum.jp
Tel: 03-3465 9421
Opening Hours: Sat–Thu

HACHIKO THE FAITHFUL

A popular rendezvous spot for the youths who throng Shibuya is a small bronze statue of a dog named Hachiko, which stands in front of the Hachiko exit at Shibuya Station. Hachiko accompanied his owner Ueda Eisaburo, a university professor, to the station each day and waited for his return in the evening, a pattern that continued until a spring day in 1925, when his master died while teaching a class. Undaunted, Hachiko returned each day to the same spot to wait, even after the professor's relatives had moved the dog to Asakusa, a distance away. In order to shorten the tireless dog's daily treks to the station, a new home was found for him in nearby Yoyogi.

Commuters grew fond of the dog and, after the newspaper *Asahi Shimbun* ran the story in 1932, Hachiko's fame as a symbol of almost samurai-like loyalty was assured. A bronze statue was unveiled in 1935, and a special ceremony is held every year on 8 April to honour Hachiko's memory. When Hachiko died at age 13, the responsibility for his immortalisation passed into the hands of taxidermists. The very life-like Hachiko can be seen encased in Tokyo's National Museum of Nature and Science (see page 167).

10am–6pm, Fri until 8pm
Entrance Fee: charge
Transport: Shinsen

The Bunkamura is located on the edge of an expensive residential district called Shoto, the site of tea plantations in the 19th century. A pleasant stroll at any time of the year, this leafy district has a number of interesting small museums and galleries. The **Shoto Museum of Art** ⑮ (Shoto Bijutsukan) – a short walk from the Shinsen Station on the Inokashira Line – features local artists in a cosy setting with a tearoom where pictures can be viewed from the comfort of armchairs.

Toguri Museum of Art

Address: 1-11-3 Shoto, Shibuya-ku; www.toguri-museum.or.jp
Tel: 03-3465 0070
Opening Hours: Tue–Thu and Sat–Sun 10am–5pm, Fri until 8pm
Entrance Fee: charge
Transport: Shinsen

Anyone with even a passing interest in ceramics will appreciate the exquisite collection at **Toguri Museum of Art** ⑯ (Toguri Bijutsukan), a short walk north of the Shoto Museum. Housed in a yellow-brick building, only a small selection from the Toguri's 3,000-strong collection is shown at any one time. Its Imari, Nabeshima and Hagi ceramic pieces, captioned in both Japanese and English, are outstanding. There are occasional tours of the museum in English – check the website for dates. On the 4th Monday of each month, there is a 'Free Talk' Day at the museum, when people can discuss the works of art loudly and freely.

Gallery TOM

Address: 2-11-1 Shoto, Shibuya-ku
Tel: 03-3467 8102
Opening Hours: Tue–Sun 11am–6pm
Entrance Fee: charge
Transport: Shinsen

The nearby **Gallery TOM** ⑰ provides a very different experience.

Owned by a constructivist sculptor, the concept gallery (the acronym stands for 'Touch Our Museum') is designed for the blind. Broad stairs and handrails lead you to sculptures, which are set at waist level. Visitors are encouraged to touch the forms and let their hands lead them around.

AROUND SHIBUYA

Japan Folk Crafts Museum

Address: 4-3-33 Komaba, Meguro-ku; www.mingeikan.or.jp
Tel: 03-3467 4527
Opening Hours: Tue–Sun 10am–5pm
Entrance Fee: charge
Transport: Komaba Todaimae

Return to Shibuya Station and go two stops on the Inokashira Line to Komaba Todaimae, where a few minutes' walk west of the station you'll find the excellent **Japan Folk Crafts Museum** ⑱ (Mingei-kan). Considered to be one of the best among Tokyo's several hundred museums, the lovely old wood and stone building, once owned by master potter Soetsu Yanagi, is a shrine to *mingei*, Japan's folk craft movement. A variety of ceramics, furniture and textiles are exhibited here and the

You will find all manner of toys along Takeshita-dori.

museum's gift shop is a great place to buy unusual souvenirs.

Komaba Park

Address: 4-3-55 Komaba, Meguro-ku
Tel: 03-3460 6725
Opening Hours: Tue–Sun 9am–4.30pm
Entrance Fee: free
Transport: Komaba Todaimae

Nearby the Folk Crafts Museum is **Komaba Park** ⑲ (Komaba Koen), formerly the estate of the Maeda family. The last *daimyo* (lord) of the Maeda clan died during World War II and the estate was requisitioned by the Occupation. Komaba Park includes the **Former Maeda Residence**, a 1929 Tudor-style structure with a separate Japanese-style building used for receiving guests. The estate interiors give a good idea of the life of a member of the Japanese nobility in the early half of the 20th century. Behind the house, in a structure dating from the 1960s, is the **Museum of Modern Japanese Literature** (Toritsu Kindai Bungakukan).

Daikanyama

One destination that can be easily accessed from Shibuya Station – most pleasurably on foot – is the fashionable residential and shopping quarter of **Daikanyama** ⑳, one stop southwest on the Tokyu Toyoko Line. Many interesting boutiques are dotted around the station, and again as you climb up the hill towards the shopping complexes Daikanyama Address and La Fuente. Daikanyama is also the location of Hillside Terrace, an architectural ensemble that took Pritzker Prize-winning architect Fumihiko Maki 23 years to complete, and which is seen as something of a model urban development.

Nakameguro

Downhill from Daikanyama is **Nakameguro**, another highly fashionable neighbourhood. Popular with courting couples, it's filled with clothing boutiques, Hawaiian restaurants and fashionable cafés. Rather incongruously, the world's largest Starbucks is also located here, with an average queuing time to get in of 1–2 hours, by the banks of the Meguro-gawa; a shallow stream whose banks are lined with cherry trees, it's deservedly one of the most popular photo and hanami targets in Tokyo during the cherry blossom season.

SHIMO–KITAZAWA

Four stops west of Shibuya, where the Keio Inokashira Line crosses the Odakyu Line from Shinjuku, is the counter-cultural hub of Shimo-Kitazawa. The word that best describes this shabby but vibrant district is eclectic. Its carefully cultivated collegiate ambience, the assorted bric-a-brac and clothing shops, used record stores and off-beat bookshops, not to mention its lively mix of restaurants and bars, suggest a kind of Ivy League junk shop. The area grew off the back of a black market that existed after World War II and also happens to be packed with tiny live music houses and theatres. Plans to create a major new road means locals fear some of the area's chaotic charm will be destroyed.

Official residence, Daikanyama.

Tokyo's love hotels

In a city where space is at a premium, it's no wonder that the love-hotel business rakes in trillions of yen each year.

While you'll find clusters of so-called 'love hotels' in all of Tokyo's major entertainment centres, it is Shibuya's Dogenzaka area that is best known for these establishments that rent rooms by the hour. Given that many couples share homes with their families or just don't want to bring their partner back to a cramped apartment that is likely to be miles from work in the centre of town, love hotels provide a valuable service for many. And not just love-struck youth; they are also commonly used by prostitutes and cheating spouses: one study found that on average 2 percent of Japan's population (2.5 million people) visit a love hotel every day.

There's a long history of such establishments in Japan, dating back to the 'teahouses' of feudal times where travellers could find prostitutes. In the post-war period the term *tsurekome yado* (bring along inn) was adopted and there's even a move today by some places to label themselves as 'fashion' or 'couples' hotels. Euphemistic, romantic or curious hotel names such as Casanova, Hotel Chez Moi, Dixy Inn and P&A Plaza abound. There's only a small chance of you stumbling into one by mistake, though, since they all have quite distinctive and common features.

First up you'll always see a sign outside that advertises rates for either a 'rest' or 'stay': the rest period can vary from one to three hours (with day-time discounts sometimes available) while the stay period usually runs from after 10 or 11pm to 10am. There's also a trend to build love hotels in various wacky kitsch styles and themes – there's a famous one in Meguro resembling a fairytale castle.

The entrance to the hotel is almost always hidden behind a wall to protect users' privacy, a level of discretion that continues inside with dim lighting and minimal contact between customers and staff. Quite often there's no receptionist at all, but instead a push button panel displaying illuminated pictures of each of the rooms available and their rates. Pay attention to this as many love hotels offer themed rooms with all manner of special features beyond the usual mirrored ceilings, waterbeds and Jacuzzi bathtubs. You may find karaoke and video game machines, all manner of sex toys and other dressing-up paraphernalia. Windows are rare – it's not the view from the hotel that you're paying for!

Knowing that it's often the woman who chooses the love hotel, some places offer luxurious boutique-hotel style rooms, making them a great place to indulge the sybarite in you whether you plan to have fun with a partner or not. Rates range from under ¥5,000 for a three hour stay to over ¥16,000 for an overnight stay; as with anything, you get what you pay for. To find out more see *Love Hotels* by Ed Jacob.

A love hotel in the Shibuya district.

ROPPONGI

The nightlife districts of Roppongi and Akasaka have both had major makeovers with big art and shopping complexes adding to their daytime attractions, which include sights such as Tokyo Tower and several important shrines.

I n the lower middle of the oval defined by the Yamanote Line, just to the southwest of the Imperial Palace, is **Minato-ku**, an area favoured by Tokyo's expatriate community. The ward is peppered with embassies and high-priced expat housing, and liberally spiced with nightclubs, bars, live music houses and restaurants. The development of mixed residential and commercial complexes such as Roppongi Hills and Tokyo Midtown, both with their own art gallery components, and shopping and business complex Tri-Seven Roppongi (added in 2016) is drawing a more diverse crowd to the area.

Up on a hill, and served by the Hibiya and Oedo subway lines, Roppongi, meaning 'six trees', was once a garrison town for the Meiji government, and later, after World War II, the Americans established barracks here. It is today the heart of Minato-ku's nightlife. Most people begin exploring Roppongi and adjacent Akasaka at the Roppongi Crossing, the intersection between Gaien-Higashi-dori and Roppongi-dori, situated underneath a raised expressway.

ROPPONGI

Ark Hills

Following this stretch of raised motorway northeast leads to **Ark Hills** ❶ (www.arkhills.com), Japan's first large-scale private redevelopment project by the construction company Mori, and a forerunner for more recent Mori projects such as Roppongi Hills and Omotesando Hills (see page 132). The **Suntory Hall** concert venue and the **ANA InterContinental Tokyo** are all within the complex.

Entrance to the Mori Art Museum and Tokyo City View at Roppongi Hills.

Okura Museum of Art

Behind Ark Hills, nestled amid a number of embassies and exclusive residential backstreets, just beyond the American Embassy, the **Okura Museum of Art** ❷ (Okura Shukokan; Bijutsukan 2-10-3 Toranomon, Minato-ku; www.shukokan.org/english/; daily 10am–4.30pm) is found in front of the Hotel Okura. Set up by Baron Okura Tsuruhiko in 1917, and housed in a Chinese-style building, the museum – renovated from 2014 to 2019 – displays a small but intriguing collection of Asian antiquities and Buddhist sculptures.

Musée Tomo

Address: 4-1-35 Toranomon, Minato-ku; www.musee-tomo.or.jp
Tel: 03-5733 5311
Opening Hours: Tue–Sun 11am–6pm
Entrance Fee: charge
Transport: Kamiyacho

A few steps away, behind the Hotel Okura, is the extraordinary **Musée Tomo** ❸. With a broad collection of the very best ceramics, from Imari vases to Raku tea bowls, the gallery also features the work of modern pottery masters.

Tokyo Tower

Address: 4-2-8 Shiba Koen, Minato-ku; www.tokyotower.co.jp/english
Tel: 03-3433 5111
Opening Hours: daily 9am–11pm
Entrance Fee: charge
Transport: Onarimon or Kamiyacho

Heading downhill from the museum towards Sakurada-dori and Kamiyacho subway station, the next sight makes itself very apparent. **Tokyo Tower** ❹, a red-and-white copy of the Eiffel Tower, dominates the skyline here. The 333-metre (1,090ft) structure, completed in 1958, was designed as a transmitting tower. Compensating for the lacklustre aquarium at the base is its Special Observatory with exceptional views of the city; if you're in luck, you may even get to see Mount Fuji out in the distance.

Zojo-ji

Address: 4-7-35 Shiba Koen, Minato-ku; www.zojoji.or.jp
Tel: 03-3432 1431
Opening Hours: daily 6am–5.30pm
Entrance Fee: free
Transport: Daimon or Shiba-koen

Just behind the tower, in the spacious grounds of **Shiba Park** (Shiba Koen), stands one of Tokyo's grandest temples, **Zojo-ji** ❺. Founded in 1393, the site was chosen by the Tokugawa clan in the late 1600s as their ancestral temple, as part of a scheme to protect Edo from evil spirits. Close to the bay and the Tokaido Road, it also served as a post station for travellers and pilgrims. Most of the temple buildings, once numbering over 100, were destroyed by fires and air raids, but its main entrance, the 1612 red-lacquered **Sangedatsumon Gate**, an Important Cultural Treasure, is original.

Pass through the gate, with its large bell made from melted down hairpins donated by the ladies of the shogun's court, to the **Main Hall**

FACT

The much-maligned Tokyo Tower sheds its shabby daytime image at night, when it is illuminated to startling effect – a sight to silence its most vocal critics.

Tokyo Tower is spectacular when lit up at night.

(Daiden). It contains many important sacred objects, including ancient sutras and statuary. The new leaders of the Meiji government showed their contempt for the outgoing Tokugawa by confiscating the temple, turning the grounds into a park and removing six of the mummified shogun to a less prestigious resting place at the rear of the Main Hall, near a row of cheerful Jizo statues, each with a windmill in its hand.

Roppongi Hills

Returning to Roppongi Crossing and heading west along Roppongi-dori

will bring you to **Roppongi Hills** ⑥. The 16-hectare (40-acre) site is impressive; its towering office blocks, luxe Grand Hyatt Tokyo, multiplex cinema, apartments, hundreds of shops and interconnecting walkways make up one of the largest developments in Japan. There's a pretty garden next to the TV Asahi building, and on the 54th floor of **Mori Tower** a first-rate contemporary gallery, the **Mori Art Museum** (6-10-1 Roppongi, Minato-ku; tel: 03-5777 8600; www.mori.art.museum; Tue 10am–5pm; Wed–Mon until 10pm) as well as **Tokyo City View** (www.roppongihills.

com/tcv; Sun–Thu 10am–11pm, Fri–Sat until 1am), an indoor observation deck with a heart-stopping 360-degree view of the city as well as access to the building's roof.

Tokyo Midtown

Address: Tokyo Midtown, 9-7-4 Akasaka, Minato-ku; www.tokyo-midtown.com
Tel: 03-3475 3100
Opening Hours: daily 11am–9pm (restaurants until midnight)
Entrance Fee: free
Transport: Roppongi

If you go northwest along Gaien-Higashi-dori from Roppongi Crossing you'll come to the area's second major development, **Tokyo Midtown ❼**. The anchor property here is Midtown Tower, the second tallest building in Tokyo, with its top floors occupied by the Ritz Carlton. Like the nearby Roppongi Hills, Midtown's several buildings are home to hundreds of shops, restaurants and offices. And just as Roppongi Hills has the Mori Art Museum, so too Midtown has its own first-rate art venues, with the **Suntory Museum of Art** and **21_21 Design Sight**, as well as numerous artworks and installations scattered around the complex.

Suntory Museum of Art

Address: Tokyo Midtown, 9-7-4 Akasaka, Minato-ku; www.suntory.com/sma
Tel: 03-3479 8600
Opening Hours: Mon, Wed, Thu, Sun 10am–6pm, Fri–Sat until 8pm
Entrance Fee: charge
Transport: Roppongi

Within Tokyo Midtown's shopping complex is the **Suntory Museum of Art ❽** (Suntory Bijutsukan). Its classy collection of lacquerware, ceramics and paintings from the 17th century to the present is housed in a very sleek and light-filled design by Kengo Kuma featuring high ceilings and louvred windows.

21_21 Design Sight

Address: 9-7-6 Akasaka, Minato-ku; www.2121designsight.jp
Tel: 03-3475 2121

TIP

The National Art Center, Tokyo, Suntory Museum of Art and Mori Art Museum form the three corners of the Art Triangle Roppongi. Keep your ticket stub after visiting any of these three museums and it will entitle you to reduced entry at each of the others. A map is also available at each museum showing other galleries in the area, or online at www.mori.art. museum/eng/atro/index.html.

Sanmon, the main entrance to Zojo-ji Temple in Shiba Park.

Opening Hours: Wed–Mon 10am–7pm
Entrance Fee: charge
Transport: Roppongi

Greenery surrounds Tokyo Midtown. Across the 10-hectare (25-acre) site are many contemporary sculptures and, in one corner, the **21_21 Design Sight** ❾. This Tadao Ando-designed space, which has fashion leader Issey Miyake among its directors, stages progressive theme-based design exhibitions in a striking gallery.

National Art Center, Tokyo

Address: 7-22-2 Roppongi, Minato-ku; www.nact.jp
Tel: 03-5777 8600
Opening Hours: Wed–Mon 10am–6pm, Fri until 8pm
Entrance Fee: charge
Transport: Roppongi or Nogizaka

Two minutes' walk southwest of Tokyo Midtown is the **National Art Center, Tokyo** ❿ . Designed by Kisho Kurokawa, this vast building is Japan's largest such gallery staging everything from blockbuster exhibitions of major artists to small-scale shows for local art groups. The atrium foyer, studded with three storey-tall conical pods, is worth a look on its own. There's also a good French restaurant, **Brasserie Paul Bocuse Le Musée**, on the third floor.

AKASAKA

Nogi-jinja

Address: 8-11-27 Akasaka, Minato-ku; www.nogijinja.or.jp
Tel: 03-3478 3001
Opening Hours: daily 'early morning'–6pm
Entrance Fee: free
Transport: Nogizaka

A five-minute walk north of Tokyo Midtown, along Gaien-Higashi-dori, and next to Nogizaka subway station is **Nogi-jinja** ⓫, a shrine named after General Nogi Maresuke, a hero of the Russo-Japanese War of 1904 who is buried, with his wife, in nearby Aoyama cemetery. Such was Nogi's loyalty to the Meiji Emperor, he and his wife killed themselves upon the Emperor's death in 1912. On the second Sunday of every month, an antique flea market is held in the shrine's grounds.

Hie-jinja

Address: 2-10-5 Nagatacho, Chiyoda-ku
Tel: 03-3581 2471
Opening Hours: daily Apr–Sept 5am–6pm, Oct–Mar 6am–5pm
Entrance Fee: free
Transport: Tameike-Sanno

Heading due east from Nogi-jinja soon brings you to Sotobori-dori and **Hie-jinja** ⓬, one of Tokyo's major shrines. Transplanted here in the 17th century in the belief that it would help to deflect evil from Edo Castle, a massive stone torii (gate) leads uphill through an avenue of smaller, red-lacquered gates to the

Cutting-edge art at 21_21 Design Sight.

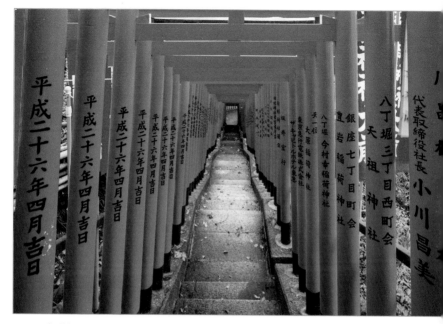

current buildings, put up in 1967. The shrine's role as protector is still evident today; look carefully at a carving to the left of the main shrine and you will see a monkey cradling its baby. Pregnant women come here to pay wishful homage to the image.

Toyokawa Inari

From Hie-Jinja, walk along Sotobori-dori to Aoyama-dori – take the street west until you reach the **Toyokawa Inari 13**, also called Myogon-ji. This combined temple and shrine has a chaotic and colourful clutter of images lining the approach to the main sanctuary: orange banners and lanterns, statues of the goddess Kannon and the child-protector deity Jizo and figures of red-bibbed foxes.

Akasaka Detached Palace

Toyokawa Inari is next to the extensive grounds of the **Akasaka Detached Palace 14** (Geihin-kan, www8.cao.go.jp/geihinkan). Completed in 1909, the palace – which is reminiscent of Buckingham Palace – is the only neo-Baroque building in Tokyo and serves as the State Guest House. It's occasionally open in summer for public visits. The palace's front gates are closest to Yotsuya Station on both the JR and Metro lines.

Meiji Memorial Hall

West of the Akasaka Detached Palace, in the extensive gardens of the Meiji shrine is **Meiji Memorial Hall 15** (Meiji Kinenkan, www.meijikinenkan. gr.jp). Its main hall is where the former Imperial Constitution of Japan was drafted and the Imperial House Act was discussed. Today, Meiji Memorial Hall serves as a venue for weddings, concerts, seminars, fairs and other functions; it was the first comprehensive wedding hall in Japan. The complex houses several restaurants and 27 banquet rooms of various sizes. The nearest station is Schinanomachi on the JR line.

Striking Hie-jinja.

Cherry blossom down the Meguro River.

SHINAGAWA

You can visit the burial grounds of the legendary 47 samurai, picnic among trees that were around when Edo was a fishing village, or drop by a massive, beautifully decorated wedding hall.

A key checkpoint and post station at the start of the great Tokaido (East Sea Road) that connected Edo with Kyoto, Shinagawa once stood on a stretch of dismal tidal flats at the edge of the city. Founded on fishing and the cultivation of seaweed, the area's main trade soon gave way to services catering to travellers, and inns and teahouses flourished. Along with these arose the inevitable facilities catering for pleasures of the flesh.

When the feudal system collapsed with the advent of the Meiji era however, railways and industry moved in. Shinagawa and its much sought after residential districts of Higashi-Gotanda, Takanawa and Shirokanedai have come up in the world since then. Shinagawa has also benefited from becoming a station on the main Shinkansen Line heading south to Kyoto, Osaka and beyond. To the east of the station is a cluster of modern office buildings and residences.

SHINAGAWA

Takanawa Prince Hotels Garden ❶

Close to Shinagawa Station's west exit amid a cluster of Prince hotels (the Grand Prince Hotel Takanawa, The Prince Sakura Tower and Grand

Prince Hotel New Takanawa) is a lovely traditional garden. The whole site was once occupied by three Imperial palaces and the gardens were created for Prince Takeda whose French-style mansion still stands next to the Grand Prince Hotel Takanawa (it's now a restaurant and used for private functions). Within the gardens is the small **Kannon-do,** a 13th-century temple relocated here in 1954.

The hotel group also owns the **Aqua Park Shinagawa** (tel: 03 5421

Graves belonging to the 47 ronin at Sengaku-ji.

The garden of the Grand Prince Hotel Takanawa.

1111; www.aqua-park.jp; usual hours daily 10am–10pm), located inside the Shinagawa Prince Hotel, about a 5-minute walk away. This modern aquarium includes high-tech displays enhanced by inventive lighting, a café bar with a tank illuminated by luminescent coral and a variety of animals, from tropical fish and jelly fish to dolphins, penguins, seals and otters.

Hara Museum of Contemporary Art

Address: 4-7-25 Kita-Shinagawa, Shinagawa-ku; www.haramuseum.or.jp
Tel: 03-3445 0651
Opening Hours: Tue–Sun 11am–5pm, Wed until 8pm
Entrance Fee: charge
Transport: Kita-Shinagawa

A fifteen-minute walk south of Shinagawa Station to the west of Dai-ichi Keihin, a broad road running beside the railway tracks, modern art finds an interesting home in the **Hara Museum of Contemporary Art ❷** (Hara Bijutsukan). Five rooms with connecting corridors are used to display the museum's changing exhibitions, which have included works by international artists such as Christo and Andy Warhol. The grandfather of the museum's founder, Hara Toshio, had the Bauhaus-style home built in 1938 and it was then transformed into today's museum in 1979. One of Japan's leading architects, Isozaki Arata, was brought in more recently to add an annexe, the **Café d'Art**.

Shinagawa Aquarium

Address: 3-2-1 Katsushima, Shinagawa-ku
Tel: 03-3762 3431
Opening Hours: Wed–Mon 10am–5pm
Entrance Fee: charge
Transport: Omori Kaigan

Hop on the Keihin Kyuko Line at Shinagawa Station and ride a few stops south to Omori Kaigan for the **Shinagawa Aquarium ❸**, where you can see dolphin and sea lion shows as well as a host of other aquatic life from sharks to stingrays displayed in giant tanks, one of which you can walk under.

Sengaku-ji

Address: 2-11-1 Takanawa, Minato-ku; www.sengakuji.or.jp
Tel: 03-3441 5560
Opening Hours: daily Apr–Sept 7am–6pm, Oct–Mar until 5pm
Entrance Fee: free
Transport: Sengakuji

North of Shinagawa Station and a short walk west of the Sengakuji Station is the **Sengaku-ji** ❹. This temple was the setting for part of one of Edo's best-known true stories (see page 157). Incense is placed every day on the graves of the 47 retainers and their Lord Asano, who are buried together here. Visitors often leave gifts for them, too, such as *sake*, snacks and small bunches of flowers. The temple was rebuilt after the war, but its entrance gate, a beautifully carved and decorated work with a dragon motif dating from 1836, remains intact. A small side building, the **Gishiken** (Hall of Loyal Retainers), contains some of the personal effects of the 47 ronin.

Tozen-ji

Directly south of Sengaku-ji is a small Zen temple with an air of purity and simplicity that is worth a short detour. **Tozen-ji** ❺ was the site of the British Legation between 1859 and 1873, its distance from the centre of Edo being considered appropriate for the Western 'barbarians'. The temple was not quite the shelter the British had envisaged. When retainers from the influential Mito clan burst in one day in 1861, Britain's first representative, Sir Rutherford Alcock, barely managed to escape death by hiding in the temple's bathtub. The minister's crime? He was spotted defiling sacred Mount Fuji by climbing to its summit. Sword marks and bullet holes from that skirmish are still

Keeping the flame alight for pilgrims to Sengaku-ji Temple.

Encounters with 'Janglish'

Be it bizarre product names or inadvertently obscene T-shirts, the Japanese flair for mangling the English language is one of the country's most endearing features.

While riding on a bus, a visitor once spotted a restaurant sign with the name 'Cheese Doll'. What an odd name for an eatery, he thought. Not long afterwards, the bus passed a second establishment with the same appellation, and at this point, he noted that both of them had been housed in matte yellow buildings. Then suddenly it all made sense: the owner had tried to emulate the name 'Chez d'Or', but unaware that it meant 'house of gold' in French, and unable to find either of these words in his English dictionary, settled for the closest equivalents he could find. The Japanese chop up the English language and reassemble it in imaginative ways that resemble the linguistic equivalent of abstract art.

Janglish manifests itself everywhere.

When English is packaged solely for domestic consumption, Japanese seem indifferent to the rules of correct usage; and when informed of this fact, they seldom care. English exists, not as a medium of international communication, but rather as decorative icing on the cake of commercialism.

In addition to names of businesses, this fractured English, known as 'Janglish' and 'Japlish', can be encountered in building signs, on T-shirts and shopping bags, in advertising slogans, menus, subway posters, product names and publications of all sorts. The internet has vastly multiplied the opportunities to disseminate this strange mutant of English around the globe, while less- than-perfect computer translation programmes have increased its prevalence in Japan.

Accurate rendering of mispronunciations are part of the problem. For example 'r' and 'l' often get confused by locals because there is no equivalent of the 'l' sound in Japanese and so 'r' is often used as a substitute – hence you may hear a flight attendant say 'We hope you enjoy your fright'. A similar mix-up happens between 'b' and 'v' (Sign in a hotel: 'Tooth Brush Bending Machine'.)

Japanese themselves refer to this linguistic phenomenon as *Wasei Eigo* (Made-in-Japan English). Indeed, rather than adopt English words as they are, they have been known to create their own unique forms. A car's windscreen is 'front glass'. A rear-view mirror is a 'back mirror'. The steering wheel is a 'handle', a hubcap is a 'wheel cover', and so on.

Some of the greatest mirth is created when these spill over into oddball product names, such as 'Creap' for a powdered coffee creamer, 'Flavour My Drip' for individual pre-mixed coffee servings and 'Pocket Wetty' for pre-moistened hand wipes.

Word borrowings seem most likely to be adopted when the subject is negative. When the 3 percent consumption tax was introduced in 1989, government posters identified it as *nyuu takusu*. Another highly unpopular subject, *risutora* – restructuring – generally implies laying off workers. And although a perfectly good Japanese word exists for sexual harassment (*seiteki iyagarase*) the media invariably refers to this as *seku-hara*.

visible on the pillars in the temple's entrance hall.

Hatakeyama Memorial Museum of Fine Art

Address: 2-20-12 Shirokanedai, Minato-ku; www.ebara.co.jp/csr/hatakeyama/english.html
Tel: 03-3447 5787
Opening Hours: Tue–Sun Apr–Sept 10am–5pm, Oct–Mar until 4.30pm
Entrance Fee: charge
Transport: Takanawadai

From the temple follow the Katsurazaka west to Sakurada-dori; follow this major road south to Takanawadai Station from where you'll head a few blocks west for the **Hatakeyama Memorial Museum of Fine Art** ❻ (Hatakeyama Kinen Bijutsukan) located on a wooded hill at the heart of an estate once owned by the Lord of Satsuma in Kyushu. A section of the old garden still remains and is overlooked by a *kaiseki-ryori* restaurant. The museum reflects the interests of its founder, the industrialist and tea ceremony master, Hatakeyama Issei. Galleries display tea utensils and bowls, hand scrolls and other tea ceremony objects, but also lacquerware and *noh* costumes. There are three tea ceremony rooms as well.

Happo-en

Address: 1-1-1 Shirokanedai, Minato-ku; www.happo-en.com
Tel: 03-3443 3111
Opening Hours: daily 10am–5pm
Entrance Fee: free
Transport: Shirokanedai

A ten minute walk north of the art museum will bring you to one of Tokyo's most beautiful stroll gardens. **Happo-en** ❼, once part of an estate owned by retainers of Tokugawa shogun, now forms the backdrop to many a Tokyoite's wedding or special celebration. The 50,000 sq metres of gardens, arranged around an ornamental pond, sport a collection of bonsai, some over 200 years old. As with any classical Japanese garden, Happo-en is designed to reflect each season to its fullest, and it's especially successful at that during the cherry blossom season in early spring. It's also possible to have green tea served in Muan, a historic teahouse reconstructed here, or dine on fine *kaiseki* at Happo-en's restaurant.

Institute for Nature Study

Address: 5-21-5 Shiroganedai, Minato-ku; www.ins.kahaku.go.jp
Tel: 03-3441 7176
Opening Hours: Tue–Sun May–Aug 9am–5pm, Sept–Apr until 4.30pm
Entrance Fee: charge
Transport: Shirokanedai

From Happo-en follow Meguro-dori west to the entrance to the **Institute for Nature Study** ❽ (Shizen-kyoikuen). This 20-hectare (49-acre) park is a valiant effort to preserve in its original form a section of the Musashino Plain that once covered much of the area Edo was built on. Among the 8,000 or more trees (160 species in all) in the park, stand moss-covered ones that were here when

TIP

One of the best points about Tokyo's Institute for Nature Study is that entrance is limited to only 300 people at a time (you will be issued with a returnable ribbon as you enter), making this one of the least crowded parks in the city.

Capsule hotels are an ingenious solution to limited space.

Janglish on T-shirts.

Edo was a mere fishing village. In a city deprived of greenery, this reserve provides an invaluable space to breathe in, not only for humans but also the aquatic flora that flourish in its ponds and wetlands, and the large variety of birds that stop by.

MEGURO

Kume Museum of Art

Address: 2-25-5 Kami-Osaki, Shinagawa-ku; www.kume-museum.com
Tel: 03-3491 1510
Opening Hours: Tue–Sun 10am–5pm
Entrance Fee: charge
Transport: Meguro

Just opposite Meguro Station's west exit on the left corner, the small **Kume Museum of Art** ❾ (Kume Bijutsukan) houses a collection of paintings by Kume Kuchiro, one of the first Japanese painters to practice Impressionism.

Daien-ji

A five-minute walk southwest of the station, down a rather steep slope,

Daien-ji ❿ is home to 500 lifelike *rakan* (Buddha disciple) images. Made as an offering to the spirits of those who died in a disastrous fire that destroyed the original temple in 1772, the stone figures stand row upon row against one of the temple's walls. Highly individualised, each pose and face is different.

Meguro Gajoen

Address: 1-8-1 Meguro, Meguro-ku; www.megurogajoen.co.jp
Tel: 03-3491 4111
Transport: Meguro

Immediately downhill from the temple is **Meguro Gajoen** ⓫, one of Tokyo's most extravagant wedding halls. Not much is left of the original building, which dates back to 1931, save for the *hyakudan kaidan* (one-hundred-step stairway), off of which are a several ornately decorated rooms that contain lovely traditional works of art. This section of the complex – which also contains a luxury hotel and several restaurants – is only open for short periods during the year when there is an entry charge.

It's well worth taking a look inside the rest of the hall, which has other beautifully decorated function halls and corridors.

Across Meguro-gawa from Meguro Gajoen is a fairy-tale castle that looks better suited to Disneyland. This is the **Meguro Emperor** (tel: 03-3494 1211), one of Tokyo's most famous love hotels and a kitsch relic dating back to 1973. The interior once sported racy rooms with all manner of decor and beds, including one shaped like a gondola; today though it is pretty much like any business hotel.

Meguro Parasitological Museum

Address: 4-1-1, Shimo-Meguro, Meguro-ku; www.kiseichu.org/e-top
Tel: 03-3716 1264
Opening Hours: Wed–Sun 10am–5pm
Entrance Fee: free
Transport: Meguro

Head west along Meguro-dori and cross Shimbashi Bridge to find one of the city's strangest institutions, the **Meguro Parasitological Museum** ⑫ (Meguro Kiseichukan). There's a morbid fascination to peering at the 45,000 parasites collected by the museum, including the remains of an 8.8-metre (29ft) tapeworm removed from the body of a 40-year-old man, but otherwise it's not one of Tokyo's must-see museums. If you want to pick up a unique souvenir, the museum's shop does a range of tapeworm T-shirts you are unlikely to find anywhere else.

Meguro Fudo

Address: 3-20-26 Shimo-Meguro, Meguro-ku
Tel: 03-3712 7549
Opening Hours: daily 9am–5pm
Entrance Fee: free
Transport: Meguro

Head south from the Parasitological Museum, following the long, straight backstreet shooting off of Meguro-dori, and in five minutes you'll be at the first of a cluster of temples. **Meguro Fudo** ⑬ (also known as Ryusen-ji) is the largest temple in the area, and is said to have been founded in the 9th century by the monk Ennin. Its main feature is a pond that stands near the main hall, into which water flows from the mouths of two bronze dragons – a

Relaxing in the Institute for Nature Study.

THE 47 RONIN

The tragic fate of the 47 ronin (masterless samurai) is a true-life event reproduced countless times in kabuki and bunraku plays. The story, often called *Chu-shin-gura* (The Story of the Loyal Retainers) is much admired by Japanese as a morality tale demonstrating the code of duty and self-sacrifice that was the highest samurai ideal. Hollywood seems to have been impressed by the story, too: a film about the 47 ronin starring Keanu Reeves was released in 2013.

The story goes like this: Lord Asano, scorned by his teacher Lord Kira, caused grave offence by drawing his sword in anger. Because the offence occurred within the castle grounds, Asano was obliged to perform seppuku (ritual suicide). Almost two years later on 14 December 1702, Asano's 47 retainers, in a carefully planned act of revenge, decapitated Kira in his mansion on the banks of the Sumida River and carried the head through the streets of Edo to their lord's grave at Sengaku-ji. Honour restored, the 47 ronin immediately turned themselves in to the authorities who, on 4 February 1703, ordered them to commit seppuku on 4 February 1703. One month later, they dutifully obliged.

Yebisu Garden Place.

(Meguro Bijutsukan), a spacious gallery in pleasant surroundings, housing a collection of craft and fine artworks by modern and contemporary Japanese artists as well as pieces from overseas artists.

Naka-Meguro

Keep following the Meguro-gawa northwards and you will soon hit **Naka-Meguro** ⑮, a station on the overland Tokyu Toyoko Line to Shibuya as well as the underground Hibiya Line. Around here are many relaxed boutiques and cafés that are great places to check out the latest trends. Cherry trees line both sides of the river, making this one of the most pleasant places in the city to celebrate *hanami* season (see page 164). The running water also has a cooling effect in summer.

EBISU

One stop up the JR Line from Meguro Station, or along the Hibiya Line from Naka-Meguro, is **Ebisu**, a district that takes its name from the beer Yebisu (an older spelling of Ebisu; Japanese no longer uses 'ye'), which was first brewed here back in 1887. The beer itself is named after one of the seven Shinto gods of good fortune. The train station here was originally a freight depot to transport beer from factories and breweries lining the Meguro and Shibuya rivers.

Yebisu Garden Place

Redesigned in the late 1990s, the south side of Ebisu Station has a long horizontal escalator that takes visitors to the **Yebisu Garden Place** (www.gardenplace.jp), a massive shopping, hotel, office and entertainment complex. Built on the site of the old Yebisu brewery, the name is a misnomer – there is minimal greenery here. Around the plaza are shops and boutiques, bars, cafés, a concert hall, the Westin Hotel and French restaurant Taillevent Robuchon, housed in a florid Disneyesque French chateau.

feel of these waters (or for the very hardy, a few minutes standing under them in midwinter) is supposed to bring religious purification.

Just to the northeast of Meguro Fudo is **Gohyaku Rakan-ji**, which like Daien-ji is known for its *rakan* (Buddha disciple) images. Some 300 of the temple's original 536 disciples, all carved by a monk called Shoun, survive today. One street southeast of Meguro Fudo is the less interesting **Joju-in**, another temple connected to Ennin and one that has become associated with Yakushi, the Buddhist deity of healing.

Meguro Museum of Art, Tokyo

Address: 2-4-36 Meguro, Meguro-ku; www.mmat.jp
Tel: 03-3714 1201
Opening Hours: Tue–Sun 10am–6pm
Entrance Fee: charge
Transport: Meguro

Returning to where Meguro-dori crosses the Meguro-gawa, head north along the riverbank to the **Meguro Museum of Art, Tokyo** ⑭

Museum of Yebisu Beer

Address: 4-20-1 Yebisu Garden Place, Meguro-ku
Tel: 03-5423 7255
Opening Hours: Tue–Sun 11am–7pm
Entrance Fee: free
Transport: Ebisu

Within the complex and celebrating the history of the beverage that the area's name and fortunes are founded on is the small **Museum of Yebisu Beer** ⑯ (Ebisu Mugishu Kinenkan). You can wander around freely or take a 40-minute tour (in Japanese) with a 'brand communicator' (charge). At the end of the tour there are samples of Sapporo's beers on offer (charge) in the tasting salon.

Tokyo Photographic Art Museum

Address: 1-13-3 Mita, Meguro-ku
Tel: 03-3280 0099
Opening Hours: Tue–Wed, Sat–Sun 10am–6pm, Thu–Fri until 8pm
Entrance Fee: charge
Transport: Ebisu

A couple in traditional Japanese wedding dress.

On the eastern side of Yebisu Garden Place is the superb **Tokyo Photographic Art Museum** ⑰ (Tokyo-to Shashin Bijutsukan), the premier exhibition space for notable photography and video art. Major Japanese and Western photographers are featured here.

Yamatane Museum of Art

Address: 3-12-6 Hiroo, Shibuya-ku; www.yamatane-museum.or.jp
Tel: 03-5777 8600
Opening Hours: Tue–Sun 10am–5pm
Entrance Fee: charge
Transport: Ebisu

Returning to Ebisu Station and walking about 10 minutes to the northeast along the main road will bring you to the interesting **Yamatane Museum of Art** ⑱ (Yamatane Bijutsukan). The museum, founded in 1966 and based around a collection of 105 works by Hayami Gyoshu, focuses on kindai nihonga, Japanese paintings from the Meiji era onward. There are around six or seven differently themed exhibitions every year featuring these delicate artworks.

Museum of Yebisu Beer.

JAPANESE WEDDINGS

Meguro Gajoen (see page 156) and Happo-en (see page 155) are two of Tokyo's most famous wedding halls where the huge parties that accompany the happy event are held. Shinto, Buddhist, Christian or non-religious ceremonies are available, but the choice may not match whatever religious affiliation the couple has; the trappings of a traditional Christian wedding, with Western-style white dresses and priests (usually just a play-acting foreigner), have become particularly popular. Back in the 'Bubble era', when money came easy, it wasn't unheard of for some couples to also hire foreign actors to be guests to make it look as if they were cosmopolitan enough to have foreign friends.

Traditional Japanese weddings, however, are held at shrines and performed to Shinto rites – a good place to see these is Meiji-jingu (see page 129). The bride wears a white *shiromuku* kimono while the groom has on *montsuki* (black formal kimono), *haori* (jacket), and *hakama* (pants). The wedding reception parties *(kekkon hiroen)* can be lavish affairs where the happy couple are expected to change outfits several times. Guests are obliged to bring a substantial cash gift, which must be enclosed in a special envelope called a *shugi bukuro*. In exchange they will leave the celebration with a gift from the couple.

Celebrating the bloom of cherry blossoms at Ueno Park.

UENO, YANESEN AND HONGO

Ameyoko's old black market alleys and Yanaka's atmospheric cemetery, temples and craft shops sandwich the rich cultural attractions of Ueno Park, including the Tokyo National Museum.

North of Tokyo Station, eight minutes on the Yamanote train, is Ueno Station (Ueno-eki). It is a subtle impression, but the area around the station seems more down to earth, if not grittier, than other parts of Tokyo. This was once the commoner's part of town, the *shitamachi*. In the post-war years, many of Tokyo's orphaned children lived in the park, and it still hosts many homeless people who live amid the trees under blue tarpaulin tents and in cardboard boxes.

Ameya Yokocho

Accessed from Ueno Station to the north and either Ueno Okachimachi or Okachimachi stations to the south, running parallel with Ueno's main street of Chuo-dori is **Ameya Yokocho** (daily 10am–8pm), one of Tokyo's liveliest street markets. **Ameyoko**, the commonly shortened name of the market, is a composite of *ame* (sweets) and *yoko* (alley). 'Confectioner's Alley' did a roaring trade in sweets, mostly made from sweet potato and beans, in the immediate post-war years. During the Korean War, it was a thriving black market for American goods. Here, under the railway tracks, among the

cheap clothes, fried noodle vendors and dried fish stalls, where young men hack blocks of ice and bellow the latest prices for strips of black seaweed, kelp and octopus, the working-class spirit of *shitamachi* lives on.

UENO PARK

Saigo Takamori statue

The centrepiece of Ueno, a meeting place for the capital's old merchant culture, is **Ueno Park** (Ueno-koen), a fine place for people watching,

Dried fruits and nuts on sale at Ameya Yokocho market.

FACT

Koban (police boxes) are a highly visible feature of Tokyo. Ranging from the tiny to the very small, the designs of these posts often mirror the mood of an area. Apart from crime prevention, its main function is to answer queries about directions.

especially on weekends. In spring, the park is cherished among Japanese for its cherry blossom trees (see page 164).

If you enter the park at the south end, near **Keisei-Ueno Station** (Keisei-Ueno-eki), it is a short walk up a slight incline to the modest 1892 **statue of Saigo Takamori** ② (1827–73). Although he was a key architect of the Meiji Restoration, Takamori led an unsuccessful rebellion against the country's new leaders and eventually committed ritual suicide. The statue shows him walking his dog, wearing a summer kimono, his sword safely sheathed.

To the left is the **Shogitai Tomb**, the resting place of loyal Tokugawa samurai who refused to accept the shogunate's collapse in 1868 and retreated to Ueno.

Kiyomizu Kannon Hall

Ahead to the left, on the edge of a small bluff, is **Kiyomizu Kannon Hall** ③ (Kiyomizu Kannon-do). Built in 1631 and moved to its present site in 1698, it is a dwarfish imitation of Kiyomizu-dera, the far grander temple in Kyoto. The main image of worship is the Senju Kannon (Thousand-Armed Goddess of Mercy), but

Ueno, Yanesen and Hongo

Statue of Saigo Takamori.

another image, the Kosodate Kannon, believed to answer the prayers of childless women, is more popular. Those who subsequently give birth return and leave a small doll as an offering of their gratitude.

Shinobazu Pond

The temple's location was partly chosen for its fine view of the **Shinobazu Pond ④** (Shinobazu-no-ike) and its tiny island, home to the **Benten Hall ⑤** (Benten-do), built in 1958 although its history dates back to the early 17th century. The abbot Tenkai dedicated the temple to Benten, patron of the arts and goddess of beauty. Now a freshwater pond, Shinobazu was once a salty inlet of Tokyo Bay. It is at its best in July and August when lotus plants bloom each morning. It is also a sanctuary for many species of birds and waterfowl, including egrets, grebes and cormorants. At weekends you will find quite a few food stalls, selling yakitori and the like, set up around Shinobazu.

Yokoyama Taikan Memorial Hall

Address: 1-4-24 Ikenohata. Taito-ku
Tel: 03-3821 1017
Opening Hours: Thu–Sun 10am–4pm
Entrance Fee: charge
Transport: Yushima

Two interesting diversions lay just to the west of the pond, across Shinobazu-dori. The **Yokoyama Taikan Memorial Hall ⑥** (Yokoyama Taikan Kinenkan) displays *nihonga* (traditional Japanese painting in a modern vein) by Yokoyama Taikan (1868–1958), one of the foremost practitioners of this style of art. Born Sakai Hidemaro (like many Japanese artists he adopted a pen name) Yokoyama lived in this house, which also has beautifully designed gardens.

Kyu Iwasaki-tei House and Gardens

Address: 1-3-45 Ikenohata, Taito-ku; http://teien.tokyo-park.or.jp/en/kyu-iwasaki
Tel: 03-3823 8340
Opening Hours: daily 9am–5pm
Entrance Fee: charge
Transport: Yushima

Kiyomizu Kannon Hall.

The Benten Temple overlooks the picturesque Shinobazu Pond.

Cherry blossoms: an excuse to party

The identification between the Japanese and the evanescent beauty of the cherry blossom, the national flower, is keen but intangible.

The springtime appreciation of the cherry blossom expresses the Buddhist notion of impermanence and transience. Japan's samurai warriors felt a special nostalgia for the cherry blossom, seeing in its brief and vivid spell a parallel with their own lives, which might end abruptly at any moment. Few nations have extracted so much pleasure and sadness from the contemplation of a single flower.

The notion of the cherry blossom's ephemerality is celebrated in countless poems. A haiku by the Japanese writer Ryota sums up the genre:

This is the way of the world –
three days pass,
you look up –
the blossom's out, or fallen.

Cherry blossoms in Ueno Park.

Far more than just a springtime rite, in many respects the blossoms mark the beginning of the Japanese year. It is also the start of the academic year, and the time new recruits enter companies. It is a season for renewal.

A national event

The progress of the flower is a national event all over Japan. The moment the first cherry blossoms, or *sakura*, bloom in Okinawa and Kyushu at the southern tip of the country in early March, television and newspaper reports follow. Until the last blossoms are blown off from the trees in the northern island of Hokkaido in early May, the media monitors the progress of the *sakura zensen*, or 'cherry blossom front', as it advances up the map.

In Tokyo, newspapers report that the flower is *sanbu zaki* (30 percent open) or *gobu zaki* (50 percent open). The most exquisite moment is when the flower is at *shichibu zaki* (70 percent open), which is considered the ideal time for a *hanami* (cherry-viewing party).

Ueno Park, one of the best-known venues in Tokyo for *hanami*, has over 1,000 trees and attracts as many as a quarter million celebrants a day at its busiest. This is when the Japanese are at their most exuberant mood. Blue tarpaulins are laid on the open spaces of the park, gargantuan quantities of food are consumed, women in kimonos dance, photos are taken in their dozens and portable karaoke sets appear from nowhere, producing a deafening beer- and sake-lubricated rowdiness. Despite the towering heaps of garbage, the sludge of discarded meat skewers, cornhusks and half-eaten fruit, no one dreams of picking a sprig of blossom, much less climbing a tree.

Purists insist the blossoms are at their best for no longer than three days. Connoisseurs seek out Tokyo's rarer species of tree, such as the wild cherries in the Hama Rikyu Garden (see page 204), or the twin-blossom cherries in the Shinjuku Gyoen (see page 122). The perfect end to a *hanami* occurs when a breeze releases a *hanafubuki* (petal storm), dusting the ground with pink and white flowers.

A couple of minutes south, the **Kyu Iwasaki-tei House and Gardens ⑦** is another quiet Meiji-era retreat, though on a grander scale. The mansion, once the residence of the industrialist Hisaya Iwasaki (son of the founder of the trading company Mitsubishi), was designed by the English architect Josiah Conder. Built in 1896, the house and estate, fine examples of fin-de-siècle Tokyo elegance and privilege, stand in immaculately kept landscaped gardens which you can observe while sipping green tea.

Shitamachi Museum

Address: 2-1 Ueno-Koen, Taito-ku; www.taitocity.net/taito/shitamachi
Tel: 03-3823 7451
Opening Hours: Tue–Sun 9.30am–4.30pm
Entrance Fee: charge
Transport: Ueno

Return to Shinobazu-dori, which runs parallel to the southern end of the pond and leads to the park entrance for the **Shitamachi Museum ⑧** (Shitamachi Fuzoku Shiryokan), one of Tokyo's most insightful museums. A transplanted tenement block and merchant house display everyday objects such as kitchenware and children's toys, many donated by people living in the area. Demonstrations of handicraft skills are regularly staged, along with videos and photo displays depicting the area up to the 1940s.

Tosho-gu

Back on the higher ground of Ueno Park, a stone torii leads to **Tosho-gu ⑨** (meaning 'Illuminator of the East'; www.uenotoshogu.com; daily 9am–4.30pm), a shrine established in 1627 (the present buildings date from a 1651 renovation) by a warlord wishing to honour the first Tokugawa shogun, Tokugawa Ieyasu. The walkway to the shrine is lined with dozens of large symbolic stone or copper freestanding lanterns – the tallest is 6 metres (20ft)

– donated by warlords to cultivate merit with the shogun.

The main shrine building is a magnificent structure; its outer hall features murals by the famous Edo artist, Kano Tanyu. Also interesting is the Chinese-style **Kara-mon,** a gate decorated with dragons that are meant to be ascending to heaven. According to local folklore, the dragons slither over to nearby Shinobazu Pond under the cover of night to drink. The good news for any thirsty dragons is that come nightfall they will find several cheap and cheerful *yatai* (food and drink stalls) around the pond where they can quench their thirst.

The 36-metre (120ft) high **Five-Storey Pagoda ⑩** (Gojuno-to), clearly visible from the grounds of the shrine, was originally a part of the Kan'ei-ji complex, much of which was burned down. You have to be within the precincts of the Ueno Zoo for a close-up look.

Ueno Zoo

Address: 9-83 Ueno Koen, Taito-ku; www.tokyo-zoo.net/english/ueno
Tel: 03-3828 5157

Penguins at Ueno Zoo.

Elaborately carved doors at the Tosho-gu Shrine.

Dinosaur display at the National Museum of Nature and Science.

Opening Hours: Tue–Sun 9.30am–5pm
Entrance Fee: charge
Transport: Ueno

Not one of the most attractive or best maintained of its kind, the **Ueno Zoo ⑪** (Ueno Dobutsuen), north of the Five-Storey Pagoda, has over 450 species of wildlife with some 2,600 animals on view, including a 'monkey mountain', where dozens of simians roam in semi-freedom. The star attraction for locals, however, are the pandas, who are most "active" at feeding time. Children will especially like the petting enclosure, where they can play with small animals like goats, sheep and ducks.

Tokyo Metropolitan Festival Hall

Address: 5-45 Ueno-Koen, Taito-ku; www.t-bunka.jp
Tel: 03-3828 2111
Opening Hours: (library) Tue–Sat 1pm–8pm, Sun until 5pm
Entrance Fee: free
Transport: Ueno

Moving across to the east side of Ueno Park, the first in a row of institutional-style buildings you'll approach is the **Tokyo Metropolitan Festival Hall ⑫** (Tokyo Bunka Kaikan). Designed in 1961 by the celebrated modernist architect Kunio Maekawa in commemoration of Tokyo's 500th birthday, its main attraction is a classical music concert hall that has a wonderful modern interior design and excellent acoustics. The hall also includes a music library with a collection of classical, ethnic and Japanese music.

National Museum of Western Art

Address: 7-7 Ueno-koen, Taito-ku; www.nmwa.go.jp/en
Tel: 03-5777 8600
Opening Hours: Tue–Thu and Sun 9.30am–5.30pm, Fri–Sat until 8pm
Entrance Fee: charge
Transport: Ueno

Ahead to the right is the **National Museum of Western Art ⑬** (Kokuritsu Seiyo Bijutsukan), consisting of two quite different buildings. The original, completed in 1959, is the work of Le Corbusier, while the new wing housing temporary exhibitions and completed in 1979 was designed by Kunio Maekawa. The permanent collection includes many works by French Impressionists such as Renoir, Degas, Monet, Tintoretto and Rubens, as well as more contemporary artists like Miro, Ernst, Picasso and Jackson Pollock. The outside courtyard has a display of 57 sculptures by Rodin.

National Museum of Nature and Science

Address: 7-20 Ueno Park, Taito-ku; www.kahaku.go.jp
Tel: 03-3822 0111
Opening Hours: Tue–Thu and Sun 9am–5pm, Fri–Sat until 8pm
Entrance Fee: charge
Transport: Ueno

Behind the art museum, on the right, the **National Museum of Nature and Science** ⓮ (Kokuritsu Kagaku Hakubutsukan) is devoted to science and technology, engineering, natural history and aerospace research. You won't be able to miss the building because it has a life-size sculpture of a blue whale in front of it. The museum's dinosaur displays and exhibits on oceanography and botany are popular with children. Two newer halls have interactive displays and simulated videos.

Tokyo Metropolitan Art Museum

Address: 8-36 Ueno Koen, Taito-ku; www.tobikan.jp
Tel: 03-3823 6921
Opening Hours: daily 9.30am–5.30pm, closed 1st and 3rd Monday of each month
Entrance Fee: free; charge for special and thematic exhibitions
Transport: Ueno

On the left side of the park, the 1975 redbrick **Tokyo Metropolitan Art Museum** ⓯ (Tokyo-to Bijutsukan) completes the set of Kunio Maekawa designs in Ueno Park. Over half the building is sunken to prevent the

Tokyo Metropolitan Art Museum.

structure from intruding on the park surroundings.

The museum's three floors are set aside for its own collection of Japanese artists, temporary exhibitions, studio space and an art school. Exhibitions range from works by established painters and calligraphers to those of promising new artists. If you need a break from exploring Ueno, there are a couple of restaurants and cafés in the museum.

Tokyo National Museum

Address: 13-9 Ueno Park, Taito-ku; www.tnm.go.jp
Tel: 03-3822 1111
Opening Hours: Tue–Sun 9.30am–5pm (Apr–Sept Fri–Sat until 9pm, Sun until 6pm)
Entrance Fee: charge
Transport: Ueno

All the previous museums are but overtures to Ueno Park's centrepiece, the colossal **Tokyo National Museum** ⓰ (Tokyo Kokuritsu Hakubutsukan). To tour this marvellous museum properly you will need to allow at least half a day.

Kannon statue at Yanaka's Daien-ji Temple.

A wide variety of rice crackers on sale.

Said to house the world's largest collection of Japanese art and archaeology, with in excess of 100,000 artefacts, the complex is divided into four main galleries. A permanent collection of paintings, textiles, calligraphy, ceramics and lacquerware are housed in the main **Honkan Gallery**. Archaeological relics from the Jomon Period right to the early 19th century can be found in the **Heisei-kan Gallery**, while the **Toyokan Gallery** has an eclectic mix of Chinese, Central Asian and Korean art treasures. The **Gallery of Horyu-ji Treasures** houses masks, scrolls, sculpture and treasures from the Horyu-ji Temple in Nara.

Kan'ei-ji

Northwest of Tokyo National Museum, running parallel to a small cemetery, the modest **Kan'ei-ji** ⑰ is all that remains of an extensive complex established in 1625 as the Tokugawa family temple. Ueno was at the northeast entrance to the shogun's city; northeast being a less than auspicious compass point, a temple was needed to metaphysically guard this approach. At its peak the complex had 68 buildings and contained an enormous image of Buddha destroyed in the Great Kanto Earthquake of 1923.

YANESEN

Exiting Kan'ei-ji onto Kototoi-dori will bring you into **Yanaka**, one of the best-preserved older quarters of Tokyo, a veritable time capsule of old wooden houses, private galleries, traditional shops, temples, bathhouses and back alleys crowded with potted plants and trellises – all easily explored on foot.

Together with the neighbouring areas of Nezu and Sendagi, quiet, low-rise Yanaka is one of the few old quarters of Tokyo to have come through both the Great Kanto Earthquake and the fire bombing of 1945 relatively unscathed. The three districts have become known by an amalgam of their names: **Yanesen**. Close to both the cultural institutions of Ueno Park and the campus of Tokyo University, this has long been the living district of choice for artists, writers, professors and intellectuals. It also sports the city's highest concentration of temples, many of which date back to the mid-17th century.

Jomyo-in

On Kototoi-dori is the entrance to **Jomyo-in** ⑱, a temple best known for its 20,000 strong army of tiny Jizo figures. A minor incarnation of the Buddha, Jizo is revered in Japan as a deity, the god of health and healing as well as protector of children. He is recognisable all over the country from his red and white bib and, in the case of the Jomyo-in, sponge gourds held in the left hand. Jizo statues are continually donated to the temple in the hope that one day they will reach their target of 84,000.

Kyu Yoshidaya Sake-ten

Address: 6-10-2 Yanaka, Taito-ku; www.taitocity.net/taito/shitamachi/sitamachi_annex/sitamachi_annex.html
Tel: 03-3823 4408

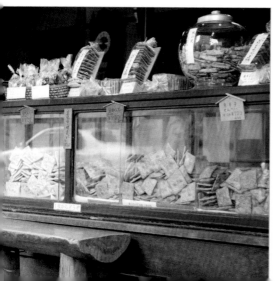

Opening Hours: Tue–Sun
9.30am–4.30pm
Entrance Fee: free
Transport: Nezu

Downhill from the temple along Kototoi-dori is the **Kyu Yoshidaya Sake-ten** 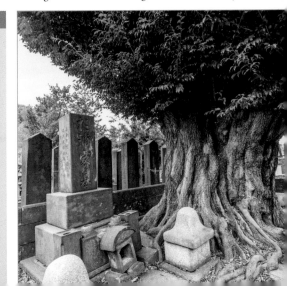, an annex of the Shitamachi Museum (see page 165) and another evocative remnant of Tokyo's past. This merchant's shop, made from wood and dating from 1910, has been preserved as a museum just like it was in its heyday, with nostalgic posters and giant glass flasks and wood barrels.

SCAI The Bathhouse

Address: Kashiwayu-Ato, 6-1-23 Yanaka, Taito-ku; www.scaithebathhouse.com
Tel: 03-3821 1144
Opening Hours: Tue–Sat noon–6pm
Entrance Fee: free
Transport: Nezu

Around the corner is the wonderfully cutting-edge art gallery **SCAI The Bathhouse** ⑳. The attractive building, dating from 1951, was once actually a neighbourhood bathhouse where the locals came to scrub up each night – you can still see the wooden lockers in the hallway where shoes would be stored before entering. Since opening as a gallery in 1993 the space has mounted exhibitions by such internationally renowned artists as Louise Bourgeois, Anish Kapoor and Genpei Akasegawa. Check they are open before going, as they sometimes close for weeks at a time between major exhibitions.

Yanaka Cemetery

From The Bathhouse gallery walk up the sloped street Sanski-zaka. As it bends to the left you'll find one of the entrances to **Yanaka Cemetery** ㉑ (Yanaka Reien) on the right, its grounds spread over a small raised plateau that can also be accessed from Nippori Station to the northeast. Many famous Tokyo personalities are buried here and, with its moss-covered tombs, leafy paths and time-eroded Buddha and Jizo bodhisattva statues, the graveyard has an almost Gothic feel about it. It's also a lovely place to linger in spring when its numerous cherry trees come into bloom.

Tenno-ji ㉒ sits in the northern corner of the graveyard, its manicured grounds filled with magnolia

FAMOUS GRAVES

Once part of a Buddhist temple, Yanaka Cemetery (Yanaka Reien) contains some 7,000 graves. At the graveyard offices (daily 8.30am–5.15pm) attendants provide a map of the graveyard (in Japanese) and direct you to some of the most famous graves in the cemetery. These include the burial places of talented composer and koto player Miyagi Michio, botanist Dr Makino Tomitaro, artist Yokoyama Taikan and the notorious female mass-murderer Takahashi Oden. Japan's last shogun, Tokugawa Yoshinobu (1837–1913), is buried here too, alongside the ignominious and destitute, whose bodies were once requisitioned by the university as teaching aids for the medical faculty.

FACT

No two *rakan* (Buddhist disciple images) are alike. If you see people placing a hand, one by one on the heads of each *rakan*, this is a search to find the warmest head, the belief being that this will be the image that most resembles you.

Yanaka Cemetery.

TIP

Travellers looking for cheap accommodation should bear in mind that in February, legions of young hopefuls descend from the provinces to take university entrance examinations. In many cases, budget rooms will have been booked weeks in advance.

trees and hydrangeas, which bloom in the June rainy season. The Great Buddha of Yanaka, a seated bronze figure dating from 1690, is the temple's pride and joy.

Asakura Museum of Sculpture

In this district of grave-makers and stonemasons, it seems natural to come across a gallery dedicated to sculpture. The **Asakura Museum of Sculpture ㉓** (Asakura Chosokan; Tue–Wed and Fri–Sun 9.30am–4.30pm), a gallery exhibiting the work of Fumio Asakura, is close to the borders of the cemetery, on the left of the road that bears right after exiting Nippori Station's west exit. The museum comprises the artist's studio-house and a lovely courtyard garden. From here, return to the road that runs from the station, turn left and continue until you see the 'Yuyake Dandan' flight of steps leading to **Yanaka Ginza ㉔**. Along this narrow, picturesque pedestrianised shopping street are several sculptures of cats peering down from the eaves of roofs or out of the corners of shop entrances – the area is famous for its feline residents.

Azaleas at Nezu-jinja Shrine.

Hebi-michi

At the end of Yanaka Ginza turn left and continue along Yomise-dori until you arrive back at Sansaki-zaka; turn right to pass the venerable rice cracker shop **Kikumi Senbei** on the way to Shinobazu-dori and the entrance to Sendagi subway station. Alternatively, cross over Sansaki-zaka to find **Hebi-michi ㉕**, a narrow residential lane that wriggles like a snake (which is what 'hebi' means) through Yanaka towards Nezu. Around here and along Sansaki-zaka you'll find several interesting craft shops including the printed-paper shop **Isetatsu**.

Daien-ji

Opposite Isetatsu set back from Sansaki-zaka is **Daien-ji ㉖**, a temple that contains a monument to the charms of Osen, a tea shop girl used by the artist Harunobu as a model for several of his woodblock prints. A statue of Kannon, the Goddess of Mercy, stands next to Osen's monument and many Tokyoites, especially the elderly, make pilgrimages here to rub a spot on the statue that corresponds to the part of their body where they are suffering an ache or pain in the hope of a cure. If this statue is anything to go by, stomach ailments and headaches are the commonest complaints among Tokyo's senior citizens.

Nezu-jinja

From Daien-ji follow Sansaki-zaka west until you reach Shinobazu-dori. Follow this south, crossing over Nichi-idai Tsutsuji-dori, and then take the next right to reach the grounds of **Nezu-jinja ㉗**. This popular shrine is known for its azalea festival in late April, when more than 3,000 bushes within the compound come into bloom. The shrine was rebuilt by Japan's fifth shogun, Tsunayoshi, in 1706. Look out for the Inari fox shrine with a row of red torii gates lining the approach and a stage for religious dances. The closest subway station to the shrine is Nezu at the junction of Shinobazu-dori and Kototoi-dori.

HONGO

Heading uphill west from Nezu is **Hongo**. Like Yanaka, this district remains stubbornly unfashionable and rather proud of the fact. Hongo's claim to have supported human settlement predating Edo is impressive. When earthen pots and other implements were found in a prehistoric mound on the high ground towards the northern section of Hongo in 1828, their design was considered sufficiently different from the preceding Jumon era to designate a new one, the Yayoi Period. The slope running down the hill from the excavation site to Nezu Station is, not surprisingly, called Yayoi-zaka.

Hongo was one of 15 wards created in 1878 for the new capital. In 1947 it was combined with the contiguous district of Koishikawa and became **Bunkyo-ku** (Culture Ward), the name reflecting its reputation as an enclave of academia and home to artists and writers. Slopes such as **Honmyoji-zaka** and **Kiku-zaka** (Chrysanthemum Slope) add interest to the Hongo district, creating a dipping and rising urban geography.

Tokyo University

At the heart of the Hongo area is the campus of **University of Tokyo** ㉘ (Tokyo Daigaku; www.u-tokyo.ac.jp/en), a pleasant place to stroll under the shade of its massive gingko trees. Founded by Imperial decree in the 1870s, this prestigious university, more popularly known as Todai, was built on the estate of the powerful Maeda feudal lords after being transplanted from Kanda in the 1880s.

Aka-mon

Just south of the main entrance to the campus on Hongo-dori is the **Aka-mon** ㉙ (Red Gate), erected in 1827 by the lord to welcome his new bride. This is the only gate of its kind remaining in Japan, a symbol for the university itself, and lends a traditional touch to the otherwise mainly prewar, vaguely Art Deco-style buildings of the campus.

The main exception is the **Fukutake Hall** ㉚ (http://fukutake.iii.u-tokyo.ac.jp), designed by Tadao Ando. The long, low concrete structure includes a 200-seat theatre, various meeting halls, the UT Café Berthollet Rouge and a shaded terrace that can also be used as a venue for art and media events.

Sanshiro Pond

Shrubbery surrounds the **Sanshiro Pond** ㉛ (Sanshiro-ike) at the centre of the campus. Once the focus of what was considered one of the most beautiful gardens of Edo, this artificial pond created in 1638 is shaped like the Japanese character for heart (*kokoro*), which explains its official name – Yutokuen Kokoroji Ike. It's more common popular name, Sanshiro, comes from its depiction in a novel of the same name by the celebrated Japanese writer Natsume Soseki.

Tokyo University students at archery practice.

ASAKUSA

This earthy area, where you'll find the city's most visited temple complex, is the heart of old Tokyo; to its west is a creaky old amusement park, a drum museum and shops which sell the kitschy plastic food models often seen at the front of Japanese restaurants.

Legend has it that on 18 March 628 two fishermen discovered a tiny image, a golden Kannon (the Buddhist Goddess of Mercy) statue in their nets in the Sumida River in the northeast of Edo. A temple – **Asakusa Kannon**, better known as **Senso-ji** – was built for the relic soon after near the river. It quickly became an important place of pilgrimage and remains Tokyo's most important Buddhist place of worship.

In his book *Tokyo Sights and Insights*, Ryosuke Kami points out that Asakusa has long been a place where worshippers came 'not just for religious purposes but for the entertainment that abounded in the temple's backyard, ranging from theatres, archery galleries, and circuses to brothels.' From the mid-1800s until World War II, Asakusa was the centre of all fine things in Tokyo, a nucleus of theatre and literature, of cuisine and other sensual delights. Its flowering, however, began with exile: first, with the banishment of the Yoshiwara, the licensed prostitution district, to Asakusa in the 1600s, and later with theatre, especially *kabuki*, in the 1800s. In the 1930s, Asakusa was the largest entertainment district in Japan, a role that was later handed to Shinjuku.

Asakusa had two prized qualities: *iki*, a sense of style and urbane polish, and *inase*, meaning chivalry or bravado, making the area, until its peak in the 1800s, *the* place to be seen in Edo Tokyo. Even samurai (banned from mixing with the lower classes) and priests (escaping strict vows of celibacy) would enter the district in disguise.

The heart of old Tokyo is still here in this quintessentially working-class district. Asakusa is a vital part of the *shitamachi* – a word that translates, literally, as 'downtown', but stands more

Main Attractions
Sumida Park
Gallery éf
Senso-ji
Asakusa-jinja
Hanayashiki Amusement Park
Edo Taito Traditional Crafts Center
Asakusa Engei Hall
Kappabashi-dogugai-dori

Map
Page 175

Geisha decked out in their finery at Asakusa Kannon.

Detail of the Senso-ji compound.

precisely for 'home of the common people' – a plebeian area synonymous in Japanese minds with hard work and equally hard play, a bustling mercantile mentality, libertine pleasures, Bohemianism and a strong sense of community. Fortunately, all these characteristics are still very much alive today.

Sumida Park

As you exit Asakusa subway station, the district's temple area lies northwest, while the **Sumida River** (see page 190) and **Azuma Bridge** (Azuma-bashi) is to the east. On the Asakusa side of the river, just north of Azuma Bridge, is **Sumida Park ❶** (Sumida Koen), a pleasant place for a stroll, especially in spring when cherry trees are in bloom. It is also one of the best spots from which to take in a view of the Philippe Starck-designed **Super Dry Hall** (see page 191) – the futuristic building of Asahi Breweries, topped by a giant gilded sculpture that is known as the 'Golden Turd' for obvious reasons – and, further away, the soaring Tokyo Skytree (see page 192), the city's communication tower across the river, which opened to the public in 2012.

The Hozo-mon gate at the Asakusa Kannon.

Gallery éf

Address: 2-19-18 Kaminarimon, Taito-ku; www.gallery-ef.com
Tel: 03-3841 0442
Opening Hours: Wed–Mon noon–7pm
Entrance Fee: free
Transport: Asakusa

Before or after exploring Asakusa it's worth dropping by **Gallery éf ❷**. The exhibition space that hides behind this hip café and bar (open until midnight) is inside a stonewalled *kura* (traditional storehouse) dating from 1868, which is just as interesting to view up close as is the contemporary artwork.

Senso-ji

The central compound of **Senso-ji** (free) Asakusa's spiritual centre, is best approached through the **Kaminari-mon ❸** (meaning 'Thunder Gate') facing onto Kaminarimon-dori, a minute's walk from the subway exit. This impressive, red-painted wooden entrance is flanked by leering, twin meteorological deities (Fujin, god of wind, on the right, and Raijin, god of thunder, on the left), and a magnificent 4-metre (13ft) -tall red

---

ASAKUSA'S FESTIVALS

The seasons are not allowed to pass by without some festival or event of purely secular invention taking place in Asakusa – flowers in January, bean throwing in February, golden dragon dancing in March and again in October, Tokyo's largest firework display over the nearby Sumida River in late July, a white crane parade in November, a kite market in December, traditional horseback archery in April as well as a relatively new innovation – a Brazilian-style carnival in August.

The biggest event is the Sanja Matsuri (Three Shrines Festival) held on the third weekend in May. Senso-ji and the roads and sinuous lanes that run around it provide the epicentre for this mammoth four-day spectacle, an important spring event for many Tokyoites. Dozens of intricate portable shrines are carried through the streets by young men and women, with much rough jostling and caterwauling. It is said the shrine gods enjoy being tossed around in this manner, something they get plenty of from the seething, swaying and chanting crowds at Asakusa. Picture opportunities abound as you will spot geisha and yakuza (gang members) sporting full-bodied tattoos – both rare sights in Tokyo these days.

paper lantern with the character for 'thunder' emblazoned across it.

Nakamise-dori

Stretching for about 250 metres/yds from Kaminari-mon to Senso-ji's main hall of worship is **Nakamise-dori** ❹; a perpetually thronged avenue of around 100 colourful stalls selling an amazing variety of products from the traditional (rice crackers and paper fans) to the bizarre (clothes for dogs). If you come at night you'll see that the stall shutters are all decorated with paintings of traditional scenes.

Denbo-in

To the left where Nakamise-dori crossed Denboin-dori sits **Denbo-in** ❺, the residence of the Senso-ji's head priest. This monastery buildings date back to 1777 but its 12,200-sq-metre (131,320-sq-ft) garden, created by the Zen landscape gardener Kobori Enshu, is around a

century older. The complex is currently closed to the public.

Hozo-mon

At the end of Nakamise-dori, pass under the grand **Hozo-mon** ❻ (Treasury Gate), with its ensemble of protective statues, to enter the main temple grounds. The upper storey of the gate contains Chinese sutras dating from the 14th century. A large bronze incense burner stands beyond the Hozo-mon where a steady stream of visitors place lighted incense sticks in the burner before offering a brief prayer. Japanese also consider it good luck to waft the incense smoke over their clothing with their hands.

Kannon Hall

The legendary golden image fished out of the Sumida River all those centuries ago is supposed to be hidden from view inside the **Kannon Hall** ❼ (Kannondo), the main building of the temple complex

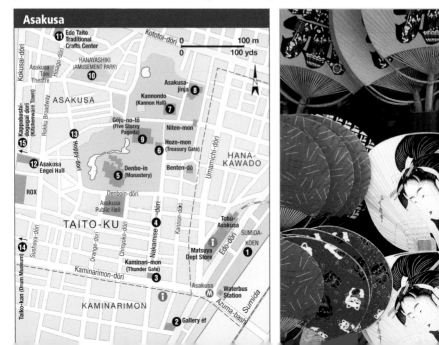
Fan shop on Nakamise.

FACT

Victorian-era traveller Isabella Bird, visiting Asakusa Kannon in 1878, noted the different approaches to faith, both the intellectual and intuitive. In her book *Unbeaten Tracks in Japan*, she observed that the temple's main hall was 'full of all the mysterious symbols of a faith which is a system of morals and metaphysics to the educated and initiated, and an idolatrous superstition to the masses.'

Japanese prayer cards (votive papers) and dolls.

that has been on this spot since 645. Kannondo has been rebuilt many times since it was first erected by the third shogun Tokugawa Iemitsu in 1648; the current structure, whose most recent major renovation was completed in 2010, dates from 1958 and has reinforced concrete walls and a dramatically sloping roof covered in titanium tiles.

On busy days, the temple resounds to the clank of money as coins are tossed into the offertory box, hands are clapped and bells, attached to thick ropes, are rung. The statue of Kannon, a mere 6cm (2ins) high, is believed to be housed in a fireproof box in the inner sanctum of this large hall, behind the golden altar. Although the original has never been seen by the public, a replica is taken out for viewing annually on 13 December. Three times a day, the temple's monks gather to chant sutras in its honour. The hall contains an important collection of votive paintings dating from the 18th and 19th centuries, while the altar, the centrepiece of the main hall, is jam-packed with religious objects.

Asakusa-jinja

Behind Kannondo and to the right is the shrine dedicated to the fishermen who found the Kannon image. **Asakusa-jinja** ❽ (www.asakusajinja.jp/english) is one of the few buildings in the complex to have remained more or less intact since it was built in the 17th century. The shrine, also known as the Sanja Sanma (Shrine of the Three Guardians), is popular for traditional weddings and is the starting place for Asakusa's most famous annual festival, the Sanja Matsuri (see page 174).

In front of the shrine is the **Niten-mon**, the main eastern gate to Senso-ji. Built in 1618 and a designated Important Cultural Treasure, the gate is usually covered with votive papers left by visitors.

Five-Storey Pagoda

The western section of the Asakusa complex is dominated by the **Five-Storey Pagoda** ❾ (Goju-no-to), an impressive reconstruction dating from 1973 of the original, first built here in 942. Opposite the pagoda is the small **Yakushido**, dating from 1649 and one of the oldest structures at the temple.

Hanayashiki Amusement Park

Address: 2-28-1 Asakusa, Taito-ku; www.hanayashiki.net
Tel: 03-3842 8780
Opening Hours: times and closures vary throughout the year; see schedule on website.
Entrance Fee: charge
Transport: Asakusa
West of the temple grounds, in the direction of Kokusai-dori and the Asakusa View Hotel, is Asakusa's

main entertainment district. This is where the endearingly old-fashioned **Hanayashiki Amusement Park** ⑩, opened in 1853 and as such Japan's oldest amusement park, is located. Not surprisingly there is a vintage quality to many of the attractions in the park, including an eerie and rather run-down *obakeyashiki* – ghost house – dating from the 1950s. Visitors to the toilet at the Hanayashiki (echoes of an old Parisian pissoir with a dented roof) will be amused – perhaps momentarily paralysed in the vitals – by a sudden, hurtling vibration as the one-minute rollercoaster, squeezed into the confines of the park, rattles 1 metre (3ft) or so overhead.

Edo Taito Traditional Crafts Center

Address: 2-22-13 Asakusa, Taito-ku
Tel: 03-3842 1990

Opening Hours: daily 10am–8pm
Entrance Fee: free
Transport: Tsukuba Express Asakusa or Asakusa

Across the street from Hanayashiki lie the back streets of Asakusa's sprawling entertainment district, centring on **Rokku Broadway**. Lurid posters outside cinemas and fleapit clubs advertise porn and *yakuza* movies, re-runs of sentimental films and sex cabarets. This area is also known for *taishu engeki*, an enduring *shitamachi* brand of popular theatre.

At the north end of Rokku Broadway, the street becomes Hisago-dori and along here you'll find the **Edo Taito Traditional Crafts Center** ⑪ (Edo Shitamachi Dento Kkogeikan) displaying around 400 items representing over 50 different crafts made in Taito Ward and elsewhere; also known as Gallery Takumi you can

Young taiko drummers during the Sanja Matsuri festival.

The decorated stalls along Nakamise.

shop for souvenirs here, and there are usually live demonstrations by craftspeople between 11am and 5pm on Saturdays.

Asakusa Engei Hall ⑫

Address: 1-43-12 Asakusa, Taito-ku; www.ntj.jac.go.jp
Tel: 03-3841 6545
Opening Hours: daily 11.40am–10pm
Entrance Fee: charge
Transport: Tsukuba Express Asakusa or Tawaramachi

South along Rokku Broadway, **Engei Hall** is Asakusa'a most prominent theatre. The daily bill here (see www.ntj.jac.go.jp for further details) includes dozens of acts, ranging from *manzai* stand-up comedy duos and acrobats to *rakugo* storytellers and magicians. Everything is in Japanese and some of the acts so rapier even fluent Japanese speakers might struggle to keep track of the gags, but much of the slapstick humour and

performances transcend language barriers. An hour or two here is a great window into Japanese culture and wit.

Hoppy-dori

Address: 2-12-4 Asakusa, Taito-ku
Transport: Asakusa

One of the most distinctive components of the Asakusa area is **Hoppy-dori ⑬**, a road named after Hoppy, a famously lowbrow "beer" – less than 1% ABV – first consumed in Tokyo during World War II, at a time when real beer was hard to come by. Recently the drink has experienced something of a retro revival, no doubt aided by the gorgeously old-fashioned bottles; the done thing, if you'd like a decent amount of alcohol in your drink, is to order a Hoppy "set", which sees your bottle served alongside a glass part-filled with sho-chu and ice. Hoppy-dori has plenty of bars selling the stuff, with most customers imbibing it on suitably rustic outdoor seats.

TIP

The Asakusa Culture Tourist Information Centre (tel: 03-3842 5566; daily 9am–8pm) is opposite the Kaminari-mon. Drop by to find out what's going on in the area and to join a one-hour guided walking tour of Senso-ji Temple and the surrounding area (Sun 11am and 1.15pm; free).

Drum Museum

Address: 2-1-1 Nishi-Asakusa, Taito-ku
Tel: 03-3842 5622
Opening Hours: Wed–Sun 10am–5pm
Entrance Fee: charge
Transport: Tsukuba Express Asakusa or Tawaramachi

South of ROX department store, at the junction of Kaminarimon-dori and Kokusai-dori, is the **Drum Museum ⓮** (Taiko-kan), on the second floor above a shop that sells drums and large items like portable shrines used in Shinto festivals. Drums from all over the world are displayed here, and visitors are encouraged to try them out (a blue dot on a drum means you can play it; a red dot means you can't). Listen out for the 1-metre (3ft) -diameter Japanese *taiko* (drum), which is popular with children.

Kappabashi-dogugai-dori ⓯

A few blocks west of the museum takes you to the kitchenware wholesale district known as Kappabashi (www.kappabashi.or.jp/en).

RYOUNKAKU

In 1890, a 60-metre (200ft) tower was erected near Senso-ji's Five-Storied Pagoda. Officially called Ryounkaku (Cloud-Surpassing Pavilion) but commonly known as Ju-ni-kai (Twelve Storeys), the octagonal tower of red bricks around a wooden frame was designed by the Scottish engineer W.K. Burton. On completion Ryounkaku was the tallest building in the eastern hemisphere and only 21.6 metres (71ft) shy of being the world's loftiest tower. Privately owned, it had the first public lift in Japan and offered visitors a view from the top, as well as shopping opportunities. Although it was later reinforced with steel, the tower was so severely damaged by the 1923 earthquake that it had to be torn down.

The intersection of Kappabashi-dogugai-dori and Asakusa-dori, where the main shops start is difficult to miss: look for the building topped with a giant chef's head, complete with a white, pleated hat. One corner of the building is decorated with several tiers of coffee cups.

Wholesale merchants sell every type of restaurant and kitchen equipment imaginable – hence its English nickname 'Kitchenware Town'. It's a great place to pick up pottery, knives and other kitchen implements as well as the plastic food samples *(sampuru)* you will see in restaurant display windows all over the city.

On the left hand side of the street also look for the golden statue of a *kappa*, the water sprite of Japanese folk stories, whom the merchants have adopted as their mascot.

TIP

You can board waterbuses at the pier beside the Azuma Bridge in Asakusa for tours of the Sumida River. It is also possible to go beyond Hinode Pier to Rainbow Bridge, Odaiba and the bay. Departures are usually every 30 to 40 minutes from 9.50am to 3.20pm for Hama Rikyu Detached Garden; until 7.15pm to Hinode Pier; and from 9.50am to 5.30pm to Odaiba.

Kappabashi kitchenware.

SUIDOBASHI, OCHANOMIZU, KANDA AND AKIHABARA

A fine Edo-era stroll garden, an obscure temple supposedly haunted by the spirits of foxes and a school turned into a contemporary arts centre are all found in these areas also well-known to lovers of books, electronics, anime and manga.

The east-west line of the Kanda River (Kanda-gawa) passes across a drained marshland from the districts of Iidabashi and Suidobashi and across to Kanda, Ochanomizu and Akihabara. This area of expanded flatlands cutting from the southern bluff of the Yamanote hills extending south of Yushima defines the area covered in this chapter.

Yushima, which means 'Island of Hot Water', an allusion to a prehistoric age when hot water bubbled up from the hills, is situated in the Soto-Kanda (Outer Kanda) district. Things have cooled down since then, but even in the late Edo and early Meiji periods, streams of clear water trickled down from the Yushima and Yamanote hills to the marshes and meadow land of the old riverine lower city. The incidental function of these *sakamichi* (areas of sloping roads), to provide drafts of fresh air and the occasional unimpeded view beyond the city, has largely been lost to high-rises and power lines, but the basic configuration remains.

Historically, the area not only marked the physical transition from the high city to the low, it was also the point where the residences, shops and trade districts of the townspeople mingled with zones set aside for the military class, the samurai and their households.

Office workers heading home through Kanda.

SUIDOBASHI AND AROUND

Koishikawa Korakuen

Address: 1-6-6 Koraku, Bunkyo-ku; http://teien.tokyo-park.or.jp/en/koishikawa
Tel: 03-3811 3015
Opening Hours: daily 9am–5pm
Entrance Fee: charge
Transport: Iidabashi

As a gentle start to your exploration of this quarter of the city pay a visit to **Koishikawa Korakuen ❶**, one of the city's finest Edo-Period stroll

Main Attractions
Koishikawa Korakuen
Tokyo Dome City
Spa LaQua
Origami Center
Yushima Tenjin
Kanda Myojin
Yushima Seido
3331 Arts Chiyoda

Map
Page 182

TIP

Yushima Tenjin holds its annual Plum Festival in February (its tiny garden is said to be one of the premier spots in Tokyo for plum viewing). In late October, admirers of the chrysanthemum throng to the shrine to see clever tableaux made from the imperial flower's petals.

gardens, the entrance of which is closest to Iidabashi Station. This is all that remains of the estate of Yorifusa Tokugawa, patriarch of the powerful Mito Tokugawa clan. Work began on the garden in 1629 and was finally completed by his heir. Stroll gardens were intended for amusement as much as aesthetic contemplation. The designers of such gardens tried to incorporate scenes from the Chinese classics as well as miniaturised Japanese landscapes.

A small stream passing through the garden is called the Oikawa River and symbolises a river of the same name in Arashiyama, near Kyoto, while two small hills, each covered in dwarf bamboo, are said to represent Mount Lu, a Buddhist pilgrimage site in China. The north end of the garden provides a completely different perspective as paddy, irises and plum trees come into view. The garden also features a large lotus pond best viewed in August when the plants are in blossom, and a section with a small pond, once a place of study for the Mito family. Apart from a Chinese gate that once graced the entrance to this inner garden, all else remains unchanged, including its original stone-paved path.

Tokyo Dome City

Address: 1-3-61 Koraku, Bunkyo-ku; www.tokyo-dome.co.jp
Tel: 03-5800 9999
Opening Hours: daily 10am–9pm
Entrance Fee: charge
Transport: Suidobashi and Korakuen

Immediately north of Suidobashi Station but also accessible from Korakuen Station is **Tokyo Dome City ➋**, an area that takes its name from the 55,000 capacity stadium at its centre. Affectionately known by its nickname the 'Big Egg', Tokyo Dome is used as a venue for major rock concerts – Madonna, Britney Spears and U2 have all performed

Suidobashi, Ochanomizu, Kanda and Akihabara

Rich autumn leaves at Koishikawa Korakuen Garden.

here – as well as professional baseball games: it's the home base for the popular Yomiuri Giants team.

The neighbouring **amusement park** was formerly known as Korakuen after the nearby garden, and some people may still call it that. Big-thrill rides, including the giant doughnut-shaped Big O Ferris wheel and the Thunder Dolphin roller-coaster which reaches speeds 130kmh (80mph), alternate with gentler attractions such as musical fountains, a carousel and a play area packed with toys for small children.

Baseball Hall of Fame and Museum

Address: 1-3-61 Koraku, Bunkyo-ku; http://english.baseball-museum.or.jp
Tel: 03-3811 3600
Opening Hours: Tue–Sun Mar–Sept 10am–6pm, Oct–Feb until 5pm
Entrance Fee: charge
Transport: Suidobashi

Also found within Tokyo Dome City, the dome's **Baseball Hall of Fame and Museum ❸** offers a comprehensive, mostly visual history of Japanese baseball. There are very good English-language pamphlets at hand to steer you through over 140 years of the game in Japan.

Spa LaQua

Address: 1-3-61 Koraku, Bunkyo-ku; www.laqua.jp
Tel: 03-5800 9999
Opening Hours: daily 11am–9am
Entrance Fee: charge
Transport: Korakuen

At the northern end of Tokyo Dome City is the shopping mall LaQua, atop of which you'll find the **Spa LaQua ❹**, a luxurious bathhouse that uses water pumped up from a natural hot spring 1,700 metres (5,577ft) below ground. The facility – one of the best in Tokyo – features outdoor baths, massage bubble baths and various type of sauna. There are also relaxation areas where you can snooze, making this a great place to pass the night

The Thunder Dolphin rollercoaster goes right through the middle of the spokeless Ferris wheel.

if you miss the last subway home and can't afford a taxi. The only drawback is a policy many bathhouses still have from when tattoos were associated almost exclusively with yakuza: nobody with tattoos is allowed entry.

TAKUZOSU INARI: THE FOX SPIRIT LAIR

In the middle of a narrow backstreet, just five minutes from Kasuga Station on the Oedo and Mita subway lines, is an old tree said to be visited by an Inari fox deity. Somehow, locals have kept town planners away from this sacred spot – incredible given how often and extensively Tokyo makes itself over. Overlooking it is the former house of the well-known Taisho-era poet and author, Rohan Koda, who predominantly wrote historical and supernatural shorts set in Edo. The tree is a signpost indicating the presence a few steps away of the **Takuzosu Inari**, a shrine that is one of the spookiest spots in the city. Shoehorned into the pinched precincts of the shrine are rows of torii gates, Jizo and Kannon statues, and fierce-looking fox messengers. Stone steps descend under blackened trees (that seem permanently wet) to an eerie cave called the Oana, its dank rock-face the home, it is believed, of the resident white fox. Credence of this comes from author Nagai Kafu who, in his short story *Kitsune* (The Fox), relates how his father spotted the bushy-tailed messenger here one afternoon. Should you spot it, count its tails. It's said the more tails an Inari has, the more powerful and wise it is.

Tokyo Wonder Site Hongo

Address: 2-4-16 Hongo, Bunkyou-ku; www.tokyo-ws.org
Tel: 03-5689 5531
Opening Hours: Tue–Sun 11am–7pm
Entrance Fee: free
Transport: Suidobashi

Head east from Suidobashi Station along Sotobori-dori. Bear left just before you reach the striking Century Tower, designed by British architect Norman Foster, to find **Tokyo Wonder Site ❺**. Set up by the Tokyo Metropolitan Government to encourage and promote exciting new works by young and up-and-coming artists, the building contains three floors of whatever is current, from paintings to video installations.

International origami center

Address: 1-7-14 Yushima, Bunkyo-ku; www.origamikaikan.co.jp/info/e_us.html
Tel: 03-3811 4025
Opening Hours: Mon–Sat 9.30am–6pm
Entrance Fee: free
Transport: Ochanomizu

From Tokyo Wonder Site continue east towards Hongo-dori. Branching off from here to the north is Kurameabashi-dori, which runs behind the Tokyo Garden Palace hotel. Along it is the **Origami Center ❻** (Origami Kaikan), set up in 1859 and considered to be the birthplace of this art of folding paper. The centre holds exhibitions of origami art and there's a workshop on the top floor where you can watch paper being made, dyed and printed. In the shop selling an amazing range of papers and books devoted to the art, the assistants also provide free origami lessons.

Yushima Tenjin

Address: 3-30-1 Yushima, Bunkyo-ku; www.yushimatenjin.or.jp
Tel: 03-3836 0753
Opening Hours: daily 6am–8pm

Entrance Fee: free
Transport: Yushima

Across the road from the Origami Center, Yokomi-zaka runs north towards **Yushima Tenjin** ➐, the city's so-called 'Shrine of Literature' dedicated to the 9th-century statesman and poet Michizane Sugawara, deified here in the form of Tenjin, patron of learning and the arts. A steady flow of students come here to pay homage throughout the year, but spring, the traditional time for entrance exams, sees inordinate numbers flocking to the shrine to seek Tenjin's intercession on their behalf.

Kanda Myojin

Address: 2-16-2 Soto-Kanda, Chiyoda-ku
Tel: 03-3254 0753
Opening Hours: 24 hours
Entrance Fee: free
Transport: Ochanomizu

Returning to Origami Center and Kuramaebashi-dori, a block to the east is one of Tokyo's most important places of Shinto worship. **Kanda Myojin** ➑ is a shrine dedicated to

rebel general Taira no Masakado, who fought for the oppressed Kantoites against Imperial forces. There is a taiko (drum) troupe attached to the shrine called Masakado Taiko. The troupe's main themes celebrate the life of Masakado, but its fame comes from being one of the few all-women taiko groups in Japan.

The temple, a concrete reconstruction of a 1616 original, enshrines two other deities besides Masakado: Ebisu, the god of commerce, family prosperity and good marriages, and Daikoku, entrusted with the care of farmers and fishermen. Side stores sell *mikoshi* (portable shrines) used during the Kanda Matsuri, one of the city's three great festivals marked by a magnificent street procession.

Yushima Seido

Address: 1-4-25 Yushima, Bunkyo-ku
Tel: 03-3201 1331
Opening Hours: daily 9.30am–5pm
Entrance Fee: free
Transport: Ochanomizu

Just across the street from the Kanda Myojin is the **Yushima**

FACT

The pachinko (Japanese pinball) arcade, with blaring sound and glitzy walls, is an industry in its own right. The 9,600 or so halls in Japan gross over 20 trillion yen per annum – spinning more profits than either the steel or auto industries.

Tokyo Dome City.

Characters and games galore in Tokyo.

Seido , a fascinating building and one of the few Confucian shrines left in Tokyo. Founded in 1632 by a scholar in the Tokugawa government, the centre moved to Soto-Kanda in 1691 when the hall became an academy for Edo's ruling elite. Drawn to Confucian teachings with their regard for hierarchy and obedience, the Tokugawa government happily set about adopting its more authoritarian aspects as a kind of unofficial state philosophy; this became known as neo-Confucianism.

OCHANOMIZU

Nikolai Cathedral

Address: 4-1 Surugadai, Kanda, Chiyoda-ku; http://nikolaido.org
Tel: 03-3295 6879
Opening Hours: daily Apr–Sept 1–4pm, Oct–Mar until 3.30pm (and services from 7.30am and 5pm)
Entrance Fee: charge
Transport: Ochanomizu or Shin-Ochanomizu

South of Yushima Seido, Hijiri Bridge (Hijiri-bashi) crosses the Kanda-gawa leading to one end of Ochanomizu Station. Ochanomizu, means 'Honourable Tea Water'. Water for the shogun's tea is said to have been drawn from the area's deep, and reportedly sweet, wells.

Two blocks south of Hijiri Bridge, the **Nikolai Cathedral** (Nikolai-do) is the main church of the Russian Orthodox faith in Japan. It is named after its founder St Nikolai Kassatkin, a Russian missionary who spent much of his life promoting the Orthodox Church's teachings in Japan. Designed by British architect Josiah Conder, the cathedral was completed in 1891, but lost the top of its original dome in the 1923 earthquake. Even though it was replaced with a smaller dome, the Byzantine-style building stands out as an exotic addition to the area.

Meiji University Museum

Address: 1-1 Kanda-Surugadai, Chiyoda-ku; www.meiji.ac.jp/museum
Tel: 03-3296 4448
Opening Hours: Mon–Sat 10am–5pm

An izakaya in Kanda.

Shinto priest at Yushima Tenjin Shrine.

Entrance Fee: free
Transport: Ochanomizu

East of the Cathedral, along Ochanomizu's main street, Meidai-dori, Meiji University has several buildings and departments. The **Meiji University Museum ⓫** (Meiji Daigaku Hakubutsukan) is located in the institute's University Hall, on the right as you descend the slope. The fourth-floor exhibition halls house an extensive collection of objects found on digs around Japan sponsored by the university's archaeological faculty, as well as items from China and Korea. Well labelled in English and Japanese, the museum has over 10,000 exhibits, ranging from stone tools of the Pleistocene Age to Kofun tomb (AD 250–538) clay haniwa figures.

Located one floor down is the best reason for a visit, a fascinating section with exhibits relating to the investigation, capture and punishment of criminals during the Edo and Meiji periods. The university, founded in 1881 as the Meiji Judicial School, draws its exhibits from a collection exceeding 250,000 objects. Woodblock prints depicting the kind of punishments given to criminals at the time hang alongside vividly real instruments of torture and execution.

Jimbocho

Continuing down Meidai-dori will lead to the intersection with Yasukuni-dori and into the heart of the area known as **Jimbocho ⓬**, named after the samurai Nagaharu Jinbo, who lived here at the end of the 17th century. In 1913, after a fire had destroyed much of the area, a university professor opened a bookshop in the area, which was the start of Jimbocho's association with the publishing industry. There are now stores specialising in art books, second-hand books, comic books and more, as well as ukiyo-e (woodblock prints) and antiques. The Japanese website http://jimbou.info provides more information on what's available in this 'book town'.

AKIHABARA

Heading east from Ochanomizu and crossing the Kanda-gawa will soon bring you to **Akihabara** (www.e-akihabara.jp), a name which translates as 'Field of Autumn Leaves'. Today, Akihabara is best known as the country's foremost commercial showcase for Japanese technology and as a mecca for those interested in anime, manga and computer games, who have nicknamed the area 'Akiba'. It's here that the craze for maid cafés (see page 188) and the J-pop dance group AKB48 (www.akb48.co.jp)

お帰りなさいませ！ご主人様・お嬢様！！

Poster advertising a maid café.

started; you'll need to be very lucky (or exceedingly unlucky, depending on your view of the group!) to find tickets to their phenomenally

MAID CAFÉS

Maid cafés, where young women dressed in costume (from French waitress in lacy pinafore and cap to nuns or 'beautiful boys') serve customers in an exaggeratedly formal manner. The phenomena kicked off in Akiba in 1991 at **Cure Maid Café** (6F Gee Store Akiba, 3-15-5 Soto-Kanda, Chiyoda-ku, tel: 03-3258 3161), founded by a cosplay outfitter, and was embraced by the otaku community of young men and later by the Japanese government who saw them as a way to sell Japan as a tourist destination to a younger demographic.

There are hundreds of different types of maid cafés now in Akiba, not all of them related to serving food and drinks; getting your ears cleaned by a girl while you lay on her lap is not something everyone would choose to experience, for example. One of the most successful operations, **@home café** (Mitsuwa Building 4F-7F, Soto-Kanda 1-11-4, Chiyoda-ku, tel: 03-3255 2808, www.cafe-athome.com) has a ¥700 cover charge before you order any drinks, food or pay to play any games (like paper, scissors, rock) with the maids, but it is lively and will give you a good idea of what these cafés are all about. If there are long lines here (there often are) and/or you're looking for a quieter experience, try **Mai:lish** (2F FH Kowa Square, 3-6-2 Soto-Kanda, Chiyoda-ku, tel: 03-5289 7310) near Suehirocho subway station.

popular shows which take place on the eighth floor of the Don Quixote store on Akiba's main thoroughfare Chuo-dori.

Despite its adoption by a generation of manga-obsessed, cosplaying otaku, Akihabara remains endearingly close to its low-life roots, with its strident shop assistants, all going hoarse hawking their goods to passers-by, and with a gaggle of unruly electronic stalls still huddled beneath the railway tracks. Hundreds of tax-free shops and discount stores, ranging from multi-storey affairs to hole-in-the-wall businesses, are shoehorned into just a few blocks. At night, the multinational throng of shoppers, smoky food stalls and giant, neon billboards, evoke street scenes from the 1982 movie *Blade Runner*.

Since the early 2000s there has been a great deal of property development in Akihabara, mainly focussed around the JR station where the

Yamanote and Sobu lines intersect and join with the Tsukuba Express Line out to the city of Tsukuba, a 'science city' planned in the 1960s, in Ibaraki prefecture. Above the Tsukuba Express entrance is a giant branch of the electronics megastore Yodabashi Camera.

Tsukumo Robot Kingdom

Japan's robot technology is famous worldwide. Robots can be viewed and played with at many museums, shows and exhibitions throughout Japan, but there's one place in Tokyo that any ardent robot fan can't afford to miss. It's **Tsukumo Robot Kingdom** ⑬, a shop based on the second floor of the Tsukumo Pasocon Honten II building, where ready-made big and small robots can be purchased. You can even choose from a multitude of robot parts and components and, at home, build your own unique robot from scratch.

3331 Arts Chiyoda

Address: 6-11-14 Soto-Kanda, Chiyoda-ku; www.3331.jp
Tel: 03-6803 2441
Opening Hours: (gallery) Wed–Mon noon–7pm; (main building) daily 10am–9pm
Entrance Fee: free; charge for exhibitions
Transport: Suehiroch

On the site of the former Chiyoda Rensei Junior High School, tucked away in the streets west of Chuo-dori, is the exciting arts centre **3331 Arts Chiyoda** ⑭. Aiming to be a hub for artistic development in the city and fostering links with other artistic communities and projects around Japan and overseas is what this place is all about. There are usually several different exhibitions going on here as well as private gallery spaces and a studio for students working on a community TV channel.

TIP

Japanese pop culture expert Patrick Galbraith, author of *The Otaku Encyclopedia* narrates the self-guided audio tour of Akihabara offered by Tokyo Realtime (www.tokyorealtime.com).

An electronics store.

SUMIDA RIVER

Relatively few tourists venture east across the Sumida River – but there's much to discover in this part of Tokyo, including lovely gardens, the sumo stadium, excellent museums and galleries and the soaring Tokyo Skytree.

Opposite Asakusa, on the northeast bank of the Sumida River (Sumida-gawa), it's difficult to imagine that the sprawling residential and small industry area of **Mukojima** was once farms and paddy fields providing food for Edo. It was here that the shoguns enjoyed the sport of falconry and planted cherry tree saplings along the river bank. Later famous for its temples and pleasure quarters, Mukojima's riverside teahouses were also the haunt of the literati and demimonde. It remains Tokyo's largest geisha district, although it's nothing like Kyoto, and without an introduction to one of the closeted *okiya* (geisha houses), or outside major festivals, you're unlikely to see one of these female entertainers on the streets.

MUKOJIMA AND AROUND

Yutoriya

Address: 2-38-7 Mukojima, Sumida-ku
Tel: 03-5247 2001
Opening Hours: daily 9am–9pm
Entrance Fee: free
Transport: Hikifune or Keisei Hikifune
Amid low-rise housing sprawl in the northeast corner of Mukojima is architect Hasegawa Itsuko's space-age **Yutoriya** ❶, a planetarium, community centre, library and media centre all rolled into one. Also known as the Sumida Lifetime Educational Center and defined as a 'microcosm of the greater media city', the building rises in a series of triangulated roofing, perforated screens and has a large central dome that has to be seen to be believed.

Mukojima Hyakkaen Gardens

Address: 3-18-3 Higashi-Mukojima, Sumida-ku; http://teien.tokyo-park.or.jp/en/mukojima

View of the Sumida River.

Tel: 03-3611 8705
Opening Hours: daily 9am–5pm
Entrance Fee: charge
Transport: Higashi-Mukojima

From Yutoriya a short walk northwest along the main road leads to **Mukojima Hyakkaen Gardens ❷**, the only Edo-era flower garden remaining in Tokyo. In the early 19th century, a wealthy antiques dealer called Sahara Kiku-u set up this garden with colleagues and named it Hyakkaen – meaning 'a garden of a hundred flowers that is in bloom throughout the four seasons'. Covering little more than a hectare (2 acres), it is intensely planted with trees, deciduous shrubs, flowering bushes and herbaceous perennials, the most notable being a beautiful, 30-metre (100ft) tunnel of bush clover that bursts into a riot of purple-rose flowers in September.

A couple of minutes' walk west of the garden towards the river, you'll come across the small shrine **Shirahige-jinja**. Although the main buildings may have been reconstructed after air raids, memorial stones dotting the grounds suggest an older site. A plaque notes that Terajima village mostly comprised paddy fields between the years 1688–1704, its fertile soil carried over from the upstream Sumida River, also ideal for growing the aubergines popularly known as *terajima-nasu*.

Chome-ji and Kofuku-ji

A short walk south of Shirahige-jinja brings you to the raised metropolitan expressway. Just before you duck under this to walk along the riverside pathway (a wonderful spot for cherry-blossom viewing in spring) you'll pass **Chomei-ji** meaning 'temple of long life'. There once was a well here that a shogun is supposed to have drawn water from and many poets, scholars and authors are also buried in the temple grounds. A few metres south from Chomei-ji, the Zen temple **Kofuku-ji ❸** was

founded in 1673. Look out for its distinctive Chinese gate and main hall. Next to Chomei-ji is the famous sweet rice dumpling shop **Chomei-ji Sakuramochi Yamamotoya**.

Ushijima-jinja

Enjoy the riverside walk between the Sakura-bashi and Kototoi-bashi where you'll head back inland along Kototoi-dori through the northern tip of **Sumida Park** (Sumida Koen). Here too is **Ushijima-jinja ❹**, a shrine dedicated to Susano-no-Mikoto, the younger brother of Japan's mythological sun goddess, Amaterasu. Ushijima means 'Cow Island', a reference that is picked up by the shrine's *Nadi-ushi* (stroking cow), a stone statue of a cow dressed in a red bib. Local folklore says the statue has the power to heal – just stroke the part of the cow's body that corresponds with the area that is troubling you.

Asahi Super Dry Hall

Exit the park to the south and head in direction of the **Azuma Bridge** (Azuma-bashi). On the left, you will see French designer Philippe Starck's

TIP

If you happen to be in Tokyo on the last Saturday in July be sure to see the spectacular fireworks *(hanabi)* display along the Sumida River.

Flags of various sumo champions.

The Asahi Beer Company dates back to 1889, but its top-selling Super Dry only debuted in 1987.

The bush clover tunnel in the Hundred Flowers Garden.

Asahi Super Dry Hall ❺. The corporate headquarters of the Asahi Beer Company is as striking a piece of architecture today as it was when first unveiled in 1989. The 22-storey, amber glass-covered tower is paired with a giant black, inverted pyramid topped with a giant sculpture that is officially called the *Flaming Ornament* but is universally known as the 'golden turd'. Almost as large as the building itself, the quirky hollow structure was built using submarine construction methods. The first and second floor of this building house a bar called Flamme d'Or, while on the 22nd floor of the tower there's another bar, the Asahi Sky Room.

Tobacco and Salt Museum

Address: 1-16-3 Yokokawa, Sumida-ku; www.jti.co.jp/Culture/museum
Tel: 03-3622 8801
Opening Hours: Tue–Sun 10am–6pm
Entrance Fee: charge
Transport: Honjo-Azumabashi

Recently relocated from Shibuya, the **Tobacco and Salt Museum ❻** (Tabako to Shio no Hakubutsukan) is less of an abnormality than you might think, in a country where tobacco consumption is distressingly high. Salt and tobacco were a government monopoly until the early 20th century. Even after sales were liberalised, it remained under strict state control until 1985.

The museum, built from the lucrative profits of Japan Tobacco Inc. (formerly the Japan Tobacco and Salt Public Corporation), traces the history of salt and tobacco production in Japan and overseas through fascinating displays that include smoking implements and salt sculptures. One highlight is the special exhibition of *ukiyo-e* woodblock prints of courtesans and other Edo Period figures in relaxed poses as they prepare their pipes.

Tokyo Skytree.

Tokyo Skytree

Address: 1-1-2 Oshiage, Sumida-ku; http://lang.tokyo-skytree.jp/en
Tel: 0570-550 634
Opening Hours: daily 8am–10pm
Entrance Fee: charge
Transport: Narihirabashi or Oshiage

Rising east of Asahi Super Dry Hall is the 634-metre (2,080ft) -tall **Tokyo Skytree ❼**, the city's latest digital communications tower, a 21st-century successor to Tokyo Tower (see page 145), opened to the general public in 2012. Apart from having the city's highest observatory (at 450 metres/1,476ft), with dizzying panoramic views over Tokyo, the tower also has another deck at 350 metres (1,148ft) with a café and restaurant. At the base, in the Sola Machi complex (www.tokyo-solamachi.jp), there is an aquarium, restaurants, shops, and other attractions, while standing just to the east is Sky Tree East Tower, a 31-storey office building that also houses some restaurants.

RYOGOKU

National Sumo Stadium and Sumo Museum

Address: 1-3-28 Yokoami, Sumida-ku; http://sumo.or.jp/En

Tel: 03-3622 0366
Opening Hours: (Museum) Mon–Fri 10am–4.30pm
Entrance Fee: free
Transport: Ryogoku

The next area of interest east of the Sumida-gawa is **Ryogoku,** primarily known for its history of sumo wrestling. Emerging from Ryogoku Station you can't miss the green roof of the enormous **National Sumo Stadium ❽** (Kokugikan), home to Japan's national sport. If you are not lucky enough to be in town when one of the main sumo tournaments are held in the months of January, May and September, there is always the small but intriguing **Sumo Museum** (Sumo Hakubutsukan) located on the same premises, boasting an extensive collection of materials related to the history of sumo.

There are several sumo stables in the area where wrestlers work out and live. It is quite normal to see stocky wrestlers walking around Ryogoku, unmistakable with their topknots, kimonos and wooden clogs. The staple diet for sumo wrestlers is a weight-inducing and nutritious stew called *chanko-nabe*, which can be sampled at several restaurants in the area. From more information about sumo, see page 198.

Philippe Starck's distinctive design is embodied in the Asahi Super Dry Hall.

Herons can be seen at Kyu Yasuda Garden.

Murals at the National Sumo Stadium.

Edo-Tokyo Museum

Address: 1-4-1 Yokoami, Sumida-ku; www.edo-tokyo-museum.or.jp
Tel: 03-3626 9974
Opening Hours: Tue–Fri, Sun 9.30am–5.30pm, Sat 9.30am–7.30pm
Entrance Fee: charge
Transport: Ryogoku

Behind the Sumo Stadium is the enormous **Edo-Tokyo Museum** ❾ (Edo-Tokyo Hakubutsukan), a must for anyone interested to learn how the city evolved into what it is today. The museum is housed in an ultra-contemporary building that looks like the bridge of a spaceship. The designers of the museum claim that their inspiration for the massive platform, raised on concrete stilts, came from the design of old Japanese rice storehouses elevated above ground to stop rats from destroying the crop. The museum does an excellent job of evoking the merchant life and culture of people living during the Edo Period, from the common people to samurai.

To reach the start of the permanent exhibition, visitors cross a reconstruction of the original Nihombashi Bridge. Exhibitions not only cover the early life of Edo, but also the years from 1868, through the post-war reconstruction years and the 1964 Tokyo Olympics. Temporary exhibitions are held in the large basement gallery. The museum shop has a good selection of traditional crafts from the *shitamachi* area. The museum also has a library and a restaurant.

Kyu Yasuda Garden

Just north of the Sumo Stadium next to the Sumida-gawa is the pretty **Kyu Yasuda Garden** ❿ (Kyu Yasuda Teien; daily 9am–4.30pm; free). This tiny, Edo Period stroll garden and the grounds of a larger estate were acquired by banker and industrialist Yasuda Zenjiro in the 1850s. Interestingly, the late Zenjiro was the grandfather of the avant-garde artist and musician Yoko Ono.

Yokoami Park and Tokyo Ireido

Across the road is **Yokoami Park** ⓫ (Yokoami Koen), a small park and the austere temple-like complex of **Tokyo Ireido**, dedicated to the 140,000 victims of the Great Kanto Earthquake, which struck just before noon on 1 September 1923 and destroyed over 70 percent of Tokyo. Incense is burnt before the three-storey pagoda and memorial hall not only to mark the earthquake, but also in remembrance of a second catastrophe, the same number who died in bombing raids that wiped out most of this largely residential part of Tokyo in March 1945. A small **museum** (Tue–Sun 9am–4.30pm; free), also within the park, displays remains from the fateful day.

Ryogoku Fireworks Museum

Address: 2-10-8 Ryogoku, Sumida-ku
Tel: 03-5608 6951
Opening Hours: noon–4pm July–Aug daily, Nov–Apr Thu–Sat, May–June and Sept–Oct Thu–Sun

Entrance Fee: free
Transport: Ryogoku

A short stroll southeast of Ryogoku Station, just past the intersection of Kiyosumi and Keiyo-dori, takes you to the **Ryogoku Fireworks Museum ⑫** (Ryokuku Hanabi Shiryokan), which focuses on the history of fireworks in Japan and the fireworks festivals held here. Ryogoku is considered to be the birthplace of Japan's evening fireworks shows. On display at this small, interesting museum are original Japanese cylindrical fireworks, photographs, traditional clothing worn by Japanese pyrotechnicians, posters advertising Japanese fireworks festivals and many other items. The museum also has a shop where postcards and souvenirs are sold.

Eko-in Temple and the Site of Lord Kira's Villa

The next two sites are for history lovers. A little way south from the Ryogoku Fireworks Museum is **Eko-in ⑬**. Rebuilt in a fairly uninspiring modern form after it was destroyed in World War II, the appeal of this small temple is its historical significance not its design, because after the devastating Long Sleeves Fire

of 1657, it was here that the ashes of the estimated 100,000 victims (almost a third of Tokyo's population at the time) were interned. In the backstreets immediately east of Eko-in there is another historical site of note, one that played a part in the story of the 47 ronin (see page 157). The remains of the **villa of Lord Kira** now form part of a small, not particularly interesting park – but this is where the 47 ronin took their vengeance on Lord Kira, the man who had caused the death of their master. You can still see the well in which the ronin are said to have washed Kira's decapitated head before they took it to Sengaku-ji temple and placed it on their master's grave.

Japanese-style split-toe socks ('tabi') are made with the 'geta' (wooden Japanese sandals) in mind.

KIYOSUMI-SHIRAKAWA AND AROUND

Basho Memorial Hall

Address: 1-6-3 Tokiwa, Koto-ku
Tel: 03-3631 1448
Opening Hours: daily 9am–5pm (closed 2nd and 4th Mon of month)
Entrance Fee: charge
Transport: Morishita

Take the subway one stop south from Ryogoku to Morishita (or just keep following the river south), from where

Recreation of ancient Tokyo at the Edo-Tokyo Museum.

FUKAGAWA HISTORY

The area gets its name from the late 16th-century local leader Fukagawa Hachiroe-mon, who was granted the land by Tokugawa Ieyasu and charged with draining and filling in the swamp that once existed here. In the late 17th century, following one of Tokyo's perennial disastrous fires, the area began to boom as lumber-yards were relocated here and new bridges over the Sumida River facilitated commerce between the two sides of the city. At the same time the area also became one of the city's 'unlicensed' quarters where brothels, masquerading as teahouses, plied their business – a trade that continued right up to and a few years beyond World War II.

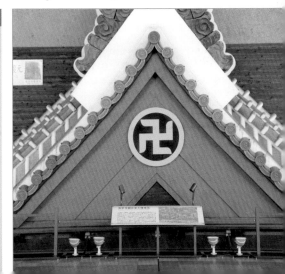

TIP

The Tokyo Mizube Line (tel: 03-5608 8869; www.tokyo-park.or.jp/english/business/index.html) waterbuses along the Sumida River, out into Tokyo Bay and over to Odaiba (see page 205), can be caught from opposite the National Sumo Stadium.

you'll head towards the river to find the next sight, just south of the Shin-Ohashi Bridge. **Basho Memorial Hall** (Basho Kinenkan) stands on the very spot from where the great haiku poet Matsuo Basho set off in 1689 for a five-month hike that would result in his masterpiece, *Narrow Road to a Far Province*. A small garden features a miniature copy of the hut in which Basho used to live. The museum contains original manuscripts and objects from the poet's journeys, but you'll need to understand Japanese to get the most out of it as there is no English labelling.

Kiyosumi Garden

Address: 3-3-9 Kiyosumi, Koto-ku; http://teien.tokyo-park.or.jp/en/kiyosumi
Tel: 03-3641 5892
Opening Hours: daily 9am–5pm
Entrance Fee: charge
Transport: Kiyosumi-Shirakawa

A short walk east from the galleries is the spacious **Kiyosumi Garden** (Kiyosumi Teien), a typical *kaiyushiki teien* or 'pond walk around garden'. Fed by water from the Sumida River, the garden was first built in 1688 by a rich lumber merchant named Kinokuniya Bunzaemon. During the Meiji era, it

was bought by another wealthy businessman, Yataro Iwasaki, the founder of the Mitsubishi Group of companies, who had the grounds restored to his own liking.

Apart from a beautiful teahouse set serenely beside the pond, a special feature of the garden is the 55 rare stones, brought from all over Japan by Mitsubishi's steamships. Stone lanterns, miniature islands, stepping stones and many species of flower, including Japanese quince, azaleas and hydrangeas, dot the grounds. In one corner of the garden is an almost separate iris garden that is absolutely beautiful in June. Near the garden entrance is a memorial hall to emperor Taisho.

Fukagawa Edo Museum

Address: 1-3-28 Shirakawa, Koto-ku
Tel: 03-3630 8625
Opening Hours: daily 9.30am–5pm (closed 2nd and 4th Mon of month)
Entrance Fee: charge
Transport: Kiyosumi-Shirakawa

A few blocks east of the subway station, follow a charming traditional shopping street (along which you'll pass an award-winning public toilet with an Edo-era facade) to find

The Fukagawa Edo Museum.

ANCIENT ART OF TATTOOS

Strongly identified with the yakuza, Japan's organised crime syndicates, tattoos *(irezumi)* were once also popular among the working class and groups like firemen, carpenters and sushi chefs. Tattooing in Japan is age-old – the indigenous Ainu used it for decorative and social purposes. In the Edo Period, skin decoration started to be influenced by ukiyo-e (woodblock prints) in their design and technique. The firemen of Edo probably had the first full-body tattoos, covering all but the hands, feet and head, as a form of spiritual protection. During the Fukagawa Hachiman Matsuri and Sanja Matsuri festivals, men with such tattoos can be seen hoisting the shrines along the streets surrounding the temples.

the **Fukagawa Edo Museum** ⑯ (Fukagawa Edo Shiryokan; daily 9.30am–5pm). Built on a small and intimate scale, it nevertheless has 11 original buildings, all taken from the Fukagawa district in around 1842, including homes, shops, a theatre, a boathouse tavern and even a 10-metre (33ft) fire tower. Volunteers, some of them English-speaking, are ready to guide tourists around the museum.

Museum of Contemporary Art, Tokyo

Address: 4-4-1 Miyoshi, Koto-ku; www. mot-art-museum.jp
Tel: 03-5245 4111
Opening Hours: temporarily closed for restoration
Entrance Fee: charge
Transport: Kiyosumi-Shirakawa or Kiba
Roughly a kilometre (0.5 miles) east of the Fukagawa Edo Museum, it is back to the present with the **Museum of Contemporary Art, Tokyo** ⑰ (Tokyo-to Gendai Bijutsukan; temporarily closed for renovations) in the north section of Kiba Park (Kiba Koen). This excellent museum features art from a stock of over 4,500 items in its permanent collection as well as new work by both Japanese and foreign artists. There are plenty of experimental and interactive displays, an extensive database in both Japanese and English, and a couple of good restaurants.

MONZEN-NAKACHO

Fukagawa Fudoson

Return to Kiyosumi-Shirakawa Station and go one stop further south to **Monzen-Nakacho**, a busy commercial strip, which retains the atmosphere of Old Tokyo. Off it, is **Fukagawa Fudoson** ⑱, a well-patronised temple of the Shingon sect of Buddhism. The original early 18th-century temple was destroyed in World War II; this one, dating from 1862, was relocated from its original home in Chiba prefecture outside of Tokyo. The narrow shopping

street leading to the temple from exit 1 of Monzen-Nakacho Station is lined with small restaurants and stalls selling *senbei* (rice crackers).

Tomioka Hachiman-gu

A minute's walk east of the temple is the **Tomioka Hachiman-gu** ⑲, the shrine that is the focus of one of Tokyo's greatest festivals, the Fukagawa Hachiman Matsuri. Held in mid-August, the frenetic festival sees over 100 portable shrines paraded around the streets amid a massive, unrelenting water fight. A 1968 reconstruction of the 17th-century original, the current shrine has impressive prayer and spirit halls and a towering, green, copper-tiled roof. It is dedicated to eight deities, including Benten, the popular goddess of beauty and the arts.

The shrine is strongly associated with sumo wrestling, and in the Edo era was the official venue for the sport. Walk to the back of the shrine and you will see the **Yokozuna Monument**, engraved with the names of long-departed sumo wrestlers who reached the rank of yokozuna, the highest in the sumo world.

TIP

For an audience with Mukojima's geisha, book one of the special tours offered by Hato Bus (www.hatobus.com) that includes dinner and geisha entertainment at the *ryotei* (banqueting restaurant) Sakura-Chaya (tel: 03-3622-2800).

Dramatic entrance to the Museum of Contemporary Art, Tokyo.

THE SPORT OF SUMO

The apprenticeship of a sumo wrestler is long and hard, but the rewards are great for those who reach the top.

Professional sumo is run by the Japan Sumo Association, who organise the six annual *basho* (tournaments) held across Japan, plus other events, and oversee the 50-odd *beya* (stables) in which wrestlers or *rikishi* live and train together. In most *beya* the day typically begins at 6am with several hours of practice. Harsh and tedious exercises work to develop the wrestlers' flexibility and strength, followed by repetitive practice matches amongst the *beya's* wrestlers (the only time they wrestle one another, as wrestlers of the same *beya* don't compete during actual tournaments).

Practice ends around noon, when the wrestlers bathe. Lower-ranked wrestlers are expected to scrub the backs of the higher-ranked *ozeki* and yokozuna (grand champion, the highest rank and rarely achieved). They will also serve meals and run errands. The food staple of the stable is *chanko-nabe*, a high-calorie, nutritious stew of chicken, fish or beef with miso. Side dishes of fried chicken, steak and bowls of rice – and even salads – fill out the meal.

Apprentice wrestlers receive no salary, only a small living allowance. A wrestler's first break comes when he reaches the *makushita* level, comprised of about 200 wrestlers nationwide, and begins to receive a more generous allowance. When a wrestler makes the next step up and reaches the *juryo* level, he becomes a *sekitori*, or ranked wrestler, and earns a salary of around US$9,000 a month. An ozeki, the second-highest rank in the uppermost *makuuchi* level, receives about US$25,000 monthly, and a *yokozuna*, US$30,000. The winner of one of six annual tournaments receives up to US$100,000.

The dohyo ring is carefully prepared ahead of a Grand Tournament.

A wrestler squats, wearing a ceremonial apron, before the bout begins.

Few people know that the sumo practice tournament at Tokyo's Kokugikan arena in the district of Ryogoku is open to the public.

The outfits sumo wrestlers wear are directed by strict tradition.

Sumo wrestlers enjoy the bulk-building stew chanko-nabe after a training session.

AN ANCIENT SHINTO SPORT

Ancient sumo painting.

Sumo has been around for at least 2,000 years. Japanese mythology relates an episode in which the destiny of the Japanese islands was once determined by the outcome of a sumo match between two gods. The victorious god started the Yamato imperial line.

While wrestling has always existed in nearly every culture, the origins of sumo as we know it were founded on Shinto rituals. Shrines were the venue of matches dedicated to the gods of good harvests. In the Nara and Heian periods, sumo was a spectator sport for the Imperial court, while during the militaristic Kamakura Period, sumo was part of a warrior's training. Professional sumo arose during the 1700s and is quite similar to the sumo practised in today's matches.

Shinto rituals punctuate the sumo match. The ritual stomping before a match *(shiko)* drives evil spirits from the ring (not to mention loosening the muscles) before a match. Salt is tossed into the ring for purification, as Shinto beliefs say that salt drives out evil spirits. Nearly 40kg (90lbs) of salt is thrown in one tournament day.

The oiled hair of sumo wrestlers is shaped into the form of an icho, or gingko leaf, before they participate in a bout.

TOKYO BAYSIDE

From a bustling fish market to serene gardens and a zippy monorail out to an artificial island stacked with futuristic architecture, plus mammoth shopping malls, a giant bathhouse and Ferris wheel – bayside Tokyo offers all this and more.

f the inlets of the Tokyo Bay area and the bluffs between them were the cradle of old Edo – the site for its great castle and the flatlands that accommodated the bustling merchant classes east of the Sumida River – then the shoreline was the crucible for newer developments. Even today, the area continues to expand. Landfills have been adding new dimensions to Tokyo's urban compression for over 400 years. Tokyo Bay is home to the euphemistically named Dream Island (Yume-no-shima), composed entirely of rubbish – an ingenious solution to dealing with the mountains of garbage generated by millions of citizens. Started in the 1960s, Yume-no-Shima has since been covered by topsoil and now hosts a sports park, tropical greenhouse and waste facility.

TSUKUDAJIMA

At the mouth of the Sumida River, a series of interlocking islands appear, the first in a number of landfills reclaimed from mudflats in the bay. The most interesting is the northern section of **Tsukudajima**, which can be reached on foot by crossing Tsukuda Bridge from Tsukiji, or by walking north from Tsukishima Station on the Yurakucho and Oedo subway lines. Meaning 'Island of Cultivated Rice

Fields' the island's name is a reference to the rural outskirts of Osaka, from where its first settlers came in the 17th century to work as fishermen, supplying the shogun's kitchens with fish as well as keeping an eye on movements in Edo's bay.

By the early Meiji Period, Tsukudajima has been combined with the reclaimed islands of Ishikawajima to the north and Tsukishima to the south into one contiguous landfill. Spared the great fires of Edo and the earthquake that struck Tokyo in 1923,

Main Attractions
Sumiyoshi-jinja
Tsukiji hongan–ji
Toyosu Wholesale
    Fish Market
Rainbow Bridge
Fuji TV Building
Museum of Maritime
    Science
National Museum of
    Emerging Science and
    Innovation
Oedo Onsen Monogatari

Map
Page 202

Apartment blocks on Tsukuda Island.

Ginza Six Dept Store
Kabuki-za
Yamaha Hall
Shōchiku Kaikan
Shimbashi-Embujō
Tsukiji Hongan-ji
Namiyoke-jinja
Sumiyoshi-jinja
Tokyo Shōsen Daigaku (Mercantile Marine University)

Uchisaiwaichō
Namiki-dōri
Ginza
Shiptomichō
MINATO
TSUKUDA KŌEN
Kiyosumi-dōri
BOTAN
Sotobori-dōri
Chūō-dōri
Showa-dōri
Harumi-dōri
Kachidoki-bashi
TSUKIJIGAWA KŌEN
AKASHICHŌ
TSUKUDA
Etchūjima
FURUISHIBA
Shimbashi
Shimbashi
Shimbashi
SHIMBASHI
Shimbashi
Higashi-ginza
Tsukiji
ETCHŪJIMA
Shiodome
Daiichi-Keihin
CHŪŌ-KU
Tsukishima
Kiyosumi-dōri
SHIO-HAMA
HIGASHI-SHIMBASHI
Expressway No 1 – Ueyosen
Shin-Ohashi-dōri
Tsukijishijō
TSUKIJI
Namiyoke-jinja
TSUKISHIMA
SHIN TSUKISHIMA KŌEN
Toyosu-bashi
KŌTO-KU
HAMA-MATSUCHŌ
Sekai Bōeki Centre Building (World Trade Centre)
KYU-SHIBA RIKYU GARDEN
Hamamatsuchō
KAIGAN
Takeshiba
Sumida
Hamateri-bashi
KACHIDOKI
Kachidoki
Nijima-bashi
Asashio Unga
Reihai-bashi
Harumi-bashi
Urban Dock LaLaport
Do Sports Plaza
Kidzania Tokyo
Gas Science Museum
HAMA RIKYU DETACHED GARDEN
Waterbus Station
Hinode
MINATO-KU
Shibaura-futō
Yurikamome
TOYOMICHO
TOYOMI KŌEN
Kagu no Hakubutsukan (Furniture Museum)
HARUMI
Autowave
Tokyo International Trading Centre
Harumi Wharf
Triton Square
Mitsume-dōri
Harumi-dōri
Shin-toyosu
TOYOSU
TOYOSU KŌEN
SHIN-ONOME
Waterbus Station
HARUMIFUTŌ KŌEN
Harumi Passenger Terminal
IHI Stage Around Tokyo
Shijō-mae
Toyosu Wholesale Fish Market
Ariake Tennis no-Mori
Shinagawa Wharf
Shuto Expressway No 11 Rainbow Bridge
Tokyo Zeikan (Tokyo Custom House)
HIGASHI SHINGAWA
ARIAKE
Ariake Colosseum
ARIAKE TENNIS-NO-MORI KŌEN
Ariake Sports Centre
Kokusai-Tenjijō
Ariake
Panasonic Center Tokyo
East Exhibition Hall
Tokyo Big Sight
ODAIBA KAIHIN KŌEN
Odaiba-Kaihin-kōen
Decks Tokyo Beach and Joypolis
Aqua City
DAIBA
Daiba
Fuji TV Building
Shuto Expressway Wangan Line
Tokyo Teleport
Tokyo Fashion Town
Palette Town
PALETTE TOWN
Venus Fort
Mega Web
Kokusai-tenjijo-seimon
Waterbus Station
West Exhibition Hall
HIGASHI YASHIO
Tokyo International Cruise Terminal
AOMI
Aomi
Miraikan (National Museum of Emerging Science & Innovation)
FERRY FUTO KŌEN
Fune-no-Kagakukan (Museum of Maritime Science)
Telecom Center
Ōedo Onsen Monogatari (Hot Spring Bath)
Telecom Center

0   500 m
0   500 yds

N

the island's cosy huddles of housing blocks, narrow alleyways full of potted plants and old-fashioned street corner lift-pumps (some still in use), lend Tsukudajima its distinct character. Many of the houses have traditionally crafted features, including black ceramic roofs, oxidised copper finials of an ancient, green patina and well-seasoned wood walls. A prime example is the shop **Tenyasu Honten**, which can be found facing the Sumida-gawa, after crossing the Tsukuda Bridge (Tsukuda-Ohashi). You'll also see here a replica of an Edo Period lighthouse.

Sumiyoshi-jinja

Less than a minute's walk to the left after crossing Tsukuda-Ohashi is the area's venerable **Sumiyoshi-jinja ❶**. Vestiges of the shrine's role as a protector of sea travellers, fishermen and sailors can be seen in carvings on beams and transoms covering some of the small outer buildings. One particularly realistic relief on the roof of the well beside the shrine's torii (gate) shows fishermen in a skiff, with firewood burning in a metal basket as they cast their nets in the bay at night.

A few steps beyond the shrine, **Tsukudako-bashi** is an attractive bridge with a red handrail that spans a narrow, tidal inlet where you can get a modest insight into the former life of this quarter. The fishermen's shacks and boathouses are less charmingly dilapidated than they were just a few years ago and the number of their vessels is depleted.

TSUKIJI AND AROUND

Retrace your steps over Tsukuda Bridge and drop back down to the river promenade on the left-hand side fronting St Luke's Hospital and continue towards the Kachidoki Bridge. One road in from the river is the entrance to **Tsukiji Jisaku**, an exclusive and expensive banqueting restaurant in the former home of Mitsubishi group founder Iwasaki Yataro. The lush entranceway is a foretaste of the traditional gardens that several of the mansion's rooms overlook.

Tsukiji Hongan-ji

Address: 3-15-1 Tsukiji, Chuo-ku; www.tsukijihongwanji.jp
Tel: 03-3541 1131
Opening Hours: daily Apr–Sept 6am–5.30pm, Oct–Mar until 5pm
Entrance Fee: free
Transport: Tsukiji

From Tsukiji Jisaku turn right onto Harumi-dori and walk northwest towards Shin-Ohashi-dori. To the right of here is the area's most imposing building, **Tsukiji Hongan-ji ❷**. Founded in Asakusa in 1617, the original temple was destroyed by fire. The current structure, a stone building designed by the architect Chuta Ito, was built in 1935. Ito, a student

Tsukiji Hongan-ji temple.

of Tatsuno Kingo, who designed Tokyo Station, travelled extensively in the Hindu and Buddhist countries of Asia. Many of the motifs incorporated into this extraordinary building, especially its lotus-shaped main facade and domes, reflect these foreign influences. Take a peek into the interior, with its opulent gold altar and elaborately carved transoms, which can seat up to 1,000 people.

Hama Rikyu Detached Garden

Address: 1-1 Hama-Rikyu Teien, Chuo-ku; http://teien.tokyo-park.or.jp/en/hama-rikyu
Tel: 03-3541 0200
Opening Hours: daily 9am–5pm
Entrance Fee: charge
Transport: Shiodome or Tsukiji-Shijo

Exiting the market on to Shin-Ohashi-dori, turn left and work your way around to the entrance of the expansive **Hama Rikyu Detached Garden** ❸ (Hama Rikyu Teien), just a 10-minute walk south. Developed in the 1650s as grounds for the Hama Palace (an estate owned by

Matsudaira Tsunashige, a lord from Kofu Province), they passed into the hands of the sixth shogun, Ienobu, who turned the grounds into landscaped gardens and a duck shooting site. The present garden, reached by crossing the Nanmon Bridge, or by waterbus from Asakusa (see page 173), were opened to the public in 1945. The highlight is a large tidal pond, with a small tea pavilion at its centre and islets connected by wooden bridges, behind which the glistening skyscrapers of the Shiodome area dominate the skyline.

Kyu-Shiba Rikyu Garden

Address: 1-4-1 Kaigan, Minato-ku; http://teien.tokyo-park.or.jp/en/kyu-shiba
Tel: 03-3434 4029
Opening Hours: daily 9am–5pm
Entrance Fee: charge
Transport: Hamamatsucho

If you have a taste for formal gardens, there is another one just a few minutes' walk south of Hama Rikyu, opposite Hamamatsucho Station. Arranged around a large pond, the **Kyu-Shiba Rikyu Garden** ❹

Tsukiji's outer market will remain at the original market site.

(Kyu-Shiba Rikyu Teien) is, along with Koishikawa Korakuen Garden (see page 181), one of the few classic stroll gardens in Tokyo to have survived intact from the feudal era. It was created in the late 17th century by Okubo Tadatomo, an official of the ruling Tokugawa shogunate.

TOYOSU

The man-made island of **Toyosu** was, until recently, little visited, but the recent relocation of the mammoth Toyosu Wholesale Fish Market changed all of that, and the place now hosts hundreds of foreign tourists most days of the week. Aside from the market, it's a nice place to stroll around and get some bay views.

Toyosu Wholesale Fish Market

Address: 6-6-2 Toyosu, Koto-ku; www.shijo.metro.tokyo.jp
Tel: 03-3520 8205
Opening Hours: daily except Sun and Wed 5am–5pm
Entrance Fee: free
Transport: Shijo-mae

Five days a week, close to 3,000 tonnes of seafood from all around the world is sorted, auctioned and dispatched at **Toyosu Wholesale Fish Market ❺**. Formerly located across the bay in Tsukiji, it was moved – lock-stock and barrel – in late 2018, putting an end to years of delays and controversy. The market was initially scheduled to move site in November 2016, but experienced serious delays after toxic waste was found in the soil beneath the new Toyosu facility. Tokyo's governor, Yuriko Koike, finally confirmed the move in June 2017; the new facility lacks the ramshackle, saline charm of the old one, but it's a safer experience for tourists, and a far more comfortable place to work for the marketfolk themselves.

Wholesalers start laying out their stalls at 3am and then begin

An assortment of knives on sale at Tsukiji.

preparing for the famous tuna auctions that start at 5.30am (there's a cap of 120 visitors per day; book ahead online). The best cuts of these rock-hard fish, lined up like frozen sputniks, labelled and marked in red paint with their country of origin and weight, sell wholesale for as much as ¥10,000 per kilo, several times the price of the most expensive prime beef. The first auction of the year traditionally sees the first tuna go for ridiculous sums, as restaurants compete for the publicity that comes with the annual marquee purchase. In 2013, 'Tuna King' Kiyoshi Kimura stumped up a record-breaking ¥333.6 million (US$3.1m) for a single 278kg (612-pound) bluefin tuna.

With all this fresh seafood on tap, Tsukiji is an excellent place to indulge in a sushi breakfast: within the market you'll find a cluster of stalls selling sushi and other dishes made with seafood. One of the best is **Sushi Bun**.

ODAIBA

South of the garden are the dock areas of Takeshiba, Hinode and Shibaura. **Hinode Station** on the Yurikamome monorail is a convenient spot to board the rail crossing over the bay to **Odaiba**. The name of this man-made island comes from the cannon emplacements placed in Tokyo Bay in 1853 to defend the city against any attack by Commodore Perry's Black Ships (see page 37). Odaiba's fortunes began to take off in the bubble years of the 1980s when the vast tracts of landfill here were used as an urban laboratory for construction projects requiring more space than downtown Tokyo can conceivably spare.

Rainbow Bridge

The remains of two of the Tokugawa's cannon emplacements can still be seen south of the multi-decked **Rainbow Bridge** ❻ that links Odaiba to the city. It's possible to walk across the 918 metre (3,000ft) -long suspension bridge in around 30

minutes rather than take the mono-rail – either way you get superb views of the city that really give an incredible sense of its vast scale. If you plan to walk, alight the monorail at Shibaura-Futo and climb up to observation gallery from where the pedestrian walkway starts.

Odaiba Kaihin Park

Alight at Odaiba Kaihin-koen Station where **Odaiba Kaihin Park** ❼ (Odaiba Kaihin Koen) offers a pleasant swathe of green abutting an artificial sandy beach that gets very busy on hot days. Although the beach is pretty on the eyes, it is best to avoid paddling in the water, as it has a reputation for being heavily polluted.

Decks Tokyo Beach and Joypolis ❽

Across the road from Odaiba Kaihin-koen are restaurants and cafés at **Sunset Beach Restaurant Row**. The line of eateries is the exterior part of the shopping mall Decks Tokyo Beach, where you'll also find the state-of-art video game arcade **Joypolis** (http://tokyo-joypolis.com; daily

Hama Rikyu Detached Garden.

10am–10), which offers the latest in virtual-reality machines alongside all manner of cutting-edge gaming cabinets. More shops and a multiplex cinema can be found next door at **Aqua City**; on the beachside of this mall a small-scale replica of the Statue of Liberty adds a surreal element to the view of the city skyline.

Fuji TV Building

Address: 2-4-8 Daiba, Minato-ku;
http://www.fujitv.co.jp/en/visit_fujitv.html
Tel: 03-5500 8888
Opening Hours: Tue–Sun
10am–6pm
Entrance Fee: charge
Transport: Daiba

Opposite the shopping malls is the unmissable **Fuji TV Building** ❾, headquarters of Fuji Television, a popular commercial TV channel and one of the most futurist-looking structures on Odaiba. Yet another Kenzo Tange design, its two 25-storey blocks are connected by a lattice of girder-like sky corridors, some of which suspend a 32-metre (105ft) -diameter, titanium-panelled sphere containing both a restaurant and an observatory.

Museum of Maritime Science

Address: 3-1 Higashi-Yashio, Shinagawa-ku
Tel: 03-5500 1111
Opening Hours: Tue–Sun
10am–5pm
Entrance Fee: free
Transport: Fune-no-Kagakukan

You can either walk or hop back on the monorail to the next station for the **Museum of Maritime Science** ❿ (Fune-no-Kagakukan), which bears the unmistakable shape of an ocean liner. Exhibits here trace the history of shipping and commercial transportation. Bringing the whole subject alive are two actual ships, the *Soya*, once used for expeditions to the Antarctic, and the *Yoteimaru*, one of a fleet of now almost obsolete ferries that carried passengers between Honshu and Hokkaido islands.

National Museum of Emerging Science and Innovation

Address: 2-41 Aomi, Koto-ku; www.miraikan.jst.go.jp

View of Tokyo from Odaiba.

KASAI RINKAI KOEN

East of Odaiba, beyond several more man-made islands, is **Kasai Rinkai Park** (www.tokyo-park.or.jp/english/park/detail_02.html#kasairinkai), the largest public recreational area in Tokyo's central 23 wards. Divided into several zones, the park includes a giant Ferris wheel, a large bird sanctuary, cycle tracks, barbecue areas and a breezy beach front. Its highlight is **Tokyo Sea Life Park** (www.tokyo-zoo.net/english; Thu–Tue 9.30am–5pm) one of the area's best aquariums, home to a massive donut-shaped tank teeming with fish and other sea creatures. Take the ferry from Ariake on Odaiba (or from Hinode Pier or Hamamatsucho on the mainland) or the Keiyo Line from Tokyo Station to Kasai Rinkai-koen.

Get tickets to the observation deck of the Fuji TV Building.

Tel: 03-3570 9151
Opening Hours: Wed–Mon 10am–5pm
Entrance Fee: charge
Transport: Fune-no-Kagakukan or Telecom Centre

A short walk further south will bring you to the fascinating **National Museum of Emerging Science and Innovation** , also known as the **Miraikan**. Tokyo's best science museum, this is where you can learn all about robotics (including seeing a demonstration of the Honda's Asimo humanoid robot), space travel, genetics, the internet and other miracles of modern technology. All the displays have English explanations and almost everything is made accessible to kids, who are given free rein to run about and bash many of the exhibits.

Oedo Onsen Monogatari

Address: 2-57 Aomi, Koto-ku; http://daiba.ooedoonsen.jp/en
Tel: 03-5500 1126
Opening Hours: daily 11am–9pm
Entrance Fee: charge
Transport: Telecom Centre

If the past has more appeal than the future, walk over to the extraordinary **Oedo Onsen Monogatari** , a traditional hot-spring bathing complex designed along theme-park lines. Sample outdoor and indoor tubs, saunas and a foot-massage bath made of sharp pebbles. Massages, spa treatments, hot sand baths and a pedicure performed by tiny 'doctor fish' who nibble the dead skin off your feet all cost extra. There are also plenty of stalls and restaurants to grab a good lunch, dinner or snack. The entrance fee to this fun complex includes towels and a choice of colourful patterned *yukata* (lightweight dressing gown). Be sure to observe local bath etiquette.

Mega Web

Address: 1 Aomi, Koto-k; www.megaweb.gr.jp
Tel: 03-3599 0808
Opening Hours: daily 11am–9pm
Entrance Fee: free
Transport: Aomi

Return to Telecom Centre Station and go one more stop east to reach the next major commercial complex

Palette Town. On the east side of this is **Mega Web** , which includes the **Toyota City Showcase**, where simulated as well as real rides on the latest models can be enjoyed, the **History Garage** and its collection of classic cars from around the world, and a giant candy-coloured Ferris wheel (charge); on the west side is the giant mall Venus Fort, part of which is lit by an artificial sky that changes back and forth throughout the day, simulating sunset, sunrise and midday.

Tokyo Big Sight

Address: 3-11-1 Ariake, Koto-ku; www.bigsight.jp/english
Tel: 03-5530 1111
Opening Hours: daily 9am–9pm
Entrance Fee: free
Transport: Kokusai Tenjijo Seimon

Take a short walk along the track to the next massive chunk of futurism – the Tokyo International Exhibition Center, better known as **Tokyo Big Sight**. Housing exhibition halls, meeting rooms, restaurants and cafés, it is used for major events such as Tokyo International Anime Fair and Comiket (see page 27). It is marked by four giant inverted pyramids and is fronted by an amusing sculpture of a huge red-handled saw sticking out of the ground.

Panasonic Center Tokyo

Address: 3-5-1 Ariake, Koto-ku; www.panasonic.com/global/corporate/center/tokyo.html
Tel: 03-3599 2600
Opening Hours: Tue–Sun 10am–6pm
Entrance Fee: free
Transport: Ariake

This centre is a giant showcase for the electronics manufacturer's latest products, including Nintendo games and audio-visual equipment. It's not all about selling though, as there is also the quite educational **Risupia** (10am–5pm) 'digital network museum', where you can learn about science and mathematics using high-tech displays.

Kidzania

Address: 2-4-9 Toyosu, Koto-ku; www.kidzania.jp
Tel: 0120-924 901
Opening Hours: daily 9am–3pm and 4–9pm
Entrance Fee: charge
Transport: Toyosu

From Ariake, the Yurikamome monorail continues east to the terminus at Toyosu. Two minutes' walk north of here facing Tokyo Bay is another mammoth 21st-century Tokyo retail experience – **Urban Dock LaLaport Toyosu**. Besides the many shops, restaurants and the multiplex cinema inside the complex, there is also **Kidzania Tokyo**, an interior theme park where children (from ages 2 to 12) get to run a small fantasy town, play-acting in roles ranging from a bank teller or fire fighter to a burger flipper. Reservations are essential (and ideally well in advance) and kids really need to understand some Japanese to get the most out of a trip here.

TIP

The best way of getting around Odaiba is to use the Yurikamome monorail (www.yurikamome.co.jp) which connects with Tokyo's metro at Shimbashi and Toyosu stations. A ¥820 one-day ticket (¥410 for kids) allows you to hop on and off at will.

The giant Ferris wheel at Mega Web.

EXCURSIONS

An efficient rail system makes nearby getaways easily accessible if you want to escape Tokyo: choose from rambunctious Tokyo Disney Resort, old-world Kawagoe, laid-back Yokohama, Zen-like Kamakura, majestic Mount Fuji and temple-crammed Nikko.

Tokyo's congestion and big city attractions may be interesting for a short period, but even after a few days the most seasoned travellers may find themselves itching to get away. And the good news is, Japan's well-established rail system makes escaping a breeze. An hour or so by rail (see page 220) is all you need before arriving at some of the country's most famous sights – the temple town of Nikko, the Edo Period merchant enclave of Kawagoe, cosmopolitan Yokohama, coastal Kamakura or exploring Mount Fuji and Hakone. Most of the attractions listed in this section can be done as day trips. However, getting out of the city can be challenging – especially on weekends, when it may seem as if all of Tokyo has the same idea.

Chiba Prefecture

The neighbouring prefecture to the east of metropolitan Tokyo is **Chiba** (http://japan-chiba-guide.com), and it's usually the first place visitors to Japan see since this where Narita International Airport is located. Closer into Tokyo you'll find the fairy-tale castle and thrill rides of Tokyo Disney Resort, while slightly further out are the old castle town of

Sakura and the surf beaches and rural delights of the Boso Peninsula.

Tokyo Disney Resort

Address: 1-1 Maihama, Urayasu-shi, Chiba-ken; www.tokyodisneyresort.jp
Tel: 045-330 5211
Opening Hours: daily but hours vary depending on season and special events
Entrance Fee: charge
Transport: Maihama

Hundreds of millions of visitors have passed through the gates of **Tokyo**

Main Attractions
Tokyo Disney Resort
Ichiban-gai
Kita-in
Minato Mirai 21
Kamakura
Enoshima
Mount Fuji
Hakone
Tosho-gu
Lake Chuzenji

Map
Page 212

Tokyo Disney Resort.

Disney Resort ❶ since it opened in 1983. As well as the original Disneyland park, a fair copy of the original in California, there's also the neighbouring DisneySea Park with attractions designed along aquatic themes. Avoid visiting on weekends and holidays when the lines for the most popular rides are invariably enormous.

Narita-san (Shinsho-ji)

Address: 1 Narita, Naritasa-shi, Chiba-ken; www.naritasan.or.jp
Tel: 0476-22 2111
Opening Hours: daily 24 hours
Entrance Fee: free
Transport: JR Narita or Keisei Narita

There is much more to Chiba prefecture than the Magic Kingdom. Most people are in a hurry to leave Chiba's Narita area after arriving at Narita Airport, which is a shame as the area has much to offer. In **Narita** ❷ is the venerable temple complex of Narita-san Shinsho-ji, a 15-minute walk from either of the town's train stations, which are themselves little more than 10 minutes from the airport. Dating back to AD 940, it is one of the most important in the entire Kanto region, drawing worshippers especially over the first three days of the New Year.

There are several reasons for Narita-san's popularity. Foremost is its image of Fudo, the Buddhist 'god of fire', said to have been carved by Kobo Daishi, the saint who founded the Shingon sect in the 9th century. The complex, with the 58-metre (190ft) -tall Great Pagoda of Peas – a beautiful three-storeyed carved pagoda that's an Important Cultural Property – and a spacious landscaped park packed with blossoming trees and a calligraphy museum, is also highly attractive.

National Museum of Japanese History

Address: 117 Jonai-cho, Sakura-shi, Chiba-ken; www.rekihaku.ac.jp
Tel: 043-486 0123
Opening Hours: Tue–Sun Mar–Sept 9.30am–5pm, Oct–Feb until 4.30pm
Entrance Fee: charge
Transport: Keisei Sakura

An overview of the nation's history can be enjoyed in the former castle town of **Sakura** ❸, on the Narita Keisei and JR Sobu lines. Within the extensively landscaped former castle grounds is the **National Museum of Japanese History** (Kokuritsu Rekishi Minzoku Hakubutsukan), which presents Japanese history from an anthropological point of view with the aid of some 200,000 well-presented artefacts.

Nokogiri-yama

The hilly Boso Peninsula (Boso Hanto), shaped like a pelican's craw separating Tokyo Bay from the Pacific, is also easily accessed from Tokyo by train lines. On the peninsula's southwest coast is **Nokogiri-yama** ❹ (translated as 'saw-tooth mountain'). A short ropeway (www.mt-nokogiri.co.jp; daily mid-Nov–mid-Feb 9am–4pm, mid-Feb–mid-Nov until 5pm, summer months until 6pm) takes visitors halfway

TIP

Other easily accessible places of interest in Chiba are the historic towns of Sawara and Itako (www.suigosanto.com/en), built on canals that meander through thousands of hectares of marshland. Tours using poled boats take visitors along the waterways, and usually include a 'traditional lunch' and even a spot of fishing.

The three-tiered pagoda of Narita-san.

Participants at the Kawagoe Festival.

The carefully preserved old godowns of Kawagoe today house shops and restaurants.

up the mountain, which affords a fine panorama of Tokyo Bay and Mount Fuji. Just as interesting is a 33-metre (110ft) image of Kannon, the Goddess of Mercy, carved into the rock face near the top of the mountain, and a cluster of 1,553 stone statues of *rakan* (disciples of the Buddha). Descend a long flight of steps to visit the Yakushi Nyorai Buddha, Japan's largest figure of the Buddha. The base to the tip of the giant lotus bud that stands behind the statue's head like a stone antimacassar measures an impressive 31 metres (100ft). The Buddha image was originally built in 1783.

Easily accessed from Chiba city, the east coast of the peninsula has some of the most underrated beaches in the Tokyo area – although Tokyo's surfing enthusiasts have certainly discovered them. **Onjuku,** with white sand, palm trees and beach-front cafés, is the most pleasant, though **Katsuura** and **Kamogawa,** both south of Onjuku, are also good for swimming. Kujukuri-hama, north of Onjuku, has over 60km (37 miles) of black, volcanic beach.

Kawagoe

Saitama prefecture, to the north of Tokyo, doesn't have an abundance of tourist offerings but one great one that it does have is the former castle town of **Kawagoe** ❺ (www.koedo. or.jp). Less than an hour northwest of Tokyo, discover this 'Little Edo' famed for its historic core of *kurazukuri* – black-walled merchant houses, some

An ornate float at the Kawagoe Festival.

constructed in the 17th century and has since been through four editions, the most recent being this one dating from after the 1893 fire. Listen out for the bell, which tolls four times daily: at 6am, noon, 3pm and 6pm. The sound of the bell has been designated by the government as one of the (oddly named) '100 best sound scenes of Japan'.

Back on the Ichiban-gai, **Osawa Jutaku,** dating from 1792, is Kawagoe's oldest *kurazukuri*. It's now a handicraft shop selling traditional products like Japanese masks and dolls. Opposite is the **Kawagoe Festival Museum** (tel: 049-225 2727; daily Apr–Sept 9.30am–6.30pm, Oct–Mar until 5.30pm, closed 2nd and 4th Wed of the month) in which you can view two more of the ornate floats paraded around in the Kawagoe festival, along with videos of past events.

At the next main intersection after the Kawagoe Festival Museum turn left and walk a block to reach the narrow stone-paved lane on the left that is **Kashi-ya Yokocho,** or Confectioners' Row. Souvenirs and trinkets have been added to the 22

The wooden bell tower of Toki-no-Kane is a distinctive landmark in old-world Kawagoe.

dating from the 18th century – and the transported remains of Edo castle.

Ichiban-gai

From Kawagoe Station it's about a 15-minute walk to reach the town's historical core, first along Crea Mall and then Taisho-roman-dori. At the end of this street, the *kurazukuri* immediately in front of you used to house the Kameya sweet shop and factory and is now the **Yamazaki Museum of Art** (Thu–Tue 9.30am–5pm), displaying screen paintings by the 19th-century artist Gaho Hashimoto. Entry includes a cup of tea and a traditional Japanese sweet (*okashi*).

Continuing down Ichiban-gai, on the left inside an old tobacco wholesaler's is the **Kurazukuri Shiryokan** (tel: 049-222 5399; Tue–Sun 9am–5pm). This was one of the first *kurazukuri* to be rebuilt after the great fire of 1893, which wiped out more than a third of the city. The displays give a good idea of what it used to be like to live in such houses.

Across the road, and down a lane to the right, is the **Toki-no-Kane**, a three-storey wooden bell tower that has become synonymous with Kawagoe. The tower was originally

*Yokohama's Chinatown
is the largest in Japan.*

nostalgically old-fashioned shops
selling traditional candies, crackers
and other sweet treats such as purple
sweet potato ice cream.

Honmaru Goten and Kita-in

Returning to the bell tower, a
10-minute walk east brings you to all
that remains of the old castle – the
entrance and main visitors' hall of the
palace **Honmaru Goten** (tel: 049-224
6015; Tue–Sun 9am–5pm) built by a
local lord Matsudaira Naritsune in
1848. Now a museum containing
beautifully painted screens and
waxwork dummies of samurai and
lords of old.

A 10-minute walk south back
towards the station brings you to
Kita-in (www.kawagoe.com/kitain;
daily 9am–4.30pm), an important
Buddhist temple-museum dating
back to AD 830. After a major fire
in 1638, the third shogun Tokugawa
Iemitsu ordered that parts of the original Edo castle be transported here to
aid in the temple's reconstruction.
From these historic wooden buildings – the likes of which do not exist

Ferris wheel in Minato Mirai.

in Tokyo itself – you can admire a
traditional Japanese garden planted
with plum, cherry and maple trees as
well as hydrangea and azaleas.

Kita-in's other crowd-pleaser is the
Gohyaku Rakan, a grove of stone
statues carved between 1782 and
1825. The name means 500 statues,
though there are actually 540 depic-
tions of the disciples of the Buddha;
no two are alike. One figure scratches
his head, a couple get drunk on wine,
others meditate, rub a sore foot or
beat drums.

Yokohama

West of Tokyo is **Yokohama ⑥**, capital of Kanagawa prefecture. An integral
part of the Greater Tokyo area, it is also
a major urban centre in its own right,
with a population of 3.7 million, as
well as one of Asia's greatest seaports.
Easily covered on foot, it has relatively
uncrowded streets (except on weekends) and a laid-back atmosphere.

Minato Mirai 21 and around

The central bay area is dominated by **Minato Mirai 21** (http://goyokohama.jp), a massive development made from reclaimed land and historic disused dock buildings. Sights here include the 70-storey Landmark Tower (www.yokohama-landmark.jp) with its Sky Garden observation deck on the 69th floor, the handsome 1930s tall ship *Nippon Maru* (www.nippon-maru.or.jp) and the **Yokohama Museum of Art** (Yokohama Bijutsukan; tel: 045-221 0300; http://yokohama.art.museum/eng; Fri–Wed 10am–6pm), with its excellent collection of modernist sculpture.

Walk through the Nippon-Maru Memorial Park and across the Kisha-Michi Promenade to **Shinko Pier,** a man-made island housing the Akarenga Park (www.yokohama-akarenga.jp). The island's old red-brick custom houses have been renovated and now serve as fashionable shops, restaurants and boutiques. Shinko Pier is also home to the **Cosmo World** amusement park (Fri–Wed 11am–9pm, weekends until 10pm), which boasts among its many attractions two roller-coasters and the 112.5-metre (369ft) -high 'Cosmo Clock' Ferris wheel; and the highly popular **Cup Noodles Museum** (Wed–Mon 10am–6pm), a modern venue charting the history of instant noodles (and a fantastic spot for souvenir purchases).

The other side of the Okagawa River from Sakuragicho Station is an area of old government buildings, banks and other institutional structures. Further on is a charming tree-lined street with red-brick pavements called Basha Michi-dori (Street of Horse Carriages). The interesting **Kanagawa Prefectural Museum of Cultural History** (Kanagawa Kenritsu Kindai Bijutsukan; tel: 045-201 0926; Tue–Sun 9.30am–5pm) is located here. The stately building, erected in 1904 as a bank, is one of the best surviving examples of the city's old commercial architecture.

Along the waterfront

In Yokohama's early days, Honcho-dori became the centre of commercial activities. The wide street is still bracketed with banks and office buildings like the handsome red-brick clock tower of the **Yokohama Port Opening Memorial Hall** (Yokohama-shi Kaiko Kinen Kaikan), which miraculously survived the 1923 earthquake and World War II fire bombings.

Also in this area are numerous prefectural offices, and near the waterfront, the Yokohama Custom House (Yokohama Zeikan). **The Yokohama Archives of History** (Yokohama Kaiko Shiriokan; tel: 045-201 2100; www.kaikou.city.yokohama.jp; Tue–Sun 9.30am–5pm), on the site of the former British consulate, houses a museum with various exhibits about Yokohama's fascinating history, and a library with related audio-visual materials.

Opposite is the Yokohama Port Opening Square, where Japan and the United States signed the Treaty of Peace and Amity in 1854. A little bit farther down the same road is the 106-metre (348ft) **Marine Tower** (tel: 045-664 1100; http://marinetower.

Skyscrapers overlook the waterfront.

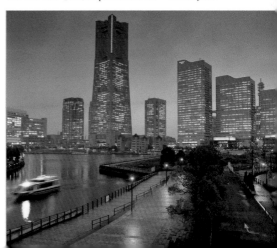

jp; daily 10am–10.30pm), featuring an observation deck, and the **Yokohama Doll Museum** (Ningyo no Ie; tel: 045-671 9361; www.dollmuseum.jp; Tue–Sun 9.30am–5pm), which displays some 3,500 dolls from Japan and around the world. **Yamashita Park** (Yamashita Koen) along the waterfront is well worth a visit. The former passenger liner and hospital ship, *Hikawa-Maru* (www.nyk.com/rekishi/e; Tue–Sun 10am–5pm), is permanently moored here and can be visited.

Yamate area

Southeast of Yamashita Park is Yamate, where the foreign merchants used to live in palatial homes. Before exploring Yamate, pause for a spectacular view of the bay and bridge from Harbour View Park (Minato-no-Mieru Oka Koen) at the top of the hill called France Yama. In the rose garden beside the park's gate, you can visit the **British House Yokohama** (Yokohama-shi Igurisu-kan; tel: 045-623 7812; daily 9.30am–5pm; July–Aug until 6pm),

One of numerous shrines tucked in the verdant hills of Kamakura.

home to the city's first British legation. Cross the road opposite the gates and go straight ahead. At the Foreigners' Cemetery (Gaijin Bochi), around 4,200 foreigners are buried. The adjacent **Yamate Museum** (Yamate Shiriokan; tel: 045-622 1188; Tue–Sun 11am–4pm), with quaint displays on the life of early foreign residents, sits near where Japan's first brewery was located. Immediately west of Yamate, on the way to Chinatown, is the lively shopping street of Motomachi (www.motomachi.or.jp).

About two kilometres south of Yamate, and best reached via bus from Yokohama Station, is **Sankei-en** (www.sankeien.or.jp; daily 9am–5pm), a traditional Japanese garden built in 1906 by a local silk merchant. Its extensive grounds have a number of historical buildings, including a farmhouse and three-storey pagoda.

Kamakura

Kamakura ❼ lies cradled in a spectacular natural amphitheatre, flanked on three sides by wooded mountains and on the fourth by the blue Pacific. For roughly 150 years from 1192, Kamakura was the de facto political and cultural capital of Japan, during which time a warrior administration based here built impressive temples and commissioned notable works of art, a great deal of it Zen-influenced.

Kamakura has no less than 65 Buddhist temples and 19 Shinto shrines, interspersed with walks through quiet surrounding hills. Most visitors customarily begin their sightseeing from Kita-Kamakura Station, nearest to the great Zen Buddhist temples of **Engaku-ji** (tel: 0467-22 0478; daily 8am–4.30pm, Dec–Feb until 4pm), **Tokei-ji** (tel: 0467-22 1663; daily 8.30am–5pm, Nov–Feb until 4pm) and **Kencho-ji** (tel: 0467-22 0981; daily 8.30am–4.30pm).

Wakamiya-dori
On the east side of Kamakura Station, where you'll also find the tourist office, is the broad boulevard of Wakamiya-dori. Parallel is pedestrian-only Kamachi-dori, a lane full of trendy shops and eating places.

Kamakura is also known for Kamakura-*bori* (lacquerware), first appearing in the 13th century as utensils used in religious ceremonies. Learn more about this art at the **Kamakurabori Kaikan** (tel: 0467-25 1502; daily 9.30am–5pm) on the right along Wakamiya-dori.

Tsurugaoka Hachiman-gu
The approach to Kamakura's main shrine, **Tsurugaoka Hachiman-gu** (www.tsurugaoka-hachimangu.jp; daily Oct–Mar 6am–8.30pm, Apr–Sept 5am–8.30pm) at the end of Wakamiya-dori, crosses a steep, half-moon bridge. Across Komachi-dori is the **Museum of Modern Art, Kamakura** (Kanagawa Kenritsu Kindai Bijutsukan; tel: 0467-22 5000; www.moma.pref.kanagawa.

jp; Tue–Sun 9.30am–5pm), with changing exhibitions by contemporary Japanese and foreign artists. The Museum of Modern Art also has another building in Hayama, along the coastline.

A little past the Genji Pond is the **National Treasure Hall** (Kamakura Kokuhokan; Tue–Sun 9am–4.30pm), where the 2,000

Statue at the entrance to the Wakamiya-dori boulevard.

Entrance to the Wakamiya-dori boulevard.

A 'forest of sculptures' in the foothills of Mount Fuji are part of the Hakone Open Air Museum.

treasures from the various temples of Kamakura are displayed.

Continuing up the avenue, cross a 25-metre (82ft) dirt track, along which every 16 September mounted archers gallop and unloosen their arrows at targets in an ancient samurai ritual. Then you reach an open area below the steps to the shrine's Main Hall. Most of the present shrine buildings are reconstructions, but the red-painted halls, lively souvenir stalls and ebullient flow of visitors make it one of Kamakura's most earthy pilgrimage spots.

The Great Buddha

Back at Kamakura Station take the Enoden Line to Hase Station, which is closest to Kamakura's famous Daibutsu (Great Buddha) in the grounds of **Kotoku-in** (www.kotoku-in.jp; daily Oct–Mar 8am–5pm, Apr–Sept until 5.30pm). At 11 metres (40ft) in height and weighing 94,000kg (93 tons), the Daibutsu is unlikely to get lost in the crowd. Stand a few metres in front of the statue to get the full impact of this artwork cast in 1252. Astonishingly, the statue has

survived some massive typhoons and tsunami – one in 1495 ripped away the wooden building then enclosing it – as well as earthquakes.

On the way back to the station, to the right, it's worth climbing up to the hillside temple **Hase-dera** (tel: 0467-22 6300; www.hasedera.jp; daily Mar–Sept 8am–5pm, Oct–Feb until 4.30pm), with its 9-metre (30ft), 11-headed Hase Kannon statue, along with thousands of small Jizo statues decked out in colourful bibs and bonnets.

Enoshima

Board the Enoden train again and get off at Enoden Enoshima Station. It's a 15-minute walk from here across the 600-metre/yd causeway to the tiny sacred island of **Enoshima**, its hilly slopes plastered with an extraordinary collection of shrines, grottos and souvenir shops. Local fishermen traditionally came to Enoshima to pray for a bountiful catch. Escalators take the faithful to higher reaches, but it's not difficult to follow the old pilgrim routes as

Climbing Mount Fuji.

GETTING THERE FROM TOKYO

Tokyo Disney Resort: 15-minute train ride from Tokyo Station on the JR Keiyo Line to Maihama, or take the Tozai Line (subway) to Urayasu, and then catch a shuttle bus.

Nokogiri-yama: 90 minutes from Tokyo Station to Hamakanaya on the JR 'Sazanami' express.

Kawagoe: The Tobu Tojo Line express from Ikebukuro takes 30 minutes to JR Kawagoe. JR trains also run on the same route, but take slightly longer.

Yokohama: Take the Tokyu Toyoko Line train (25 to 35 minutes) from Shibuya, or the JR Tokaido Line (25 minutes) from Tokyo Station to Yokohama.

Kamakura: An hour's journey from Tokyo Station (or 30 minutes from Yokohama) on the JR Yokosuka Line to Kita-Kamakura or Kamakura.

Mount Fuji and Hakone: The Odakyu Line from Shinjuku serves Hakone. JR Pass holders can access the area from Odawara on the Shinkansen (bullet train) Line.

Nikko: A two-hour train ride to the north of Tokyo – by direct local or Tobu Line express train from Asakusa to Tobu Nikko.

Racks of padlocks near the bell tower in Enoshima.

they wind up through this island of the gods. Apart from its shrines and sacred caves, the island boasts a yachting harbour, a botanical garden containing more than 300 species of tropical plants and several cafés with fine views of Mount Fuji.

MOUNT FUJI AND HAKONE

It would be hard to find a mountain more highly praised for its beauty than Fuji, or a lake more often photographed than Hakone's Ashi-no-ko. Most of the region is a designated national park, but due to Japan's rather weak laws at protecting and restricting commercial exploitation of such assets, national parks are more often than not considered 'nature' amusement parks.

Climbing Mount Fuji

Sweeping up from the Pacific to form a nearly perfect cone, 3,776 metres (12,388ft) above sea level, **Mount Fuji** ❽ (Fuji-san) is said to watch over Japan and her people. Like many natural monuments held to be sacred and imbued with a living spirit, Fuji was considered off limits to women until 1867, when an English woman broke the taboo and scaled the mountain.

According to a Japanese saying, there are two kinds of fools: the ones who never climb Mount Fuji and the ones who climb it twice in a lifetime. The ascent to Mount Fuji's summit can take anything from five to ten hours, depending on the route, so don't attempt the climb unless you are reasonably fit.

For those who wish to see the rising sun from Fuji's peak, start in the afternoon, stay overnight at one of the cabins near the top, and complete the climb while it is still dark. Or start at about 9pm and climb through the night. On a mountain

TIP

The 'official' climbing season for Mount Fuji begins on 1 July and ends on 31 August. The mountain huts along the trails to Fuji's peak are open only then, and casual hikers are advised, despite the crowds, to pick this period to make the ascent. Full details about the huts can be found at www.fujisan-climb.jp/en/index.html.

Lake Ashino with the snow-capped Mount Fuji in the background.

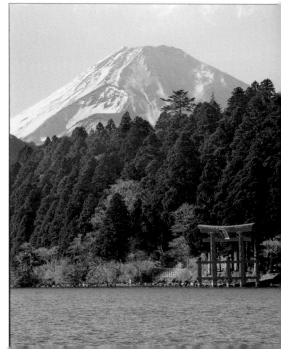

TIP

See www.odakyu.jp/global_
site for details about
Odakyu Electric
Railway's two and three-
day Hakone Passes
(¥5,140/¥5,640), both of
which cover a return trip
on the Odakyu Line from
Shinjuku to Odawara,
plus unlimited use of the
Hakone Tozan Railway,
the Sounzan funicular,
Hakone Ropeway, boats
on Ashi-no-ko and most
local buses. It also gets
you discounts at many of
Hakone's attractions.

this high you need to be prepared for extreme changes of temperature and rain, so bring along a sweater, gloves and a waterproof jacket, plenty of water and a torch.

Fuji Five Lakes

The **Fuji Go-ko** (Five Lakes) district skirts the northern base of Mount Fuji and provides an ideal year-round resort, offering a range of outdoor recreational activities such as camping and water sports during the summer months, and skiing and skating in the winter.

From east to west, the lakes are Yamanaka-ko, Kawaguchi-ko, Sai-ko, Shoji-ko and Motosu-ko. Yamanaka-ko, which is the largest in the group, and the picturesque Kawaguchi-ko, are the most frequented of the five, but some of the most picturesque and tranquil spots are hidden near the smaller and more secluded three other lakes.

Hakone

Hakone ⑩, set against the backdrop of Mount Fuji, has long been a popular place for rest and recreation. Tours usually start at Hakone-Yumoto Station, where the Hakone Tozan Railway begins its 9km (6-mile) zigzag route up all the way to the terminus at Gora. The gateway to Hakone's 16 hot springs, Hakone-Yumoto nestles in a shallow ravine where the Hayakawa and Sukumo rivers flow together. If on a day trip, the luxurious onsen complex **Tenzan Tohji-kyo** (tel: 0460-86 4126; daily 9am–11pm), a five-minute taxi ride from Hakone-Yumoto Station, provides an exquisite hot spring treat.

Some 20 minutes from Hakone-Yumoto on the Hakone Tozan lies **Miyanoshita,** the oldest and most thriving of the spa towns. Miyanoshita is home to the famous **Fujiya Hotel** (tel: 0460-82 221; www.fujiyahotel.jp). Opened in 1878, it is a veritable time capsule, with a 1930s-style wood-panelled dining room, a library full of old books and waitresses in Agatha Christie-period uniforms. Look out for the guest book with comments from personalities like Margaret Thatcher, John Lennon and Yoko Ono, among others.

The Hakone Tozan train also stops at **Hakone Open Air Museum** (Chokoku no Mori Bijutsukan; tel: 0460-82 1161; www.hakone-oam.or.jp; daily 9am–5pm), an outdoor sculpture garden that has few parallels elsewhere in the world. The works of Picasso, Rodin, Leger, Takamura Kotaro and many others are on display at this stunning location.

At the Gora terminal, change over to the funicular to Mount Soun (Soun-zan) and transfer to the cable car headed for Togendai, which lies on the shore of **Ashi-no-ko,** a beautiful caldera lake

Torii gate and Five-Storey Pagoda at Nikko.

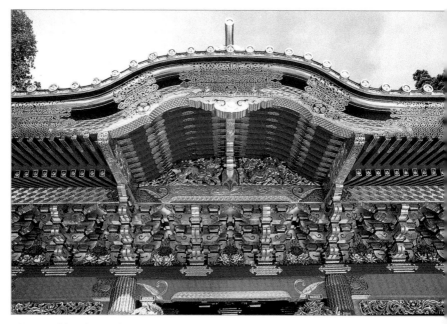

Heavily gilded rooftop of the Toshogo-jinja shrine in Nikko.

crisscrossed by pleasure boats. On the way up is **Owakudani** (Valley of the Greater Boiling) in the old crater of Mount Kami. It is an interesting place but the sulphurous fumes coming out of the lunarscape can be overwhelming; the most active area is often closed to visitors, sometimes for years at a time.

Nikko

A couple of hours north of Tokyo is the delightful mountain town of **Nikko** ⓫, a treasure house of religious art and architecture produced during the Tokugawa era and set among dense cedar forests. In 1617 Nikko was chosen by the Tokugawa as the burial place of their first shogun, Ieyasu. **Tosho-gu,** an astonishingly elaborate memorial shrine, was completed in 1636.

The ideal way to approach the complex is via the steps opposite the vermillion bridge **Shinkyo** (daily Apr–Sept 8am–5pm, Oct–Nov until 4pm, Nov–Mar 9am–4pm), spanning the Daiya River at the top of the main street, around a 20-minute gentle uphill walk from both the JR and Tobu Nikko stations. From there, follow the cedar avenue to the temple **Rinno-ji** (daily Apr–Oct 8am–5pm, Nov–Mar until 4pm). Rinno-ji's Sanbutsudo Hall houses three gigantic images: Bato Kannon (protector of horses), Amida and the thousand-armed Kannon, the Goddess of Mercy.

Continue along the main Omotesando path towards the Five Storey Pagoda (Goju-no-to). Just before the main entrance to the **Tosho-gu** (daily Nov–Mar 8am–4pm, Apr–Oct until 5pm), the Buddhist-style gate Omote-mon is guarded by two mythical kings. The adjacent Sacred Horse Stable is carved with scenes illustrating the life cycle of humanity. Past the torii gate at the top of the stone steps is Tosho-gu's most famous feature, the

TIP

Edo Wonderland is a cultural theme park in Nikko where tourists can explore the history of the Edo era (1603–1868), engage in various kinds of activities, watch live performances, dress in Edo style and even try the period food (http://edowonderland.net; Thu–Tue mid-Mar–Nov 9am–5pm, Dec–mid-Mar 9.30am–4pm).

Lake Chuzenji.

Yomei-mon, beyond which only the highest-ranking samurai could once pass. Standing 11 metres (35ft) high, this gate is covered with hundreds of intricate carvings – children at play, clouds, pine trees, bamboo and animals – all painted in a riot of brilliant colours.

More treasures await inside: the east and west corridors surrounding the main building are also covered with carvings, among them the celebrated but difficult to find Nemuri-Neko, or Sleeping Cat, on the side of the Sakashita-mon gate. Beyond this gate are the 200-odd steps to Tokugawa Ieyasu's mausoleum.

Retrace your route to the exit of Tosho-gu, bear right at the pagoda and walk along a path lined with stone lanterns, to reach the grounds of **Futarasan-jinja** (daily Apr–Oct 8am–5pm, Nov–Mar until 4pm). Dedicated to nearby Mount Nantai, the simplicity of this red-lacquered shrine, and its pleasant garden, is a welcome relief after the highly accomplished but ostentatious Tosho-gu shrine.

Lake Chuzenji

From Nikko, take the 30-minute bus ride up the winding mountain road to **Lake Chuzenji** ⑫ (Chuzenji-ko), 1,270 metres (4,170ft) above sea level. From there, savour the clear air and lakeside scenery: a sightseeing boat leaves the pier just across the road from the bus stop, for a one-hour tour of the lake.

Five minutes' walk in the opposite direction is the observatory of the 100-metre (320ft) -high **Kegon Falls** (Kegon no Taki); a lift descends right to the bottom of the gorge where a platform allows views of the thundering falls.

The mighty Kegon Falls.

The streets of Tokyo.

TRAVEL TIPS

TOKYO

TRANSPORT

GETTING THERE AND GETTING AROUND

GETTING THERE

By air

Tokyo is served by two main airports: **Narita International Airport** (Narita) about 66km (41 miles) east of the city; and the **Tokyo International Airport** (Haneda), 20km (12 miles) to the south of the city centre. The airports are usually simply referred to as Narita and Haneda.

Traditionally most international flights to Tokyo arrive at Narita, while Haneda is primarily for domestic flights. However, with the addition of an international terminal and four runways, there is now an increasing number of international flights to Haneda, too.

Narita airport

Although rather inconveniently located, Narita is an efficiently run airport with three terminals and two runways. Two terminals have currency exchange counters, restaurants and cafés, internet facilities, post offices, health clinics, and a range of shops. Terminal 2 has a children's playroom, day rooms for taking a nap and showers. Terminal 3 is dedicated to low-cost carriers.
General and flight info: 0476-34 8000; www.narita-airport.jp/en

Tourist info: 0476-34 5877 (Terminal 2); 0476-30 3383 (Terminal 1)

Haneda airport

Haneda Airport is Tokyo's main hub for domestic flights including those of the main domestic airlines – Japan Air Lines (JAL; www.jal.com) and All Nippon Airways (ANA; www.ana. co.jp).

The addition of a runway and international terminal has also seen more international flights operating at Haneda. A regular shuttle bus service links the international terminal to the domestic terminal.

Haneda's three terminals are comfortable and well designed, with many restaurants, cafés,

shops, post offices and information desks.
Airport info: 03-5757 8111; www.tokyo-airport-bldg.co.jp.

Flying from UK and US

The three big-name airlines serving Tokyo from the UK are British Airways, JAL and ANA. Flying time direct from London is 11 to 13 hours.

Coming from the US or Canada, you are spoiled for choice. Besides JAL and ANA serving the US and Canada, among the better known airlines that fly the Tokyo route to the US are American Airlines, Delta and United Airlines and to Canada – Air Canada and Qantas Airlines. Flying time from the US west coast is 12 to 13 hours; from the

KEY AIRLINES

Air China
2-5-2 Toranomon, Minato-ku
Tel: 03-5251 0711
www.airchina.com.cn/en
American Airlines
Tel: 03-4333 7675
www.aa.com
British Airways
Tel: 03-3298 5238
www.britishairways.com
Japan Airlines
Yurakucho Denki Building, 1-7-1 Yurakucho, Chiyoda-ku

Tel: 03-6733 3062
www.jal.co.jp
Qantas Airways
3-5-1 Toranomon, Minato-ku
Tel: 03-6833 0700
www.qantas.com.au
Singapore Airlines
1-10-1 Yurakucho, Chiyoda-ku
Tel: 03-3213 3431
www.singaporeair.com
United Airlines
Tel: 03-6732 5011
www.united.com

east coast it's 18 to 20 hours, including stopovers.

Tokyo is an increasingly important transportation hub for direct flights to major destinations like Beijing, Shanghai, Hong Kong, Bangkok and farther afield to Singapore, Bali and Sydney.

While fares vary from airline to airline, late April to early May, August and December tend to be the most expensive times to fly to Japan from the UK or US as they coincide with the country's Golden Week, O-bon and Year End-New Year holidays. Flying even a few days on either side of these peak periods can result in huge savings.

By road

The expressways that connect major cities throughout Japan are of extraordinarily high quality. Like the British, the Japanese drive on the left, and the signs are generally self-explanatory. All major expressways charge a toll fee, so apart from traffic-congested roads, the option of using a train or bus is much more appealing. See 'Driving' (see page 231) for details on car hire.

Japan has an excellent system of inter-city buses. They offer a comfortable and sometimes cheaper alternative to trains. Buses often include destinations not covered by trains, and many operate direct services, unlike trains. Night buses are cheaper than trains, but leave late and arrive in the early hours.

The main **JR bus office** is located on the south side of Tokyo Station (tel: 03-3215 1056). **The Tokyo Bus Association** (tel: 03-5360 7111) has information on buses arriving and departing from the city. A good discount long distance bus service is **Willer Express** (www.willerexpress.com).

By sea

Although few people arrive by sea, Japan's ferry services are quite extensive, at least in their connections with South Korea and China.

There is a regular boat service between South Korea's port of Busan and Shimonoseki in Japan. Hydrofoils and ferries also ply between Busan and Fukuoka in Japan.

Ferries from China (Shanghai and Tanggu) arrive in Osaka and Kobe respectively, from where passengers travel either by rail or air to Tokyo.

By train

The majority of train lines entering Tokyo from major Japanese cities, whether JR or shinkansen (bullet train), terminate or make a stop at Tokyo Station on the JR Yamanote Line. Travelling to places like Hakone and Nikko usually involves taking a private line. Major non-JR line terminals are Asakusa, Shibuya and Shinjuku stations, and these last two on the useful Yamanote Line.

Information on train connections to the places of interest outside Tokyo are found on page 220.

GETTING AROUND

From Narita airport

Because of its distance from Tokyo, you should allow at least one hour to reach the city centre, depending on the time of day and your mode of transport.

There are a few ways to get into Tokyo: taxi, bus, limousine bus, the Access Narita or Tokyo shuttle and the train – either express trains such as JR's Narita Express or Keisei's Skyliner Express, or the slower regular trains.

By taxi

This is the most expensive option, and usually the slowest. The fare to or from downtown Tokyo is ¥25,000 to ¥30,000 and one is often sitting in a traffic jam, watching the meter spin inexorably higher.

Expect the 66km (41-mile) ride to central Tokyo to take anywhere

between 1.5 and 3 hours depending on traffic density. Signs indicating taxi ranks are clearly posted at exit points throughout the terminals.

By bus

Convenient, frequent and comfortable airport 'limousine' buses are much cheaper than taxis. They connect Narita Airport with most parts of the city, including major hotels and railway stations as well as Haneda Airport, Tokyo Disneyland and Y-CAT (Yokohama City Air Terminal). Tickets (around ¥3,000, depending upon destination) can be bought in the arrival lobby after clearing immigration and customs. Estimated travel time to central Tokyo is 1 hour and 15 minutes, barring major traffic jams. For enquiries, call 03-3665 7220 (www.limousinebus.co.jp).

The frequent Access Narita buses depart from Terminals 1, 2 and 3 to Ginza and Tokyo Station. The estimated travel time is 1 hour (¥1,000). There's no need to buy tickets in advance as they're available on board. For information, see http://accessnarita.jp.

Another transport option is the Keisei Bus Tokyo Shuttle, which goes to Tokyo Station from the airport. The ticket costs ¥900 if reserved in advance and ¥1,000 without a reservation.

By train

Between the two express trains – **JR's Narita Express** and **Keisei's Skyliner Express** – the Keisei service is the fastest, taking just 36 minutes to reach the city centre. Both train companies also offer slower and cheaper train services into Tokyo. The stations for both lines are found on the basement level of each of the two terminal buildings.

Narita Express connects with the JR railway network at Tokyo, Shinagawa, Shinjuku, Ikebukuro, Omiya, Yokohama and Ofuna stations. It takes one hour to travel to Tokyo Station, and costs ¥3,020

(¥4,560 for first class; although the seats are more than comfortable enough in standard class).

For JR East train information (in English), call 03-3423 0111; www.jreast.co.jp/e.

Keisei's Skyliner Express runs to Tokyo's Ueno Station, stopping first at nearby Nippori; you can connect with JR lines at either station, as well as the subway at Ueno. It takes 41 minutes to Ueno (36 to Nippori) and costs ¥2,470. Contact Keisei Ueno Information Centre at tel: 03-3831 0131; www.keisei.co.jp.

Note: Using the train and subway can involve long walks. If you have more baggage than you can carry, make use of the fast and reliable baggage delivery services at the airport. Look for counters in the arrival lobby. JAL's ABC service is recommended (tel: 03-3545 2800 or 0120-919-120). For about ¥1,500 to ¥2,500 per piece, they deliver your baggage by the following day to anywhere in Japan. Similarly, they pick up bags from anywhere and deliver to Narita.

T-Cat Departures

Passengers of selected airlines taking the airport limousine bus to Narita can complete check-in and passport control procedures at **Tokyo City Air Terminal** (T-CAT) in downtown Tokyo. To find out if your airline offers this service, call T-CAT at 03-3665 7271, www. tcat-hakozaki.co.jp/en. T-CAT can be accessed by taxi (most taxi drivers know it just as Hakozaki) or by subway from Suitengumae Station on the Hanzomon Line.

TRAVEL PASSES

Active sightseers can save by buying a Tokyo Furii Kippu, a one-day pass that entitles you to use all JR, subway and bus lines in the Tokyo region. Pass offices (look out for a triangle symbol on subway maps) at major stations sell the tickets for ¥1,590.

From Haneda airport

By taxi

By taxi, it should take about 30 minutes to central Tokyo, and cost around ¥8,000, but expect to encounter traffic congestion.

By limousine bus

An airport limousine bus service connects Haneda with central Tokyo. Fares range from ¥1,000, depending on which part of the city you're heading to. There is also a service from Haneda to Narita that takes about 75 minutes and costs ¥3,100.

By train

Most people opt for the cheaper, slower trains. Frequent services run from the Keihin Kyuko Railway Station in the airport basement. The train takes 13 to 25 minutes to Shinagawa Station, depending on the exact service, and costs ¥410.

By monorail

If travelling light, another alternative is the Tokyo Monorail, which connects Haneda with Hamamatsucho Station on the JR Yamanote Line. It takes only 15 minutes and costs ¥490, but can be very crowded during rush hour.

Orientation

Central Tokyo is divided into 23 *ku* (wards), which are sub-divided into *cho* (districts), then numbered *chome* (blocks) – see page 233. Japanese people tend to think in terms of city blocks, often finding their way from one block to the next by using landmarks such as shops, restaurants and architectural features as markers. Even taxi drivers get confused once they depart from the main thorough-fares and sights. Maps are essential for navigating the city. Good English-language city maps which show major landmarks along with railway and subway lines can be picked up for free from major hotels or Tourist Information Centre (TIC) offices (see page 239).

ASKING FOR HELP

Japanese people are generally very helpful when quizzed about addresses and, if nearby, may even on occasion escort you to your destination. When in doubt, ask at the local *koban* (police box). The police are generally very helpful and will consult maps on your behalf and even phone to confirm an address.

Exits at train stations are usually clearly signposted overhead. Landmarks like museums, department stores and government offices are marked in English on yellow boards, which should be visible as you exit the ticket barriers. Train stations usually have maps near their exits. Though often in Japanese, they provide some sense of orientation.

Public transport

The public transport system in Tokyo is unrivalled anywhere in the world. A sophisticated and highly efficient network of railway lines, subways and bus routes serves the city. During rush hour, services run every one to two minutes on some lines, at a degree of reliability inconceivable elsewhere.

Both trains and subways are notoriously crowded during the morning and evening rush hour, and sometimes run at 300 percent of the seating capacity.

Subway (Metro)

The subway system is clean, safe and convenient. It is also the fastest and most economical means of getting across town. There are 13 lines crisscrossing central Tokyo, nine operated by Tokyo Metro and four by Toei Subway.

Subways run to precise schedules, indicated on timetables posted at each station. Services run from 5am to around 12.30am at intervals of two to three minutes during rush hours, with frequencies dropping to around every five to ten minutes at off-peak periods. The frequency is slightly reduced on weekends.

All subway and train stations have a route map indicating fares for each stop near the ticket machines, usually in English.

The fares for both subways and trains are regulated on a station-to-station basis, so if you cannot determine the fare required, just purchase the cheapest ticket available (¥170 for Tokyo Metro lines) at the ticket machine. If you have not paid the correct fare, simply top up the difference on arrival – either at designated fare adjustment machines or at the station office.

PASMO magnetic smart cards (www.pasmo.co.jp), valid for any public transportation line in Tokyo can be bought at subway stations (¥500 deposit), and recharged when depleted. These are simply passed over sensors of the automated ticket gates as you enter, with the fare deducted at your destination. Japan Railway's **Suica** cards act in exactly the same way and both this and PASMO cards can be used on subways, trains and buses. If you are going to be out and about a lot, it's well worth getting one these cards to avoid the hassle of fare adjusting and fiddling with ticket machines.

Train

Above ground, **Japan Railways** (JR) operates an equally efficient service, with equivalent frequency and operating hours (5am–1am) on commuter lines. Like the subways, the lines are colour coded.

The **Yamanote Line** (green) makes a long, 35km (21-mile) oval loop around central Tokyo, with other lines branching out to the suburbs. These are either JR lines or several private train lines, like Keio and Tobu, radiating out to the suburbs from hubs situated around the Yamanote Line.

Taxis

Taxis are a convenient but pricey way of getting around town. The

TAXIS' AUTO DOORS

There is no need to touch the doors at all when getting in or out of a taxi. The doors are opened and closed by the driver, who operates a lever at the front. After hailing a taxi, wait for the door to open; on arrival, the door will be opened again for you.

standard flagfall is ¥410 for the first 1km (0.65 miles) and ¥80 for every 237 metres/yds after that. Short trips typically run to ¥2,000. No tipping is expected.

Taxis are readily available on almost every street corner, and at every major hotel and railway station. A red light in the front window signifies that the taxi is available. Roads are narrow and rush hour traffic appalling – especially on Fridays or before a holiday.

Most taxi drivers speak only Japanese, so it can be helpful to have your destination written out in Japanese. Many drivers are not native Tokyoites, and are only familiar with central Tokyo and the main landmarks. Having the address of your destination handy also means they can input it into their car navigation systems and avoid getting lost! Do not be surprised if taxis fail to stop when you hail them, particularly at night. Drivers will be looking for profitable long runs out to the suburbs rather than stranded foreigners wanting to return to their hotels. Recommended taxi operators are:
Hinomaru: tel: 03-3814 1111; https://hinomaru.tokyo
Nihon Kotsu: tel: 03-5755 2336 (English language); www.nihon-kotsu.co.jp/en.

Buses

There are no English signs on Tokyo buses, but imminent stops are announced by a recorded voice. Passengers pay on entry, dropping the flat fare (usually ¥210) into a box located next to the driver; there's a machine in the box for changing notes if you don't have the coins. Tourist information centres and hotels can give you bus maps with the major routes

marked. Buses generally run from 5.30am to midnight.

River buses

For river cruises, enquire at **Tokyo Cruise Ship**, tel: 0120-977 311; www.suijobus.co.jp. The most popular itinerary is the trip up the Sumida River to Asakusa from Hinode (or vice versa; 40 minutes). Other routes include a 45-minute cruise around Tokyo Harbour, starting at Hinode and going past the Rainbow Bridge and the Odaiba Seaside Park (55 minutes); and to the Shinagawa Aquarium (35 minutes). Hinode Pier is located near Takeshiba and Hinode stations on the Yurikamome New Transit System (five and seven minutes from Shimbashi, respectively).

Look out for the striking, sci-fi-esque *Himiko* vessel, designed by *manga* artist Leiji Matsumoto, which morphs into the floating bar Jicoo at night.

Driving

Tokyo is not an easy place to drive in, even when you know the city layout. Except on the crowded expressways, there are few road signs in Romanised Japanese. For getting out of town, it is usually faster to take public transport. If you do need to hire a car try **Toyota Rent-a-Car** (https://rent.toyota.co.jp/eng), which has branches at the airports and across the city.

Cycling

Intrepid travellers may want to try cycling around Tokyo. Major roads can be perilous, but if you stick to the back roads bikes offer a great way to get intimate with the city at surface level.

A – Z

AN ALPHABETICAL SUMMARY OF PRACTICAL INFORMATION

A

Accommodation

Choosing a hotel

There is never a shortage of places to stay in Tokyo. Accommodation ranges from deluxe Western-style hotels and no-frills business lodgings to budget 'capsule hotels'. Tokyo's top hotels are among the finest in the world in terms of facilities and service. The older establishments especially exude a distinctive Japanese ambience. Business hotels target Japanese salarymen rather than foreign businessfolk, providing bedrooms that are clean and functional, but usually quite small.

Traditional Japanese inns, or ryokan, provide a very different experience. At their best (and most expensive), they epitomise the essence of Japanese hospitality. You sleep on futon mattresses on tatami mats, bathe in a traditional bath, and are served exquisite *kaiseki ryori* meals in your room by attendants in kimono.

On an altogether different level, there are budget Japanese-style inns (minshuku) that give a taste of the traditional but at a fraction of the cost of a top ryokan. These simple family-run lodgings offer personalised service and simple accommodation, and give a close-up view of how many Japanese live.

Capsule hotels offer basic bunk-style accommodation in enclosed cabins just big enough to sit up in. They are not an option for long-term stays (you can't store luggage), but are good in an emergency. There are capsule hotels in most areas where salarymen go carousing. Most are for men only, but a few have floors reserved for women.

Hotel areas

For the sake of simplicity, many visitors choose to stay at places close to the circular Yamanote Line, where many of the main sights are located. Many of the bigger Yamanote stations like Shinjuku, Ikebukuro and Tokyo are transportation hubs linked to overground and subway lines that will take you to other sights within or outside the city.

Stations like these are mini-cities in their own right, offering a vibrant package of activities that include shopping, restaurants and nightlife. Each has its own distinctive character. While you may choose an area for a notable feature that interests you (Ueno

CLIMATE CHART

°C / J F M A M J J A S O N D / mm

Maximum temperature
Minimum temperature
— Rainfall

for museums, Shibuya for fashion, Roppongi for nightlife), these micro-cities work hard at providing something for everyone. Central Tokyo (Roppongi, Akasaka, Nihombashi and Ginza) tends to be more expensive and cater to the business market, while areas such as Shinjuku, Shibuya, Ueno and Ikebukuro tend to have a greater choice.

Prices and bookings

Western-style hotels charge on a per-room basis, but at traditional ryokan inns and pensions, customers are charged per person, with the rate usually including dinner and breakfast. Many larger hotels also offer non-smoking rooms and women-only floors. Most stipulated hotel rates include ten percent consumption tax. Luxury hotels may impose a 10 to 15 percent service charge. If your room costs over ¥10,000 per person per night, there's also a Tokyo Metropolitan Government tax of ¥100 per person per night (¥200 per person if the room costs over ¥15,000).

Useful websites include **Japan Hotel Association** (www.j-hotel. or.jp), **Japanican** (www.japanican. com), **Japan Ryokan and Hotel Association** (www.ryokan.or.jp) and **Japan Guest Houses** (www.japaneseguesthouses.com).

Note: budget travellers should book in advance for February, when thousands of students descend on the city for university entrance exams.

Addresses

Tokyo is one of the most complex cities in the world. Even the Japanese get confused when trying to get from A to B, which is why businesses often print little maps out on cards, websites and advertisements.

However, with a little knowledge of how the streets are laid out and numbered, you should be able to negotiate the city without too much frustration. Apart from main roads, very few streets have names. Addresses traditionally follow a big-to-small system, with the *ku* (ward) listed first, then the *cho* or *matchi* (district) and then the *chome* (an area of a few blocks), the block itself and the number of the building within that block. A typical address rendered in Japanese might read like this: Minato-ku, Hamamatsucho, 3-8-12, Riverfield Hotel, 4F. However, the English rendition of Japanese addresses often follows a different order, most commonly the one used throughout this guide: Riverfield Hotel, 4F, 3-8-12

Hamamatscho, Minato-ku; here, 3 is the number or the *chome*, 8 is the number of the block and 12 is the number of the building within that block.

Note: in Japan the ground floor equals the first.

Admission charges

Practically all museums and public galleries in Tokyo charge an admission fee – anything from ¥200 to ¥1,500 depending on the size and nature of the institution. If you are planning on visiting a lot of museums then investing in the GRUTT Pass (www. rekibun.or.jp/grutto) is recommended. This ¥2,200 ticket provides free or discounted entry to 80 public, national and private institutions, including all of Tokyo's major museums. It is valid for two months after first being used and can be bought at participating venues and the Tokyo Metropolitan Government tourist information centre in Shinjuku (see page 241).

Age restrictions

The age of consent is 18, the same age it is legal to drive. If you are hiring a car in Japan, though, you must be over 21 and have an international driving licence. The legal age for drinking alcohol is 20, but this is not strictly enforced. For smoking the legal age is also 20.

B

Budgeting for your trip

Tokyo has a reputation for being one of the most expensive cities in the world, but after over 15 years of economic stagnation, the cost of living index in capitals like London and Paris have caught up, and in some cases exceeded, that of Tokyo. Compared with other Asian capitals though, Tokyo remains the most costly.

Accommodation can run from as little as ¥2,000 in a dorm bed at a hostel, ¥5,000 in a modest inn, to over ¥50,000 in one of its top-class hotels. Food is better value than you would think, especially lunch sets, where there is fierce competition for customers. A lunch set at a decent restaurant can be had for as little as ¥800. Japanese fast food restaurants have all-hours fixed sets from only ¥500. Expect to pay ¥2,000 to ¥4,000 for a two–three-course dinner without drinks. Drinking alcohol, though, can boost the bill substantially. Reckon on ¥500 to ¥700 for the cheapest beer or glass of house wine at a good restaurant or bar. Cheaper *izakaya*, however, often have beer for as low as ¥200.

Public transport is inexpensive with single metro tickets starting off at ¥170. Taxis have a base fare of ¥410 but rise quite quickly if you get stuck in a traffic jam.

C

Children

Tokyo may be crowded, but with a little forward planning, travelling with children is both feasible and enjoyable, and the options, ranging from science and nature museums to amusement parks, toyshops, aquariums and zoos, are quite broad.

On trains, buses and subways, children up to age 12 travel for half-fare; those under six ride for free. Try to avoid trains during rush hour, especially when using strollers.

Department stores and malls usually have family rooms or areas set aside for mothers to nurse infants or change nappies. The malls are also good places to eat, since their restaurant floors offer a variety of food, often with child-size portions. Many restaurants, especially those in malls, offer good value set meals for kids (ask for *okosama setto*).

Cycle police on patrol.

Some of the larger hotels offer babysitting services. Several have outdoor swimming pools that are open to the public at specific hours during summer.

Climate

In Tokyo, spring is ushered in with the cherry blossoms in early April, and the temperature starts to rise. By May, the weather will become warm and pleasant, still without any great humidity. June brings rather grey, drizzly weather, known poetically as *tsuyu* (dew), a rainy spell that lasts about a month.

Midsummer is hot and sticky, with the mercury rising to around 35°C (100°F) – occasionally up to 40°C – and hovering overnight at around an uncomfortably sticky 25°C (72°F). Typhoons (tropical storms) occur between August and October (though Tokyo is affected far more rarely than Okinawa and western Japan).

From mid- to late September, there is usually a late summer, with hot days that cool when the humidity level drops at night.

During October and early November, there are many mellow autumn days – this is many Tokyoites' favourite time of the year.

After a month or so of rainy, changeable weather, winter arrives, with clear blue skies and low humidity. The harshest cold sets in in January and February, although Tokyo only receives occasional snowfalls. The weather in March is usually chilly, overcast and changeable.

All this, naturally, is subject to global climate change.

Periods to avoid

There are three times in the year when almost all of Japan is on holiday and travelling en masse. It is unwise to pass through Narita Airport or plan any train trips during these periods:
New Year Around 28 December–4 January
Golden Week 29 April–5 May (avoid weekends at either end)
Obon Seven to 10 days centring on 15 August.

What to wear

Japanese people place importance on appearance and dress accordingly. For visitors, casual clothes are acceptable in almost all situations, except on business, for which a suit is de rigueur.

The weather is relatively predictable, so dress for the season. Bring a thick jacket or overcoat for winter weather in January and February; in summer, wear light fabrics (cotton or linen); in spring and autumn, a light jacket will prove handy as will waterproof clothing and an umbrella for showers. At any time of year you'll be walking a lot to see the city, so wear comfortable shoes.

Crime and safety

For a city its size, Tokyo has a low incidence of petty theft, and personal security is far higher than in most cities in Europe and North America. Theft of luggage and money is rare, though not unheard of in Tokyo.

Organised crime is another matter, and it can turn violent. The police try to keep a lid on prostitution, gambling, ticket touting, illegal immigration and the protection rackets operated by the yakuza gangs, conducting sporadic crackdowns only when inter-gang warfare spills onto the streets.

However, visitors need never come into contact with the underbelly of Japanese society. If an incident occurs, report it to the nearest *koban* (police box). These are located in every neighbourhood, especially in busy areas and outside major railway stations. If possible, go with an eyewitness or a Japanese speaker. For police contact details, see 'Emergencies'.

Customs regulations

Non-residents entering the country are given a duty-free allowance of 400 cigarettes or 500 grams of tobacco (going down to 200 cigarettes and 250 grams in 2021); three 760ml bottles of alcohol; 2oz of perfume; and gifts and souvenirs whose total value is not more than ¥200,000. If you are carrying the equivalent of over ¥1 million, you must declare it.

Japan bans the import and use of illegal drugs, firearms and ammunition, as well as swords – and strictly punishes anyone caught with the above items. Pornographic magazines and videos showing pubic hair are also forbidden in Japan. It is also illegal to bring in endangered species or products containing them.

For further information, see www.customs.go.jp.

E

Electricity

Japan's power supply is 100 volts AC. Tokyo and Eastern Japan run on 50 cycles (Western Japan uses 60 cycles). Plugs are two-pin. Most hotels have adaptors.

Embassies and consulates

Embassies and consulates open Monday through Friday. Call ahead to find out the hours, as these vary.
Australia: 2-1-14 Mita, Minato-ku; tel: 03-5232 4111; http://japan.embassy.gov.au
Canada: 7-3-38 Akasaka, Minato-ku; tel: 03-5412 6200; http://www.canadainternational. gc.ca/japan-japon
New Zealand: 20-40 Kamiyama-cho, Shibuya-ku; tel: 03-3467-2271; www.nzembassy.com/japan
UK: 1 Ichiban-cho, Chiyoda-ku; tel: 03-5211 1100; http:// ukinjapan.fco.gov.uk
US: 1-10-5 Akasaka, Minato-ku; tel: 03-3224 5000; https://jp. usembassy.gov

Etiquette

There are points of etiquette for doing just about everything in Japan (blowing your nose in public for instance, especially at high volume which is considered rude). Although as a visitor you may be blissfully unaware of most of them (and will be immediately forgiven for almost any faux pas anyway), the cardinal rule is to try to be courteous at all times.

At work and in most formal situations, the Japanese may seem reticent and lacking in spontaneity. But when drinking and having a good time, Japanese, especially the men,

can become very raucous and often let out their real opinions and feelings.

Bathhouses

Whether at a hot spring resort, a local *sento* (bathhouse) or a traditional inn, the procedure is the same. Disrobe, enter the bathroom (in public a small washcloth is usually used for modesty), wash and rinse off thoroughly under a shower before easing into the hot bath – which is for soaking, not washing yourself. Do not pull the plug after you've finished: others will use the same water.

Dining

Drinking: When having beer or sake, one always pours for the other party, who will hold up the glass while it is filled. It is polite to keep the glasses filled; if you have had enough, leave your glass full.

Eating: Soup is sipped directly from the bowl in which it is served. So is the broth of hot noodles, except for ramen, which comes with a spoon. When sipping soup, tea or other hot liquids, it is customary to draw in a good amount of air at the same time. Slurping sounds for noodles and other soup dishes are quite acceptable (in fact, almost obligatory at times), but should be kept to a minimum in polite company.

Footwear

There is a strong distinction in Japan between the areas inside and outside the home. Just inside the entrance to homes (and many restaurants, ryokan and some museums and galleries) is an area where you are expected to remove your shoes. From here, you step up into the living area either wearing the slippers provided or in your stockinged feet. This keeps the house clean and increases the amount of useable space, since you can sit on the floor without worrying about

getting dirty. (Men sit cross-legged and women sit with their legs tucked under.) Slippers are never worn on tatami mats. Go barefoot or in socks instead. Note that there will be a separate pair of slippers to be used in the toilet.

Invitations

It is rare to be invited to someone's home. Most people live too far out of town or find their homes too cramped to invite guests. If you receive an invitation, take along a small gift with you: flowers, a food item or something from your own country.

Trains/subway

On rush-hour trains you may find yourself being pushed and bumped around. You do not need to be polite here; just push along with everyone else.

H

Health and medical care

No vaccinations are required before entering Japan, except if arriving from certain countries in Africa, Asia or South America. Hygiene levels are high, and you are unlikely to become ill as a result of eating or drinking. Tokyo's tap water is safe to drink.

Hospitals/clinics

Although some doctors speak English, it is likely the receptionist and nursing staff will not. When seeking medical aid, go with a Japanese-speaking companion.
Tokyo Medical Information Service (tel: 03-5285 8181; www.himawari.metro.tokyo.jp/qq/ qq13enmnlt.asp; daily 9am–8pm) can provide emergency medical translation services over the phone and can help you find English-speaking doctors and dentists.
Most hospitals and clinics do not have an appointment system for outpatient treatment, and visits

TRANSPORT

A – Z

LANGUAGE

usually entail a long wait. The following facilities are accustomed to dealing with foreign patients.

Japanese Red Cross Medical Centre, 4-1-22 Hiro-o, Shibuya-ku; tel: 03-3400 1311; www.med.jrc.or.jp

St Luke's International Hospital, 10-1 Akashicho, Chuo-ku; tel: 03-3541 5151; http://hospital.luke.ac.jp

Tokyo Medical and Surgical Clinic, 2F 32 Shiba-koen Bldg, 3-4-30 Shiba-koen, Minato-ku; tel: 03-3436 3028; www.tmsc.jp.

Pharmacies

The American Pharmacy (B1F, Marunouchi Building, 2-4-1 Marunouchi, Chiyoda-ku; Mon–Fri 9am–9pm, Sat 10am–9pm, Sun 10am–8pm; tel: 03-5220 7716) has English-speaking pharmacists. Alternatively, try one of the Koyasu pharmacies: in the Hotel Okura (tel: 03-3583 7958), Roppongi (tel: 03-3401 8667) and Hiroo (tel: 03-3446 4701).

Travel insurance

All Japanese subscribe to national or company health insurance schemes, and charges for hospitals, consultations and drugs are high. Make sure you buy a travel health insurance policy.

Internet

Broadband and/or Wi-fi internet access is common at Tokyo's hotels and either free or available for a charge of around ¥1,000 a day. Most convenience stores have Wi-fi (7-Eleven is best in such regards), as do almost all subway stations. You can also get online at the 24-hour *manga* cafés found around the capital such as the chains **Gera Gera** (www.geragera.co.jp) and **Gran Cyber Cafe Bagus** (www.bagus-

99.com/netcafe). Other places include:
Apple Ginza Store, 3-5-12 Ginza, Chuo-ku: daily 10am–9pm and **Wired Cafes** (www.cafecompany. co.jp/brands/wiredcafe).

L

Left luggage

There are 24-hour counters offering storage facilities in both Terminals 1 and 2 at Narita Airport (tel: 0476-34 5000) and in the arrival lobby of the international terminal at Haneda Airport. There's also a baggage room at Tokyo Station (daily 9am–8pm).

LGBTQ travellers

Despite the presence of a few token transvestite personalities on prime-time television, the LGBTQ community in Japan keeps a relatively low profile. In Shinjuku's Nichome district there are around 300 bars and clubs catering to all age groups and sexuality. For information see:
Out Japan Co Ltd (www.out-japan. com): LGBTQ information portal for overseas visitors.
Tokyo Wrestling (www. tokyowrestling.com) for the latest information on Tokyo's lesbian scene.
Utopia (www.utopia-asia.com/ tipsjapn.htm): an Asian site with Tokyo contacts and information.

Lost property

JR trains and subways: Items left behind on trains and subways are usually kept for a few days at the station where they were handed in. After that, they are sent to one of the major stations where they are stored for another five days. Call any of the following for help:
JR East English-language InfoLine at tel: 050-2016 1603; Tokyo Metro, tel: 03-3834

5577; Toei trains and buses don't have a lost and found number: report any lost items to your nearest station.
Police: The Tokyo Metropolitan Police Department, tel: 03-3814 4151 (lost and found centre).
Taxis: All taxi companies in Tokyo report unclaimed items to the **Tokyo Taxi Kindaika Centre**, tel: 03-3648 0300.

M

Maps

Tourist offices provide adequate maps of Tokyo for free. Visitors requiring more in-depth coverage will find Tuttle's Getting Around **Tokyo: Pocket Atlas and Transportation Guide** very useful.

Media

Newspapers/magazines

There are two daily newspapers in English: the *Japan Times* (www.japantimes.co.jp) and the *Japan News* (http://the-japan-news.com). The *Nikkei Asian Review* (http://asia.nikkei.com) is a financial digest in English.

The quality of the English-language magazines in Japan isn't great, but the free monthly *Metropolis* (metropolis.co.jp) sometimes includes interesting features and reviews and also has up-to-the-minute listings. Also look out for the quarterly *Tokyo Journal* (www.tokyojournal. com).

Radio

Tokyo's main foreign language radio station is **Inter FM** (76.1 MHz; www.interfm.co.jp), which broadcasts news and music mainly in English. **J-Wave** (81.3 MHz; www.j-wave.co.jp) also has some shows in English. Try also **Radio Japan Online** (www.nhk. or.jp/nhkworld/english/radio/ program), which streams programmes in 17 languages from Japan's national broadcaster NHK.

Television

There are seven terrestrial TV channels. Two are from the quasi-national **Japan Broadcast Corporation (NHK)** and the other five are private-sector commercial networks. NHK also broadcasts on two satellite channels. A small percentage of the programmes – including news bulletins such as NHK's 7pm and 9pm broadcasts – is bilingual, offering English on the sub-channel. Ask your hotel

Carry some cash as credit cards are not always accepted.

reception which button to press to see if the programme has a bilingual service.

Overseas networks, such as CNN and BBC, are available on satellite and cable TV at most large hotels.

Money

The unit of currency is the yen (indicated as ¥). Coins are issued in denominations of ¥500, ¥100, ¥50, ¥10 and ¥1. There are bank notes for ¥10,000, ¥5,000, ¥2,000 (quite rare) and ¥1,000.

Cash machines

Major credit cards and cash cards linked to Cirrus, PLUS, Maestro and Visa Electron networks can be used at post office ATMs. Most convenience store ATMs also accept these cards.

Changing money

Yen can be purchased at branches of major Japanese banks and authorised moneychangers on presentation of your passport. Besides the airport, authorised moneychangers can be found in the major hotels.
At Narita Airport, bank counters remain open during airport hours.

International transactions (eg remittances) are best conducted at major branches of Japanese banks, which have English-speaking staff.

Credit cards

Major credit cards (eg American Express, Diners Club, Visa, MasterCard) are accepted at most establishments in and around Tokyo without surcharges. However, credit cards are not accepted in some restaurants and small bars; this is still a cash society.

Credit cards issued by foreign banks cannot be used to make cash withdrawals, except at a few selected ATMs around central Tokyo. Check with your card issuer.
American Express: 0120-020 120
Diners Club: 0120-074 024
MasterCard: 03-5728 5200
Visa: 0053-144 0022.

Tipping

'No tipping' remains the rule in Japan, except for unusual or exceptional service. At more upmarket restaurants, a service charge of 10 to 15 percent is included on the bill.

Opening hours

Standard business hours for government offices and private sector companies are Mon–Fri, 9am–5pm. They are closed on national holidays. Banks are open 9am–3pm. Department stores and larger shops usually operate from 10am–8pm (sometimes later); all are open on Sundays and perhaps closed another day of the week. Convenience stores are open 24 hours. Most restaurants serve lunch from 11.30am–2pm and dinner from 6–9.30pm. Pubs, bars and *izakaya* usually remain open much later. Museums often close on Mondays.

PUBLIC HOLIDAYS

1 January *Ganjitsu* (New Year's Day)
January, second Monday *Seijin-no-Hi* (Coming of Age Day)
11 February *Kenkoku Kinen-no-Hi* (National Foundation Day)
23 February *Tenno Tanjobi* (Emperor's Birthday)
Around 21 March *Shumbun-no-Hi* (Vernal Equinox Day)
29 April *Showa-no-Hi* (Showa Day)
3 May *Kenpo Kinenbi* (Constitution Memorial Day)
4 May *Midori-no-Hi* (Greenery Day)
5 May *Kodomo-no-Hi* (Children's Day)
July, third Monday *Umi-no-Hi* (National Maritime Day)
11 August *Yama-no-Hi* (Mountain Day)
September, third Monday *Keiro-no-Hi* (Respect for the Aged Day)
Around 23 September *Shubun-no-Hi* (Autumnal Equinox Day)
October, second Monday *Tai-iku-no-Hi* (Sports Day)
3 November *Bunka-no-Hi* (Culture Day)
23 November *Kinro Kansha-no-Hi* (Labour Thanksgiving Day)

TRANSPORT

A – Z

LANGUAGE

The Japanese postal system is efficient but expensive.

P

Photography

Although there are no restrictions on what you can photograph, use your discretion in religious places. Millions of Japanese are avid amateur photographers so camera stores are plentiful everywhere. The best prices for cameras and film are found at discount chains such as **Bic Camera** (www.biccamera.com), **Laox** (www.laox.co.jp) and **Yodobashi Camera** (www.yodabashi.com). The main stores for these are in Akihabara and Shinjuku, with outlets in the other main shopping districts.

Postal services

Post offices are open Mon–Fri 9am–5pm; some are also open Sat 9am–3pm. For English-language information about postal services, including postal fees, call tel: 0570-046 111 or go to www.post.japanpost.jp.

Express mail/courier

Larger post offices offer express mail services. International parcel post cannot exceed 30kg per package to any international destination. For heavier packages use a commercial courier service. **Federal Express**: tel: 0120-003 200, www.fedex.com/jp

Yamato Transport: tel: 0120-179 625, www.kuronekoyamato.co.jp/en.

R

Religious services

Most Japanese follow both the indigenous animist religion Shinto as well as Buddhism, which was imported to Japan from Korea around the 6th century. About one percent of the population is Christian (with a higher percentage in Tokyo).

Catholic

Azabu Church: 3-21-6 Nishi-Azabu, Minato-ku, tel: 03-3408 1500, http://azabu-catholic.jp.
Franciscan Chapel Centre: 4-2-37 Roppongi, Minato-ku, tel: 03-3401 2141, http://franciscanchapelcentertokyo.org.

Jewish

Jewish Community of Japan: 3-8-8 Hiroo, Shibuya-ku, tel: 03-3400 2559, www.jccjapan.or.jp.

Muslim

Islamic Centre Japan: 1-16-11 Ohara, Setagaya-ku, tel: 03-3460 6169, http://islamcenter.or.jp.

Protestant

United Church of Christ in Japan, Ginza Church: 4-2-1 Ginza, Chuo-ku, tel: 03-3561 0236, www.ginza-church.com.
International Christian University Church: 3-10-2 Osawa, Mitaka-shi, tel: 0422-33 3323, www.icuchurch.com.

S

Smoking

Smoking is banned on all public transport and in most public buildings. There are sometimes separate smoking sections in bars and restaurants; few eating and drinking places are fully smoke free and many do not police their policies too strictly. Smoking on the street is being clamped down on in certain central wards such as Chuo-ku, Chiyoda-ku and Shinjuku-ku – you'll see smokers in these places clustered in designated smoking spots.

Student travellers

If you have an International Student Identity Card (ISIC) you will usually qualify for the student discount at sights.

T

Taxes

At present a consumption tax (VAT) of ten percent is applied to all retail transactions (including at hotels and restaurants).

Telephones

Public phones are available throughout Tokyo, though the number is dropping because of the prevalence of mobile phones. The minimum cost of a local call is ¥10 per minute. Telephone cards – not coins – are the primary form of payment for public phones, though you can still find machines that accept ¥10 and ¥100 coins. Be aware that change isn't given if you use a ¥100 coin to make a short call.

Area codes

Tokyo 03
Yokohama 045
Narita 0476
Nikko 0288
Hakone 0460
Fujiyoshida 0555
Kamakura 0467
Kawagoe 049

Note: Local telephone numbers that begin with 0120, 0088 or 0053 are toll-free calls that can be dialled only within Japan.

Directory assistance

Local: 104. Ask for an English-speaking operator.
International: (English-speaking) 0057.

Domestic calls

Long-distance domestic calls (over 60km/37 miles) are cheaper after peak hours by up to 40 percent. If calling from one province to another in Japan, be sure to dial the area code first (including the zero) before the phone number. When calling within Tokyo, do not dial the city's area code.

International calls

International Dialling Code for Japan is 81: if calling Tokyo from overseas, dial +81-3 and then the local number.
International operator, dial 0051 to make a person-to-person, collect, or credit-card call from anywhere in Japan. To make overseas calls from Tokyo, first dial the access code of one of the international call service providers below (they each have their own cards which can only be used at the appropriate telephone booth), then the country code and the number.
KDDI 001
NTT 0033
Softbank Telecom 0041

International calls are possible from some grey and green public telephones; look for the globe logo.

Mobile phones

Most phones work in Japan, either via roaming or (if the phone is unlocked) a Japanese SIM card, but it's always worth checking with your home service provider if unsure; the alternative is to rent a handset, which can be done most easily at one of the international airports. Buying a prepaid phone in Japan requires you to show proof of local residency.

The major mobile phone operators are **NTT Docomo** (www.nttdocomo.co.jp) and **Softbank** (www.softbank.jp/en).

Most mobile phone numbers begin with 090 or 080.

Time zone

Tokyo (like the rest of Japan) is +9 hours GMT; +14 hours EST (New York); and +17 PST (Los Angeles). Japan does not have summer daylight savings time.

Toilets

Public toilets are reasonably common on Tokyo's streets, in its parks and most of its subway and railway stations. People use the facilities in department stores, convenience stores or coffee shops, too. Most toilets are Western style but you'll also come across the traditional squatting type. Carry tissues, as toilet paper isn't always available. The same goes for soap in public toilets in parks and stations.

Tourist information

The Japan government is vigorously implementing advertising and other programmes aimed at attracting more tourists to the country. This has resulted in more information available on the Internet, and at tourism offices both within the country and overseas.

The **Tourist Information Centres (TIC)** run by the **Japan National Tourism Organisation (JNTO)**, not only have massive amounts of information on Tokyo, but can also organise hotel reservations. The multilingual counter staff found in the tourism offices are exceedingly well trained and helpful. The main one in Tokyo is at 4-4-1 Yotsuya, Shinjuku-ku, tel: 03-6691 4850, www.jnto.go.jp.

For Tokyo-specific tourist information the best office to head for is **Tokyo Tourist Information Centre** (1F Tokyo Metropolitan Government No. 1 Building, 2-8-1 Nishi-Shinjuku; tel: 03-5321 3077; daily 9.30am–6.30pm). It has branches at Haneda Airport (tel: 03-6428 0653; 24/7) and in the Keisei Line station at Ueno (tel: 03-3836 3471; daily 9.30am–6.30pm).

Overseas tourist offices

See JNTO's website (www.jnto.go.jp) for a full list of overseas offices.
Australia
Suite 1, Level 4, 56 Clarence Street, Sydney NSW 2000, tel: 02-9279 2177, www.jnto.org.au
Canada
481 University Avenue, Suite 306, Toronto, ON M5G 2E9, tel: 416-366-7140, www.ilovejapan.ca
UK
1st Floor, 28 Leman Street, London, E1 8ER, tel: 020-7398 5670, www.seejapan.co.uk
US
New York: 60 East 42nd Street, Suite 448, New York, NY 10165, tel: 212-757-5640, www.us.jnto.go.jp
Los Angeles:
340 East Second Street, Little Tokyo Plaza, Suite 302, Los Angeles, CA 90012, tel: 213-623-1952, www.us.jnto.go.jp.

Travellers with disabilities

Although Tokyo is still behind most Western cities in wheelchair accessibility, major strides have been taken over the past decade to improve access and facilities for the disabled.

TRANSPORT

A – Z

LANGUAGE

A bilingual sign.

Wide doors and special toilets are being designed into new buses and trains, including the Narita Express, *shinkansen* bullet trains and some local commuter lines. Most major JR stations have elevators and/or escalators with special attachments for wheelchairs.

Similarly, consideration is given to those with visual impairments in some parts of the city, with markers built into the pavements, braille signs on newer JR ticket machines and speakers emitting jingles at pedestrian crossings.

Nevertheless, it is still a struggle for the disabled to get around Tokyo, and don't contemplate using a wheelchair in trains or subways during rush hours from 7.30 to 10am and 5 to 7.30pm.

It is possible to reserve a special seat for wheelchairs on the *shinkansen*. For more information, call the JR East English InfoLine at 050-2016 1603.

Find out up-to-date information at http://accessible. jp.org/tokyo/en, the website of the **Japanese Red Cross Language Service Volunteers**, 1-1-3 Minato-ku, Shiba Daimon; tel: 03-3438 1311. Reliable information about accessibility in Japan is also available at www. accessible-japan.jp, the website

operated by the **Japan Accessible Travel Organisation**. The 24-hour Japan Helpline is also a great source of information and is able to help out in emergencies (tel: 0570-000 911).

V

Visas and passports

Visas are required only for visitors from some countries; most may stay for up to 90 days with just a valid passport. A visa is necessary for foreigners living in Japan and engaged in business or study. Check with the Japanese embassy or consulate in your own country, or go to the website www.mofa.go.jp, before making travel plans.

Extension of stay

Anyone wishing to extend their stay should visit the Tokyo Regional Immigration Bureau office (5-5-30 Konan, Minato-ku; tel: 5796 7111; www.moj.go.jp).

W

Weights and measures

Japan follows the metric system, except in cases governed by strong

tradition. For example, rice and sake are measured in units of 1.8 litres and rooms are measured by a standard tatami mat size.

Women travellers

Tokyo is not a dangerous place for women on their own. However, instances of harassment do occasionally occur, and incidents of women being groped on crowded trains are not uncommon. Western women, while less likely to be targeted, are not completely exempt.

The idea of the independent career woman has slowly gained acceptance over the past two decades, however, a deep, occasionally aggressive streak of sexism still runs through Japanese society. This is evidenced in degrading TV shows (not all late-night), tabloid 'sports' newspapers featuring explicit pictures, plus thinly veiled ads for prostitution services and cartoon books which glorify sexual violence towards women.

That said, it is safer to walk, travel, eat and drink anywhere in Tokyo than it is in most world cities. Areas like Shinjuku's Kabuki-cho are not advisable if you are alone, but two women together will generally suffer nothing more unpleasant than leering.

LANGUAGE

UNDERSTANDING THE LANGUAGE

GENERAL

Japanese is the main language, but in the conduct of international business, English is used. Signs on streets, stations and public buildings in Tokyo are generally written in Roman letters as well as Japanese text, sometimes with English translations. The level of spoken English is generally poor.

Japanese uses three different forms of writing (four, including Roman letters): two simple homegrown syllabaries (phonetic scripts) known as hiragana and katakana, each of which consist of 46 basic characters plus the Chinese characters (kanji). Knowledge of just under 2,000 of these (plus their numerous compounds) is required to read a daily newspaper.

While it is unnecessary to memorise more than a very few simple kanji characters (those for

TERMS OF ADDRESS

Japanese do not usually use first names, but the family name, followed by '-san,' which can stand for Mr, Mrs, Miss or Ms. The suffix '-chan' may be used by close friends, or the suffix '-kun' when talking to boys or close male friends.

'man' and 'woman' are useful at hot spring resorts and public toilets), it is not so daunting to learn the two kana scripts. This will help you read some establishment names and menu listings.

Hiragana is used for transliterating most kanji and for connectors that cannot be written with kanji. Katakana is used primarily for representing foreign names and loan words (eg *takushi*/taxi).

PRONUNCIATION TIPS

Apart from a few consonants, Japanese is easy to pronounce. The vowels in standard Japanese are always regular. The most important aspect is to give each syllable equal stress and to avoid the intonation patterns of English and other Western languages.

Consonants do not exist on their own, with the exception of 'n', which only follows a vowel, but are always accompanied by one of the five basic vowel sounds. These are pronounced much as they would be in English, with the following notes:
chi – as in cheese
g – always hard (as in get)
ji/ju/jo – as in jeans/June/joke
n – pronounced like m before b or p (*tenpura*) is read tempura *shinbun* (newspaper) is pronounced shimbun

tsu – like 'it's' (without the i)
The basic vowel sounds are pronounced much as in Spanish.
a – like the a in about
e – like the e in egg
i – like the i in ink
o – like the o in orange
u – like the u in butcher
In combination the vowels are pronounced as follows:
ai – like 'eye'
ae – almost the same as ai, but with a slight e sound at the end
ao – like the ow in cow
au – almost the same as ao, but with a slight u sound at the end
ei – like the ay in way
io – like an elision 'ee-yo'
iu – like an elision 'ee-yu'
ue – like an elision 'oo-e'
uo – like an elision 'oo-oh'
When i and u occur in the middle of words, they are sometimes almost silent. For example, *shitamachi* (Tokyo's 'low city') is actually pronounced 'sh'ta-machi', while *sukiyaki* sounds more like 's'kiyaki'. A final u is also pronounced so imperceptibly as to be unnoticeable: thus *desu* is always pronounced 'dess'.

Vowels are sometimes elongated (doubled), and this is indicated in Roman letters by a macron (a line over the said vowel), by an extra h (after o), or by writing a double vowel (in the case of i). The spelling in English, however, does not always reflect the double vowel.

WORDS AND PHRASES

Essential phrases

Do you speak English? *eigo ga dekimasu ka?*
Please write it down *kaite kudasai*
Pardon? *sumimasen*
I understand *wakarimashita*
I don't understand/I don't know *wakarimasen*
Yes/No *hai/iie*
OK *okee*
Please *onegai shimasu*
Thank you (very much) *(domo) arigato*

Greetings

Good morning *ohayo gozaimasu*
Hello (afternoon) *kon-nichi-wa*
Good evening *konban-wa*
Good night *oyasumi nasai*
Goodbye *sayonara (shitsure shimasu for formal occasions)*
How are you? *ogenki desu ka?*
My name is…… *..to moshimasu*
I'm Mr/Ms Smith *watashi wa Smith desu*
Are you Mr/Ms Honda? *Honda-san desu ka?*
I'm American *Amerika-jin desu*
I'm British *Igirisu-jin desu*
I'm Australian *Osutoraria-jin desu*
I'm Canadian *Kanada-jin desu*

Asking for directions

Excuse me, where is the toilet? *sumimasen, toire wa doko desu ka?*
Excuse me, is there a post office near here? *sumimasen, kono chikaku ni, yubin-kyoku wa arimasu ka?*
on the left/right *hidari/migi ni*
bakery *pan-ya*
stationer's *bunbogu-ya*
pharmacy *yakkyoku*
bookshop *hon-ya*
supermarket *suupaa*
department store *depaato*
restaurant *resutoran*

hotel *hoteru*
station *eki*
taxi rank *takushii noriba*
bank *ginko*
hospital *byoin*
police station *koban*

Out shopping

This one *kore*
That one (near the other person) *sore*
That one (near neither of you) are
Do you have…? *…(wa) arimasu ka?*
How much is it? *ikura desu ka?*
I'll take this *kore o kudasai*

Boarding the train

Ticket (office) *kippu (uriba)*
reserved seat *shitei seki*
unreserved seat *jiyu seki*
first-class car *guriin sha*
Which platform does the train for Nagoya leave from? *Nagoya yuki wa namban sen desu ka?*
Thank you (very much) *(domo) arigato gozaimasu (informally, domo is enough)*
Don't mention it *doitashimashite*
Thanks for the meal *gochisosama deshita*
Here you are *doozo*
After you *doozo*

Days/time

Sunday *nichi-yobi*
Monday *getsu-yobi*
Tuesday *ka-yobi*
Wednesday *sui-yobi*
Thursday *moku-yobi*
Friday *kin-yobi*
Saturday *do-yobi*
Yesterday *kino*
Today *kyo*
This morning *kesa*
This evening *konya*
Tomorrow *ashita*

Months/seasons

January *ichi-gatsu*
February *ni-gatsu*
March *san-gatsu*
April *shi-gatsu*
May *go-gatsu*
June *roku-gatsu*

July *shichi-gatsu*
August *hachi-gatsu*
September *ku-gatsu*
October *juu-gatsu*
November *juu-ichi-gatsu*
December *juu-ni-gatsu*

At the hotel

Western-style hotel *hoteru*
business hotel *bijinesu hoteru*
love hotel *rabu hoteru*
Japanese-style inn *ryokan*
guesthouse *minshuku*
temple accommodation *shukubo*
youth hostel *yuusu hosuteru*
I have a reservation *yoyaku shite arimasu*
Do you have a room? *heya wa arimasu ka?*
I'd like a single/double room *shinguru/daburu ruumu o onegai shimasu*
I'd like a room with …… *tsuki no heya o onegai shimasu*
twin beds *tsuin beddo*
double bed *daburu beddo*
bath/shower *furo/shawa*
air-conditioning *eakon*
TV/telephone *terebi/denwa*
How much is it? *ikura desu ka?*
Can I see the room please? *heya o misete kudasai*

At the restaurant

A table for two, please *futari onegai shimasu*
The bill, please *o-kanjo onegai shimasu*
tsukemono **pickled vegetables**
sashimi **raw fish served with soy sauce and Japanese horseradish** *(wasabi)*
sushi **rice balls topped with fish/seafood**
tempura **battered vegetables, fish or seafood**
okonomiyaki **pizza/savoury pancake**
gyoza **meat or vegetable dumplings**
soba **buckwheat noodles**
udon **thick wheat-flour noodles**
tonkatsu **breaded deep-fried pork**
yakitori **grilled chicken on skewers**

FURTHER READING

FOOD AND DRINK

Drinking Japan, by Chris Bunting. An entertaining and detailed look at everything on the bar menu in Japan, from sake and shochu to Japanese whiskey and wine.

The Insider's Guide to Sake, by Philip Harper. A foreigner, who has become a full-time sake brewer, explains what makes the trade so special.

Izakaya: The Japanese Pub Cookbook, by Mark Robinson. Profiling some of the author's favourite izakaya in Tokyo with over 60 associated recipes.

The Sake Handbook, by John Gauntner. Explains the intricacies of Japan's national tipple, and includes favourite Tokyo drinking holes.

What's What in Japanese Restaurants, by Robb Satterwhite. Invaluable for deciphering menus.

HISTORY AND CULTURE

Embracing Defeat, by John Dower. Pulitzer prize-winning study of Japan under the American Occupation.

Inventing Japan, by Ian Buruma. Looks at the period 1853 to 1964 and how Japan changed itself after opening up to the outside world.

Low City, High City: Tokyo From Edo to the Earthquake, by Edward Seidensticker. The best history of how the city changed from shogun's capital to a modern metropolis.

My Asakusa: Coming of Age in Pre-War Tokyo, by Sadako Sawamura. A delightful and frank memoir of one of the city's best-loved districts by the late actress-writer Sawamura.

Speed Tribes, by Karl Taro Greenfeld. Profiles of Tokyo's subterranean youth culture.

Tokyo: 29 Walks in the World's Most Exciting City, by John H. Martin and Phyllis G. Martin. Guided walks around Tokyo and its environs that delve deep into the city's history and development.

Tokyo Megacity, by Donald Richie and Ben Simmons. Thirty-one fascinating essays on Tokyo, accompanied by slick photography, by one of the city's foremost expat writers.

Tokyo Underworld, by Robert Whiting. Fascinating biography of an American gangster in the post-war era.

Tokyo Vice, by Jake Adelstein. An entertaining and revealing account by an American journalist about his years on the crime beat for the Yomiuri Shimbun, Japan's top-selling newspaper.

Wrong About Japan, by Peter Carey. Tokyo as seen through the eyes of the Australian author who visits with anime-obsessed 12-year-old son.

LITERATURE

Blind Willow, Sleeping Woman, by Haruki Murakami. Twenty-four stories by Japan's best-known author, several of them set in Tokyo.

Green Tea to Go: Stories from Tokyo, by Leza Lowitz. Superior stories of Tokyo life, love and cultural orientation.

Idoru, by William Gibson. Futurist fantasy but strangely accurate rendering of Japanese youth in the digital age. Parts of his novel Pattern Recognition are also set in Tokyo.

Number9Dream, by David Mitchell. Booker Prize-nominated novel that is partly set in Tokyo and paints a vivid picture of the contemporary city.

Out, by Natsuo Kirino. Slick thriller about a group of women who commit murder and how they go about covering it up. If you like this also check out the follow-up novel Grotesque, about the deaths of two Tokyo prostitutes.

Samurai Boogie, by Peter Tasker. Private eye Kazuo Mori investigates the underbelly of the city in Tokyo-based Tasker's noir novel. Check out also the more recent Dragon Dance, also set in Tokyo.

MISC

A Flower Lover's Guide to Tokyo, by Sumiko Enbutsu. Includes 40 walks that take advantage of all seasonal blooms.

Twenty-first Century Tokyo: A Guide to Contemporary Architecture, by Julian Worrall and Erez Golani Solomon. Illustrated survey of some of the city's most striking modern buildings and structures.

OTHER INSIGHT GUIDES

Among nearly 200 companion books to this one are several titles covering Japan, including Insight Guide Japan, Experience Tokyo, Explore Tokyo and Fleximap Tokyo, an indispensable map of the city.

INSIGHT ⊙ GUIDES

OFF THE SHELF

Since 1970, INSIGHT GUIDES has provided a unique perspective on the world's best travel destinations by using specially commissioned photography and illuminating text written by local authors.

Whether you're planning a city break, a walking tour or the journey of a lifetime, our superb range of guidebooks and phrasebooks will inspire you to discover more about your chosen destination.

INSIGHT GUIDES

offer a unique combination of stunning photos, absorbing narrative and detailed maps, providing all the inspiration and information you need.

PHRASEBOOKS & DICTIONARIES

help users to feel at home, when away. Pocket-sized with a free app to download, they go where you do.

CITY GUIDES

pack hundreds of great photos into a smaller format with detailed practical information, so you can navigate the world's top cities with confidence.

EXPLORE GUIDES

feature easy-to-follow walks and itineraries in the world's most exciting destinations, with our choice of the best places to eat and drink along the way.

POCKET GUIDES

combine concise information on where to go and what to do in a handy compact format, ideal on the ground. Includes a full-colour, fold-out map.

EXPERIENCE GUIDES

feature offbeat perspectives and secret gems for experienced travellers, with a collection of over 100 ideas for a memorable stay in a city.

TOKYO STREET ATLAS

The key map shows the area of Tokyo covered by the atlas section. An index of street names and places of interest shown on the maps can be found on the following pages. For each entry there is a page number and grid reference.

Map Legend

Motorway with Junction	⊖ Border Crossing	Motorway	Ⓜ Subway
Motorway (under construction)	✈ ✈ Airport	Dual Carriageway	🚌 Bus Station
Dual Carriageway	✝ ✝ Church (ruins)	Main Roads	❶ Tourist Information
Main Road	✝ Monastery		✉ Post Office
Secondary Road	🏰 🏰 Castle (ruins)	Minor Roads	✝ Cathedral/Church
Minor road	∴ Archaeological Site		☾ Mosque
Track	∩ Cave	Footpath	✡ Synagogue
International Boundary	★ Place of Interest	Railway	🗿 Statue/Monument
Province Boundary	🏛 Mansion/Stately Home	Pedestrian Area	⛩ 🏮 Shrine
National Park/Reserve	※ Viewpoint	Important Building	
Ferry Route	⚑ Beach	Park	

NORTHWEST CENTRAL TOKYO

NORTHEAST CENTRAL TOKYO

SOUTHWEST CENTRAL TOKYO

SOUTHEAST CENTRAL TOKYO

MINAMI-IKEBUKURO KŌEN
MINAMI-IKEBUKURO

HIGASHI-IKEBUKURO Y10 東池袋駅
HIGASHI-IKEBUKURO

Higashi-Ikebukuro

SHIN-ŌTSUKA

Kanju-in

Expressway No 5 – Ikebukurosen

Kasuga-dōri

Shinobazu-dōri

Hōmyō-in

Zōshigaya-mae

SENGOKU

kyo Folkcraft Antiques Hall

Y10 雑司ヶ谷駅

ŌTSUKA

KOISHIKAWA SHOKUBOTSU-EN

Kishimoj-In

Funeral Hall

ZŌSHIGAYA REIEN

HIMA-KU

Zōshigaya Kyu-senkyoshiksan (Missionary Museum)

Nio-mon (Gate)

Gokoku-ji

Shinobazu-dōri

Serikawa-dōri

Kishimojinmae

GOKOKUJI M23 護国寺

Kasuga-dōri

ZŌSHIGAYA

Shinobazo-dōri

Tokyo University Hospital

Ochanomizu University

MYŌGADANI M23 茗荷谷

KOISHIKAWA

Kinjō-in

Nihon Joshi Daigu (Japan Women's University)

Shinko-ji

Kishimojinmae

MEJIRODAI

Takushoku University

TAKADA

Mejiro-dōri

Tōkyō Katedoraru Sei-Maria Daiseido (St Mary's Cathedral)

OTOWA

BUNKYŌ-KU

Nanzō-in

SHI EDOGAWA KŌEN

KOHINATA

Omokagebashi

Ryōcho-in

Waseda

SEKIGUCHI

Shōmio-ji

KASUGA

Waseda-dōri

EDOGAWABASHI Y12 江戸川橋

SUIDŌ

NISHIWASEDA

TŌTSUKA-MACHI

Waseda University

WASEDA-TSURUMAKICHŌ

YAMABUKICHŌ

Kanda

Expressway No 5 – Ikebukurosen

Suwa-dōri

Ana Hachiman

TŌTSUKA-MACHI

WASEDA T04 早稲田駅

ENOKICHŌ

TEMJINCHŌ

KITAI-TŌ

NISHI-GOKEN-CHŌ

HIGASHI-GOKENCHŌ

TŌYAMA

Waseda Memorial Hall

BARASHITA-CHŌ

Waseda-dōri

HIGASHI-CHŌ

NAKA-ZATOCHŌ

TSUNOHAZU-SHIMMACHI

AKAGI-SHIMMACHI

SHI OGAWAMACHI

Kokuritsu Kokusai Iryo Centre (International Medicine Centre of Japan)

KIKUICHŌ

WASEDA MINAMI-CHŌ

Sōsan-ji

KAGURAZAKA T05 神楽坂

TSUKIDO-HACHIMANDHO

Waseda-dōri

TSUKUDO-CHŌ

U

HARAMACHI

SENTEN-CHŌ

Yarai Noh Theatre

YARAICHŌ

YOKO-TERAMACHI

KAGURAZAKA

WAKAMATSUCHŌ

MINAMI-ENOKICHŌ

USHIGOME-KAGURAZAKA E05 牛込神楽坂

OMOTOCHŌ

FUKURO-MACHI

Waseda-dōri

Ōkubo-dōri

ICHIGAYA-YAMABUSHICHŌ

KITA-YAMABUSHI-CHŌ

Ōkubo-dōri

KŌTAMACHI

Tokyo Rika Daigaku (Science Univ. of Tokyo)

INJUKU

Shinon-yan-dōri

WAKAMATSU-KAWADA E03 若松河田駅

ICHIGAYA-YANAGICHŌ

ICHIGAYA-KŌRACHŌ

NIJUKKIMACHI

SAIKI-MACHI

NAKACHŌ

WAKAMIYACHŌ

Nukebenten

Tokyo Women's Medical College & Hospital

KAWADACHŌ

MINAMICHŌ

FURAKAWABA MACHI

en-ji

YOCHŌMACHI

SUMI-YOSHICHŌ

ICHIGAYA-KAGACHŌ

NANDO-MACHI

HARAKATA-MACHI

FUJIMI

Hōsei University

Galen-Higashi-dōri

ICHIGAYA-YAKUOJI-MACHI

ICHIGAYA-SADOHARACHŌ

ICHIGAYA-TAKAJŌ-MACHI

Sotobori-dōri

Tokyo Medical College

ICHIGAYADAI-MACHI

AKEBONOBASHI E02 曙橋駅

ICHIGAYA-KŌEN-JI

ICHIGAYA-TAMACHI

Yasukuni-jinja

TOMIHISACHŌ

ICHIGAYA-NAKANO-CHŌ

ICHIGAYA-HONMURACHŌ

Ichigaya Hachiman-gū

ICHIGAYA-YAKUOJI

KUDANKITA

AIZUMI-CHŌ

FUNA-MACHI

Yasukuni-dōri

ARAKI-CHŌ

SAKAMACHI

Yasukuni-dōri

Ichigaya

ICHIGAYA S04 Y14 N09 市ヶ谷駅

Yasukuni-dōri

Ōzuma Women's University

KUDANMINAMI

GOBANCHŌ

SANBANCHŌ

D

E

TOMIHISACHO

ICHIGAYADAI-
MACHI

ICHIGAYA-
NAKANO-
CHO

ANEBONOSASHI
S03 姉ヶ崎町

KATAMACHI

ICHIGAYAHONMURACHŌ

KUDANKITA

Yasukuni-dōri

KUDANMINAMI

FUNA-
MACHI

AIZUMI-
CHŌ

ARAKI-
CHŌ

YOTSUYA-
SAKAMACHI

ICHIGAYA
Y14 N09 S04
市ヶ谷駅

SANBANCHŌ

JUKU-SANCHŌME
S02 M09
三丁目

Galen-Nishi-dōri

Shinjuku-dōri

YOTSUYA-SANCHŌME
M11 四谷三丁目

SAMONCHŌ

YOTSUYA-
SANCHŌME

SANEICHŌ

HONSHIOCHŌ

GŌBANCHŌ

YONBANCHŌ

ROKUBANCHŌ

NIBANCHŌ

ICHIBANCHŌ

YOTSUYA
M12 N08
四谷駅

KŌJIMACHI
Y15
麹町

HANZOMON
Z05
半蔵門

EN

DAIKYŌCHŌ

Hozo-ji

Shin-ei-ji

Aisen-in

Oiwainari

Shinsei-in

Seio-ji

Sofuku-ji

WAKABA

KŌJIMACHI

Galen-Higashi-dōri

SUGACHŌ

NAITŌMACHI

SHINANO-
MACHI

Keio
University
& Hospital

MINAMIMOTO-
TOMACHI

ndagaya

Shinanomachi

Geihin-kan
(Akasaka Detached
Palace)

SHIMIZUDANI
KŌEN

HIRAKAWACHO

essway No 4 Shinjuksen

KIOICHO

Aoyama-dōri

kyo Taiikukan
Gymnasium

National Olympic
Stadium
(under construction)

Seitoku
Kinen Kaigakan
(Meiji Memorial
Picture Gallery)

Meiji Kinenkan
(Memorial Hall)

Tōgū Gosho
(Crown Prince's Residence)

Suntory Building

NAGATACHŌ
N07 Z04 Y16
G05 M13
永田町駅

-ji

Senju-in

JINGŪ GAIEN
(MEIJI JINGŪ
OUTER GARDEN)

MOTOAKASAKA

Toyokawa
Inari

Akasaka-
Fudōson

Hie-jinja

Galen-Nishi-dōri

Galen-Higashi-dōri

Jingū
Baseball
Stadium

KITAAOYAMA

Aoyama-dōri

ASAKASA-MITSUKE
N07 Z04 Y16
G05 M13
赤坂見附駅

Jōdo-ji

Jōgen-ji

Akasaka
Musical Theatre

Sotobori-dōri

Kumano-
jinja

Kōtoku-ji

Chichibunomiya Rugby-jō
(Prince Chichibu Memorial
Rugby Football Ground)

AOYAMA-ITCHŌME
N04 Z03 G04
青山一丁目駅

Sannō
Hospital

AKASAKA
C06 赤坂駅

Akasaka-dōri

Roppongi-dōri

en-ji

Jiho-ji

GAIEMMAE
G03 外苑前駅

Gyokusōzen-ji

MINATO-KU

i-um Bijutsukan
ari-um Museum)

Kaizō-ji

Baisō-in

AOYAMA
KŌEN

Ryūsen-ji

Nogi-jinja

21_21
Design
Sight

Hikawa-
jinja

Ark
Hills

Reinansaka
Church

enkoku Dentōteki Kōgeihin
pan Traditional Crafts Centre)

Galen-Nishi-dōri

MINAMIAOYAMA

AOYAMA

NOGIZAKA
C05

Tokyo
Midtown

Myōzo-ji

Suntory
Hall

ae

OMOTESANDO
Z02 C04 G02
表参道

ling

Tessenkai Nohgaku
Kenshujo
(Noh Institute)

REIEN

Kokuritsu Shin
Bijutsukan
(National Art
Centre)

Suntory Bijutsukan
(Suntory Museum
of Art)

Haiyū-za
(Actor's Theatre)

Koun-ji

ROPPONGI-
ITCHŌME
N05
六本木一丁目

Kotto-dōri

Nezu Bijutsukan
(Nezu Museum)

AOYAMA
KŌEN

Galen-Nishi-dōri

Daian-ji

Jigan-in

Expressway No 3 Shibuyasen

ROPPONGI
H04 E23
六本木駅

ROPPONGI

ersity

Chōkoku-ji

NISHIAZABU

ROPPONGI

Galen-Higashi-dōri

AZABUDAI

Kotto-dōri

Roppongi-dōri

Myōzen-ji

Sakurada-jinja

Mori
Tower
Roppongi Hills

Torizaka
Church

Senshō-ji

Tōyōeiwa
Jogakuin

Seikei-dōri

AZABU-
NAGASAKA-
CHŌ

Shibuyasen

Galen-Higashi-dōri

D

E

SUMIDA-KU
RYŌGOKU

Keiyō-dōri

Ryōgoku-bashi

D   E

WAJICHO
M19

TSUKASA-
MACHI

KAJICHO

D. TOMIYAMACHO
8 KANDA KONYACHO
9 K. KITANOMÔN-CHO
10 K. KITAJIMA-MOMOCHO
11 K. KONYACHO
12 K. NISHIKONYACHO
13 K. MIKURACHO
13 KANDA-HIGASHI-MATSUSHITA-CHO

Bakurochō

Kanda

UCHIKANDA

Kandanishiki-dōri

IWAMOTOCHO

Sotobori-dōri

Chuo-dōri

KAJICHO

Edo-dōri

HIGASHI-
NIHOMBASHI

HIGASHI-NIHOMBASHI
A15 S09

CHŪŌ-KU

Ryōgoku-bashi

CHITOSE

Eshima-
sugiyama-jinja

Yoshin-ji

nen
Hall

Nikkei
Hall

kei
Hall

Nippon Ginkō
(Bank of
Japan)

Kahei
Hakubutsukan
(Currency Museum)

ŌTEMACHI

Maru Ōazu
ing Building

nouchi
ng

Tokyo
17

RUN
BE
—

ō Yūbinkyoku
tral Post Office

a Kokusai Forum
o International

akarazuka 1000
sekijo (Theatre)
yo Kotsu
■

onnier
kai
Ginza
□
M

■ H08
Matsuya
Dept Store

Mitsukoshi
Dept Store

Kabuki-
za
tore

Shimbashi-
Embujō

Expressway No 1 Ueno-sen

Shin-
Ōhashi-dōri

TSUKIJI

NIHOMBASHI-
NIHOMMACHI

NIHOMBASHI
HONCHO

Shinnihombashi

Mitsui Bijutsukan
(Mitsui Memorial Museum)

Takarada
Ebisu-jinja

NIHOMBASHI-
MUROMACHI

MITSUKOSHIMAE
G16 Z09 三越前
MITSUKOSHIMAE
G12 Z09 三越前

Mitsukoshi
Dept Store

Kesodutoshinkanjosen

Tako no
Hakubutsukan
(Kite Museum)

Coredo

NIHOMBASHI
G11 T19 A13
日本橋

NIHOMBASHI

Takashimaya

NIHOMBASHI
KYŌBASHI

KYŌBASHI
G10 京橋

TAKARACHO
A12 宝町

HATCHŌBORI

Bridgestone
Bijutsukan
(Bridgestone
Museum of Art)

Tokyo Kokuritsu
Kindai Bijutsukan
(National Film Archive
of Japan)

GINZA-ITCHOME
Y19 銀座一丁目

The Magazine
House

Shōchiku
Kaikan

Namiyoke-
jinja

Kokuritsu Gan Centre
(National Cancer Centre)

Eitai-dōri

Sotobori-dōri Yaesu-

Chuo-dōri

Shōwa-dōri

Shōwa-dōri Ōkura-dōri

Harumi-

Kachidoki-bashi

Kesodutoshinkanjosen

HIGASHI-GINZA
A11 H09 東銀座

GINZA

Daimaru
Dept Store

Chuo-dōri

Yaesu-dōri

Expressway No 1 Ueno-sen

Shin-Ōhashi-dōri

Shirakawa-dōri

SHINTOMI

SHINTOMICHO
Y20 新富町

IRIFUNE

TSUKIJIKAWA
KŌEN

TSUKIJI
H10

TSUKIJI
Hongan-ji

CHŪŌ-KU

NIHOMBASHI-
KODEMMACHO

NIHOMBASHI
KODEMMACHO

NIHOMBASHI-
HORIDOMECHO

Kabuto-jinja

Tōkyō
Shōken Torihikijo
(Tokyo Stock Exchange)

KAYABACHO
H12 T11

Hakozaki

NIHOMBASHI-
KAYABACHO

HATCHŌBORI
H11 八丁堀

Hatchōbori

MINATO

AKASHICHO

NIHOMBASHI
HISAMATSUCHO

HAMACHO
S10

HAMACHŌ
KŌEN

NIHOMBASHI-
HAMACHO

Meiji-za

Kiyosubashi-dōri

Shin-Ōhashi-dōri

NIHOMBASHI-
NINGYOCHO

NIHOMBASHI-
KAKIGARACHO

SUITENGUMAE
Z10 水天宮前

Kiyosubashi

NIHOMBASHI-
YOKOYAMA
A15 S09

HACHŌ

HIGASHI-
NIHOMBASHI

HAMACHŌ
KŌEN

Expressway No 7 Komatsugawasen

TOKIWA

NIHOMBASHI-
NAKASU

Kiyosubashi

KIYOSUMI

Kiyosubashi-
dōri

KIYOSUMI
TEIEN

Tokyo City
Air Terminal

Kiyosubashi-dōri

HAKOZAKI
KŌEN

Hakozaki

NIHONBASHI-HAKO-
ZAKICHO

SAGA

FUKUZUMI

SHINKAWA

KŌTŌ-KU

EITAI

TOMIOKA

MONZEN-NAKACHO
E15 T12 門前仲町

BOTAN

FURUISHIBA

Etchūjima

TSUKUDA
KŌEN

TSUKUDA

Tsukuda-bashi

TSUKISHIMA

TSUKISHIMA
E16 Y21 月島

Kiyosumi-dōri

ETCHŪJIMA

TOYOSU

HARUMI

Sumida

Kachidoki-bashi

Harumae-bashi

Nishinaka-
bashi

Tsukishima-
bashi

Reihei-
bashi

KACHIDOKI
E17 勝どき

KACHIDOKI

Shin-
Ōhashi-dōri

Sumida

A RIKYŪ
TEIEN

D   E

1

2

3

4

STREET INDEX

ART AND PHOTO CREDITS

INDEX

INSIGHT ⊙ GUIDES

TOKYO

Editors: **Tom Fleming & Zara Sekhavati**
Author: **Rob Goss**
Head of DTP and Pre-Press:
Rebeka Davies
Updater: **Martin Zatko**
Managing Editor: **Carine Tracanelli**
Pictures: **Tom Smyth**
Layout: Aga Bylica
Cartography: original cartography
Berndtson & Berndson, updated by Carte

Distribution

UK, Ireland and Europe
Apa Publications (UK) Ltd
sales@insightguides.com

United States and Canada
Ingram Publisher Services
ips@ingramcontent.com

Australia and New Zealand
Woodslane
info@woodslane.com.au

Southeast Asia
Apa Publications (SN) Pte
singaporeoffice@insightguides.com

Worldwide
Apa Publications (UK) Ltd
sales@insightguides.com

Special Sales, Content Licensing and CoPublishing

Insight Guides can be purchased in
bulk quantities at discounted prices.
We can create special editions,
personalised jackets and corporate
imprints tailored to your needs.
sales@insightguides.com;
www.insightguides.biz

Printing

Inerak-Poland

All Rights Reserved
© 2020 Apa Digital (CH) AG and
Apa Publications (UK) Ltd

First Edition 1991
Eighth Edition 2020

ABOUT THIS BOOK

What makes an Insight Guide different? Since our first book pioneered the use of creative full-colour photography in travel guides in 1970, we have aimed to provide not only reliable information but also the key to a real understanding of a destination and its people.

Now, when the internet can supply inexhaustible (but not always reliable) facts, our books marry text and pictures to provide that more elusive quality: knowledge. To achieve this, they rely on the authority of locally based writers and photographers.

This new edition of *City Guide Tokyo* was copyedited by **Tom Fleming** and **Zara Sekhavati**.

The book was updated by **Martin Zatko**, building on work by travel writer **Rob Goss**.

This edition builds on the success of earlier editions produced by **Simon Richmond, Francis Dorai** and **Low Jat Leng**. The text of writers who contributed to previous editions include **Stephen Mansfield, Angela Jeffs, Alexandra Waldman, Mark Schreiber, Dan Grunebaum** and **Robbie Swinnerton**.

Among the prominent photographers whose images bring Tokyo to life are **Stephen Mansfield, Richard Nowitz** and **Ming Tang-Evans**.

The book was indexed by **Helen Peters**.

SEND US YOUR THOUGHTS

We do our best to ensure the information in our books is as accurate and up-to-date as possible. The books are updated on a regular basis using local contacts, who painstakingly add, amend, and correct as required. However, some details (such as telephone numbers and opening times) are liable to change, and we are ultimately reliant on our readers to put us in the picture.

We welcome your feedback, especially your experience of using the book "on the road". Maybe we recommended a hotel that you liked (or another that you didn't), or you came across a great bar or new attraction that we missed.

We will acknowledge all contributions, and we'll offer an Insight Guide to the best letters received.

Please write to us at:
Insight Guides
PO Box 7910, London SE1 1WE
Or email us at:
hello@insightguides.com

Tokyo Subway